Peter Wortsman

Talking in Tongues

Peter Wortsman

Talking in Tongues

Essays on
Language and Literature

PalmArtPress
Berlin

Without translation, we would be living in provinces bordering on silence.

– George Steiner

To Claudie

Contents

Smuggling Secrets Across Time and Space
A Foreword

You taught me language and my profit on't is I know how to curse.
– William Shakespeare, *The Tempest*

As I pass through my seventh decade of consciousness, I listen all the more attentively to the Morse code crackle of the synaptic circuitry. Not being conversant in C++, C, JAVA, FORTRAN, Pascal, Perl, Ruby, Visual Basic and other high-tech tongues, I remain beholden to English, German and French, the three languages through the lens of which I receive and transmit meaning and thereby make some sense out of the muddle of life.

*

People sometimes ask me if I made up my surname Wortsman (German for "man of words") as a penname to fit my profession. Let me assure you that I was born a Wortsman. The only alteration my grandfather (father's father), a native of Krakow, Poland, transplanted to Vienna, and later a refugee from Nazi-occupied Austria, made upon his arrival in New York was to shave off the second "n" at the tail end of his surname, a nominal trim to make it sound less Teutonic in the wake of the atrocities committed by some speakers of German.

Among my forbears, I imagine, there must surely have been a blabbermouth or a scribe, or an ancestor who paid through the nose for a respectable surname. Jews have historically gone by Hebrew patronymic names, i.e. So and so, the son/daughter of So and So, until 1787, when Emperor Joseph II issued a decree compelling all those Jews living in German lands to adopt German surnames. The better-off were able to bribe bureaucrats to assign them respectable appellations, like Goldmann or Silverstein, to suit their calling and social status. But the impecunious were beholden to bureaucratic whim and oftentimes saddled with embarrassing surnames. There is a Jewish joke about a well-to-do merchant who comes home and announces to his wife: "Our name is now *Schweiss*." (*Sweat*, as in blood, sweat and tears). "You're so rich," his wife objects, "couldn't you have bought us a better name?" To which the husband replies: "You can't imagine how much I had to pay for that "w!"

*

Whales whale, birds twitter, cats purr, dogs bark, and lions roar, evoking hunger, lust and a limited roster of other crude cravings, but only homo sapiens can dissect sound into terse parcels of intent, and deploy complex symbol systems to be spoken, etched in stone, inscribed on parchment scrolls, bound in books, and flashed on computer screens, to register impressions of the present, capture memories of the past, and project visions of the future.

*

Words have mattered to me for as long as I can remember. Writing and translation have always gone hand in hand in my experience as parallel practices, the one fortifying the other. The New York-born son of Viennese-Jewish émigrés, I was raised in a bilingual (German-English) household.

My father was equally conversant in German, French, English, Italian, Spanish, and Portuguese, not to speak of Latin, ancient Greek and Hebrew, and the Turkish and Arabic he was studying at the time of his death. In England, where my parents spent the War years, my father mastered the King's

English to such an extent that when someone stopped him on the street to complain of "those damn refugees taking our jobs," he smiled and stunned his interlocutor: "I know, I'm one of them." And in America, where my parents emigrated after the War, he skillfully and convincingly peppered his business English with baseball metaphors, that being the idiom of commerce, though he had never, to my knowledge, set foot in a ballpark. These were no mere charades, but rather the verbal accoutrements of personae he could slip on and into, and which subsequently proved inseparable from himself—or should I say, him-selves?

Following a talk I gave some years ago in Washington D.C. as a guest speaker at the fiftieth anniversary gathering of the Northeast Modern Language Association (NEMLA), an incensed member of the audience took issue with my tongue-in-cheek metaphoric and altogether laudatory reference to my late beloved father as a "cultural schizophrenic." "The appropriate term is mentally challenged," she chided me. Not being presently employed as an academic, and therefore not beholden to the Orwellian newspeak of the moment, and so free to let my tongue wag as I please, I refused to comply.

*

Having grown up with two mother tongues: German, the vernacular of my communion with my parents from the time I started talking until my father's death in 1979 and my mother's in 2007, and English, the vehicle of public palaver—as well as French, as a third, adoptive, "step-mother" tongue tailor-made for romance; and having been nourished from an early age with a heaping helping of Jewish angst—raised to be ready to leap at a moment's notice and land like a talking cat—I am heir to my father's benign cultural split-personality, a precious gift which my French wife and I took pains to pass on, albeit in a different combination (that is, in French and English), to our bilingual, bi-national, bi-cultural children. But the cost for me was and remains to this day a certain linguistic and cultural confusion.

*

I have not always been comfortable with my forked tongue and divided identity. For the longest time, I felt as though my voice and the words I uttered, or jotted down in English, German, and French, were not really my own, but a puppet's parroted lines.

Upon my return to New York, after four years at a liberal arts college in New England, and two post-graduate years abroad—the first in Freiburg, Germany, where I studied fairy tales on a Fulbright Fellowship; the second in Vienna, Austria, and Eastern Europe, on a Thomas J. Watson Foundation Fellowship, tracking down the unhappy history that sent my parents running for their lives, I remember making an emotional scene. Momentarily flummoxed, and emotionally drained after having been obliged for the last two years to mentally translate every menu listing, street sign, and remark addressed to me; unable to find the right words to express the confusion I was feeling, I lashed out at my poor speechless progenitors: "Why didn't you raise me in a single language with a single identity I can call my own!? At least then I would belong somewhere."

Pulling myself together the very next day, in part to please my parents, I set out to look for a job. Daring myself to knock at the door of every international news service, I paced the corridors of the Associated Press Building, at 50 Rockefeller Plaza. Turned away everywhere else, I hesitated momentarily at the last door in the corridor, the office of Springer News, a German news outlet best known for publishing the tabloid daily *Die Bild Zeitung*, a picture-rich, sensationalist gossip rag. I swallowed my pride and knocked. Busy painting her fingernails, the gatekeeper was about to turn me away with a perfunctory backwards sweep of the left hand, on which the fresh coat of nail polish was still wet, when a booming baritone chimed in from behind a glass partition: "*Was will er*? What does he want?" And rising like a magic stalk, a head sprouted like a pumpkin, almost colliding with the ceiling, and a pair of eyes peered out at me through thick-lensed glasses, as if through the sight of a submarine periscope.

"*Ich suche Arbeit.* I'm looking for work," I replied. The interview was perfunctory, just long enough for me to spin a few coherent sentences to convince my interlocutor that I was sufficiently conversant in German, whereupon I was promptly hired.

The boss, the late Alfred von Krusenstiern (1929-2007), himself an émigré, born in Prague of Baltic-German nobility, was grace and kindness incarnate. And while our political views surely differed, his tilted to the right of center, mine more to the left, and the assignments I was given did not quite suit my temperament, most memorable among them to conduct telephone interviews with the world's crawling champion in Tennessee and the boxing promoter of a fight between a man and a killer shark in the water off Manila Bay, and I didn't last long on the job, I remain forever grateful to "Ank," as he was affectionately known in the business, for giving me my first professional break in the world of words.

*

To be conversant in several tongues is to live and breathe divided selves. There are cultures and countries where bilingualism, and even multilingualism, are the norm. Most Swiss master at least French and German, with Italian and Romansch added to the mix in some cantons. Educated Indians read Sanskrit, and depending on where they're from, speak either Hindi, Bengali, Marathi, Telugu, Tamil, Gujarati, Urdu, Kannada, Odia, or Malayalam, in addition to English, the language of the colonizer. In Senegal, where my wife and I spent a memorable summer, Mami, a five-year-old girl with whom I conversed in French took it upon herself to instruct me the rudiments of Mandingo, while switching off to Wolof, another tribal tongue, to scold the neighbor's boy. But in the U.S., in the Fifties, when I came of age, monolingualism was the norm. Even in the ethnically diverse hotpot of New York City, where the parents or grandparents of most natives hale from diverse nations, and mothers chide their offspring in every language and dialect under the sun, all essential communication was conducted in homogenized English.

*

The effort to clarify, focus, and yes, to celebrate the stereophonic nature of my thinking was at least one of the determinant factors in my becoming a writer. Whereas English, the language I learned in school and on the street, is undoubtedly my primary, multi-purpose vernacular for calculating, cursing and cajoling; and French (the language I speak at home with my French wife and bi-cultural children) is my present domestic lingua franca; German, the dialect of my childhood, remains my real mother tongue, the language I spoke with my mother, and in which I still think and feel most emotionally.

The primary quandary I face as a writer, or what used to be called a man of letters, is how to combine the various linguistic strands and weave them into a single intelligible wreath.

My early attempts to write in English, though syntactically correct, seemed somehow bloodless, omitting much, emoting little. It was during my year abroad in Freiburg, Germany, where I studied German *Märchen* on a Fulbright Fellowship, that I dusted off my childhood German and began to tease out its literary possibilities, to translate and to write for real. The subsequent year in Vienna, on a fellowship from the Thomas J. Watson Foundation, and two years of graduate study in German at New York University further reinforced my grasp of German.

*

I started translating to bridge a psychic gap inside myself and to clear my mind, as a meditation and warm-up exercise before writing. I still translate to study up close, breath to breath, as it were, the voices of writers I revere.

*

A translator is essentially a double-agent impersonating others, whose task it is to smuggle the poetic essence of one culture to another.

In France, they take their language so seriously as to have a government-appointed body, the Académie Française, comprising a group of 40 so-called "immortals," decked out like prize peacocks in brocaded jackets, tasked with maintaining the purity of the mother tongue. In addition, self-appointed Gallic vigilantes take it upon themselves to reprimand and correct erring strangers. I have received unsolicited corrections of my spoken French from waiters, concierges, and gas station attendants. Such rebukes, I should add, are not restricted to the foreign-born. My wife, a respected university professor of French literature who hails from the South of France and attended the elite École Normal Supérieur, once asked for onions at a restaurant in Paris, pronouncing the word in the southern French manner as "*oignons,*" (pronounced *wa-nyaw*) and was promptly and rather curtly reprimanded by a waiter: "*Madame, on dit 'ognons!'*"

To the utilitarian American mindset, for which language is a primarily a tool deployed to conduct business, and sentences are preferably short, sweet and to the point, this French concern for linguistic purity borders on manic compulsion.

I finally got my revenge for all those unsolicited corrections. After stopping at a gas station in France to "*faire le plein,*" (fill 'er up), I politely requested the promotional offer of a complimentary DVD of the English language, animated classic "Chicken Run" for my children.

"*Monsieur, on dit 'Chicken Rrrrun!'*" (Sir, we say 'Chicken Rrrrun!') the gas station attendant corrected my pronunciation, stressing the guttural 'r'.

But this time it was my turn to set him straight. "*Non, Monsieur, on dit 'Chicken Run!,'*" I retorted, softening the 'r.' "*C'est de l'anglais, et c'est comme ça qu'on le prononce!*" (It's English, and that's the proper way to pronounce it!")

"*Ah, bon?!*" (Is that so?) the chastened gas pumper cum Gallic grammarian was obliged to bite his tongue.

*

In Russia, pre- and post-revolution, whichever autocrat happens to be running the show simultaneously reveres and fears language and literature, going so far as to apprehend poets and writers who refuse to conform, sending them to Siberia as a "finishing school," to silence and literally finish them off.

In America, on the other hand, words don't really matter, except when employed in instruction manuals, cookbooks, and the lingo that leads directly to financial gain, competitive sports or political victory. Like all erstwhile colonial nations, the U.S. has an ambivalent relationship to its mother tongue. Born on the battlefield at Hastings, in 1066, where the army of the victorious William, Duke of Normandy, formerly known as William "the Bastard," following his army's victory, dubbed William the Conqueror, beat the army of the Saxon king, Harold Godwinson, English is a hybrid tongue, with the palaver of the victorious French henceforth dominating that of the defeated Germanic tribes. At table, the refined Englishman dines with knife and fork on pork (from the French *porc*), but the farmer labors in the pigpen raising swine (from the German, *Schwein*). Our forebears spilled English tea in protest into the Boston harbor. As their heirs, we Americans excel at manhandling the mother tongue. For us, words are primarily utilitarian instruments. If your words don't make a buck, you might as well shut up.

*

My first book-length translation, *Posthumous Papers of a Living Author*, by Robert Musil, put me on the literary map. Parts appeared in the literary journal *Antaeus*, and thereafter were excerpted in *Pictures*, a slender volume edited by Megan Ratner, of the Echo Press, and published by the Coalition of Publishers for Employment, Cooper Union, New York, in 1983. The book subsequently appeared in its entirety as Volume One of the Eridanos Library, published in Hygiene, CO, in 1988; was republished in a second edition by Penguin 20th Century Classics, Penguin U.K., London, in 1995; in a third edition by Archipelago Books, NYC, in 2006; and excerpted yet again in *Flypaper*

(Penguin Mini-Classics, Penguin Books, London, UK, 2011). Vincent Kling, writing in *Modern Austrian Literature*, dubbed it "a kind of classic in its own right."

But the success of that first translation proved a double-edged sword. Lauded as I was by the literary establishment, I was immediately pigeonholed by mainstream American publishers as a literary translator first and foremost, with my own writing taking second rung. Let me remind the reader that translation was a respected literary sideline for the likes of Charles Baudelaire, Gérard de Nerval, Samuel Beckett, Paul Bowles, Julio Cortazar, Julien Green, Vladimir Nabokov, Ngugi wa Thiong, Alexander Pope, and Bruno Schulz, to name only a few of the most notable practitioners. Short fiction writer and translator Lydia Davis is a notable contemporary case of a writer who also translates.

*

What follows is a selection of literary essays, the first part theoretical, comprising reflections on language, translation, and writing in a second tongue; the second part analytical, comprising mostly the introductions or afterwords I wrote to accompany my translations.

I

Talking in Tongues

'Gwrhyr, Interpreter of Languages,' said Arthur, 'it will be proper for you to go on this errand, for you know all tongues and can speak with some of the birds and animals.'

– The Mabinogean

I Harbor a Stillborn Scribe of the German Language[1]

Once, after heartily and gamely shooting the breeze over Russian bubbly at a congenial gathering in the former German Democratic Republic, the Polish wife of a German friend asked me what, in fact, my mother tongue was. The conversation, in which I took a lively part, vigorously affirming and defending my points of view about this and that, was conducted entirely in German, while I communicated shreds of the essential gist in French to my French wife, and every now and then scolded, in English, my young son, who, two years of German instruction notwithstanding, made not the slightest effort to exchange a few German words with the neighbors' delightful little daughter.

Reflecting for a moment, I gave the following answer: "My mother tongue is actually a kind of linguistic wrap, with German, the language I spoke for my entire life with my mother, enveloped by English, whereby I am quite sure that there are forgotten Yiddish sentiments slipped into my eccentric German; the Yiddish, in turn, studded with Hebrew longings smuggled out of the desert, the whole generously salted with tears and seasoned with screams.

Given that I learned German as a first language, albeit only orally, from my mother and father, it is and remains for all intents and purposes my mother tongue. But I grew up in English. And since I only learned to read and write German much later, as an adult, German remains for me the language of childhood, or rather a delinquent dialect in which I pull no punches. As such, he who bears the name Peter Wortsman keeps stumbling on a

1 First published in *Stimme und Atem/Out of Breath, Out of Mind, Zweizüngige Erzählungen / Two-Tongued Tales*, by Peter Wortsman, PalmArtPress, Berlin, 2019, this essay was excerpted in *The Yale Review Online*, May 2019.

second self in the clang of German syllables, the Mr. Hyde to his Dr. Jekyll, a shamelessly impertinent creature who allows himself to take liberties that my well brought-up, adult, English-speaking self would never have let slip.

Let me lay it on the line, even if it sounds a bit bizarre: I harbor a stillborn scribe of the German tongue in me, who, despite everything, belongs to the literary tradition from Kleist to Kafka. As a translator, I have a very intimate relationship with that tradition. Every word is an air bubble, every sentence a breath, an exhalation burdened with meaning. With his ear pressed to extinguished lips, the translator acts as a kind of medium who literally derives inspiration transmitted by strange syllables. Translation from one language into another, particularly the words of the dead, is a kind of mouth-to-mouth resuscitation in which you breathe new life into expired syllables.

But German for me, if I can be perfectly frank, also harbors a dark subtext. The language of the *Dichter* and *Denker* (poets and thinkers), to whom I, in my own modest way, feel a certain kinship, is also the language of the *Richter* und *Henker* (judges and executioners). In Auschwitz and Buchenwald, they not only murdered people, they also once and for all time erased the tenuous borderline between nightmare and reality, and thereby devised a new marginal tongue in which consciousness and the subconscious blabber like undivided Siamese twins. Sayings like "*Jedem das Seine*" (To Each His Own) and "*Arbeit Macht Frei*" (Work Makes You Free) and concentration camp jargon like *Muselmann* (a walking dead man) and *Kanada* (the depot in Auschwitz-Birkenau where the last possessions of the slaughtered were saved and stored, thus the epitome of limitless riches and boundless possibilities) bespeak a black humor that arouses a tickle in the throat that can never be stilled by easy laughter. I am also heir to that German tongue.

*

A word about my conflicted identity. Once upon a time there was a turbulent cultural melding, a marriage of two peoples that exploded again and again in outbursts of violence, nevertheless bearing rich fruits, a marriage that finally fell apart in a terrible divorce.

This tenuous German-Jewish union, in the braded double helix of which the souls of the North Sea and the Mediterranean, of mountain climber and nomad met, a union dating back to Roman times, when the Jews first established small settlements along the Rhine, led to some of the cultural heights and the depths of our modern era. One can only imagine a Marx, a Freud, a Kafka, a Wittgenstein, or an Einstein, among many other pathfinders of modernity, at the crossroads of strict German syntax, logic, and idealism coupled with Talmudic justice and idealism, qualities that on the one hand tend to secularized messianism, and on the other, in the case of some Jews, is bound with a seemingly contrary readiness—namely, systematically to break all rules. An elective affinity perhaps. I would rather call it a productive symbiosis, like that of the bird that lives on the back of the bison and feeds on the insects in its fur before flying on. Only the fleas lose out in the deal.

*

The Biblical term *Ivri* (Hebrew) means "to cross over." Abraham left his birthplace Ur to seek his fortune elsewhere. Moses led his enslaved minion out of Egypt, through the desert, and rolled-back waves of the Red Sea to find freedom on the far shore.

I belong to a tribe of wanderers. Perhaps I carry the nomadic drive of my ancestors in my toes and retain their anxious breath patterns in my lungs. The Germans were also once a wandering people, or group of peoples. Modern movements like the *Wandervögel* and the Kibbutzniks are essentially not all that dissimilar. Perhaps German and Jewish Wanderlust came together in the joints of my knees. Already as a young man, my father, a native Viennese, was often underway somewhere, preferably Paris. Later my parents were expelled from their homeland. My father, who spoke seven languages fluently, turned his refugee status into an *art de vivre*. From early on, he raised his offspring to be travelers. But beneath the pleasure of experiencing the big wide world and of rediscovering oneself again and again in foreign climes, there was always the underlying notion that we had to learn to leap like a cat, since you could never know when it would once again be time to pick up and go.

For me, being Jewish means, above all, bearing a deeply engraved question mark in my brain as a badge of honor, to be certain only in uncertainty, and as soon as I arrive anywhere to look around already for the exit door.

It always seemed to me as if I'd been born in the shadow of the flames that engulfed my parents' world, as if everything meaningful and significant had already happened before my birth, and that, in fact, I had no right to my own experience, because it would always be considered inconsequential in comparison to what my parents lived through.

Then in 1973, I landed as a Fulbright fellow at the Albert Ludwig University in Freiburg im Breisgau, to study fairy tales, the literary love of my childhood. And the following year, as a fellow of the Thomas J. Watson Foundation, I went to Vienna, where I conducted interviews with survivors of the concentration camps. Today they comprise "The Peter Wortsman Collection of Oral History" at the U.S. Holocaust Memorial Museum in Washington. Back then I tried to seek out the ghosts in the shadows.

These interviews inspired a few songs, and many years later became the basis of my first play *The Tattooed Man Tells All* (PalmArtPress, Berlin, 2024).

My father died in 1979. Despite the heavy burden of grief, his death also freed me, as if a second, metaphoric umbilical cord had been cut. Only after his death did I one day begin to write short original texts in German. I dedicated my first book of short prose *A Modern Way to Die* (Fromm Publishing International, New York, 1991), parts of which I composed in German, and then translated, or rather adapted into English, to my father, and as an epigram graced it with the Viennese saying he was fond of repeating: *Nichts dauert ewig, der schänste Jud wird schäbig.* (Nothing last forever, the nicest Jew grows shabby.)

Strangely enough, it was only on the now canonical date of September 11, 2001, when the great peril appeared to draw near and I saw the Twin Towers tumble outside my window, that I was freed from the phantoms of the past. The geopolitical ground rules of the game seemed to be changing all around me.

My mother, with whom I spoke mostly German, died in 2007. After that I fell into a great depression and for a time stopped sleeping, which also had serious consequences for my state of mind. On the verge of madness, I contemplated giving up on everything, my marriage, my profession, my middle-class life. I wrote next to nothing. Fortunately, I am blessed with the love of a wise woman, who suffered my caprices until they played themselves out.

Then in 2010, everything suddenly changed again. As a Holtzbrinck Fellow at the American Academy in Berlin, I had the opportunity to experience, not only the city of Berlin in all its cultural complexity, but also to sound the depths of my prickly relation to German culture and to the German language. I collected and worked up my observations, experiences and memories in the book *Ghost Dance in Berlin: A Rhapsody in Gray* (Travelers' Tales, Palo Alto, 2013), in which I finally got to dance with the ghosts of my childhood.

Do the Jewish and German pieces of my puzzle of self actually still fit together at all?

If one can and may still speak of national characteristics, a supposition that I sometimes doubt, one runs the risk of falling into empty clichés, as, for instance, that the Germans are hard-working, dreamy, and idealistic, somewhat like the dwarfs in Snow White. Normalcy, either of the European or whatever variety, is a quality I wish on no individual and no nation. The norm draws downwards. Let us rather remain abnormal, eccentric, quirky, and odd, each in our own way, a gathering of harmless lunatics who take pleasure in everything and anything.

Perhaps we Germans and Jews of the postwar generation, as children of that shattered cultural union, can still achieve something productive together; perhaps we can pick a few rags of reason from the ruins of the past and therewith pitch a tent big enough to hold all our dreams.

Of Sublime Ecstasy and Guttural Disgust: My German Language[1]

I would rather decline two drinks than one German adjective.
– Mark Twain

What is it about the German language that so moves me? That push and pull of contradictory impulses, that never-ending string of nouns and adjectives in search of a predicate verb to bind meaning, that strange amalgam of superlatives and expletives exuding sublime ecstasy and guttural disgust! German curses and cajoles, belches, farts and philosophizes with boundless delight, then retreats suddenly, tightening its belt, squelching its own wild urges with the syntax of discipline and restraint. German sentences are chiseled, each a miniature Gothic cathedral, replete with grinning gargoyles, stained glass and flying buttresses; each a catacomb of neatly stacked bones crowding the unconscious.

How much German infuses every fibril of my being!

Two tongues tugged at my childhood heart and mind, two takes on the world, two flavors of consciousness.

English was the public channel of communication at school and on the street, a peppermint tongue that stung and excited. German, all chocolaty, viscous and sweet, was the private funnel of intimacy in my first-generation German-speaking, Jewish, immigrant family. And though I'm a native New Yorker, my emotional grounding is still and always will be in German, the dialect of that tiny city state of five afloat in the teeming megalopolis.

---

1 An earlier version of this essay was first published under the title "Double Take: The Bilingual Family," a memoir of linguistic conundrums in my immigrant family, in *Family: A Celebration, An Anthology*, edit. Margaret Campbell (Peterson's Publ., Princeton, NJ, 1995). The text in its entirety was subsequently published as a chapter of my travel memoir, *Ghost Dance in Berlin, A Rhapsody in Gray* (Travelers' Tales, 2012).

English meant business, sharpened Number-2 pencils, white shirt and tie; commerce: "I'll trade you a Roger Maris for a Mickey Mantle!"; and diplomacy: "If you don't, I won't be your best friend anymore!"

German coddled, cursed and cajoled. "*Wir sind jung, die Welt ist offen*!" (We are young, the world is open!) my mother invoked a Socialist marching song from her youth between the World Wars to rally the ranks at reveille and again at bedtime and buck us up when spirits were down. My father fondly referred to us kids as his "*Affengesindel*" (monkey mob) or "*Arschgesichter*" (ass faces), depending on our manners and his mood—language the like of which we wouldn't dream of using outside the home. While English called for good behavior, German was a license to relax, in the spirit of father's favorite schoolboy verse:

Salomon der Weise spricht:
Laute Schasse stinken nicht,
Aber jene leisen die unhörbar durch die Hose schleichen,
Mensch, vor denen hüte dich,
Denn die stinken fürchterlich!

(Roughly):

Solomon the Wise once said it:
Loud farts smell not, but hear me now.
Those quiet ones that slither through,
Beware of them, I'm telling you.
Hold your nose, or you will dread it!

The cost of my linguistic split personality was a certain confusion. At times I felt off-kilter, an alien at home plate. There was something perennially out-of-sync in the swing of my baseball bat, as there was, and still is, something not quite kosher about my English, a tendency to over-articulate, "public speak" it, which in the slurred "slanguage" of *Nooyawk* amounted to an accent.

It was the early Fifties, and the terrible cataclysms of World War II and the Holocaust were still fresh in everyone's mind, so fresh nobody wanted to be reminded. German was taboo, the tainted tongue of evil. And that a Jew should speak it seemed particularly inimical. Yet despite considerable pressure from relatives and peers, my parents refused to blame the language and stop speaking it. For to excise German would have been to cut out their own tongues and grant the nasty little man with the mustache a second victory.

Years later I found it difficult to get intimate in English. In a college writing workshop, the instructor prodded us to speak and write frankly and openly about our private life, such as it was. With my girlfriend of the moment seated beside me, I put my foot in my mouth. We were discussing the colorful language in one of Henry Miller's "Tropics," and I awkwardly referred to the sexual organs as the stick and the hole, because my tongue was locked in a pre-adolescent limbo and, believe it or not, the English words penis and vagina were not a part of my vocabulary. I can still feel the sting of the All-American laughter.

*

For me, the big abstractions, like "*Liebe*" (love), "*Traum*" (dream) and "*Tod*" (death), will always resonate in German and somehow fall flat in English. For me the English word "remembrance" has a vaguely vulgar ring, like groping around in the flea market of the mind and subsequently reassembling the cracked and broken bric-a-brac; whereas the German word "*Erinnerung,*" (literally a turning inward) raises the conceptual bar, upgrading those haphazard knickknacks into precious antiques.

Sometimes, indeed, I doubt my own identity. Am I myself, or a blatant case of identity theft, a ventriloquist or a ventriloquist's dummy? Are the words I speak my own, or is my subconscious merely taking dictation in a secret code and automatically translating the original German before I wake, superimposing my exhalations with borrowed English meaning? To this day, I often feel like one of those plump, round, hand-painted, Russian, wooden Martryuschka dolls, with German imbedded in my English, Yiddish hidden inside the German, Hebrew pulsing in the Yiddish, and the universal cry of the newborn echoing within.

I am a French Irregular Verb[1]

(To my father, Alfred Wortsman, 1914-1979)

Speak in French when you can't think of the English for a thing ...
– Lewis Carroll

Forgotten is the pain of memorizing all those irregular French verbs, the torment of rounding the mouth just right and skewing the glottal apparatus so as to emit a fair approximation of the proper nasal inflections. The Gallic syllables are honey on my tongue, a mastered password that lets me pass, if not as a native, then as a presumed Luxembourger, French Swiss, Belgian, or perhaps an Alsatian, a useful trick for traveling incognito in these troubled times.

In my own private atlas of the heart, the Old World is divided down the middle by an imaginary Maginot Line, a border which, I readily admit, bears little, if any, relation to today's geopolitical reality, but which bisects Europe along a tenuous fault line riddled with psychic land mines along which the phantasms of inherited memory stand guard. While the European Union dropped its national borders, according to the Schengen Agreement of 1995, the dividing line on my internalized roadmap has a serrated edge that roughly runs along the Rhine.

On one side they speak German, a loaded language, burdened for me, as the son of German-speaking Jewish refugees, with contradictory associations, since it is both my mother tongue (the language I spoke with my mother) and the guttural grunt of asphyxiation. On the other side they speak *Liberté, Egalité, Fraternité* (Liberty, Equality, Fraternity). The French have a sense of humor about their national slogan. I recently

1 First published in *Catamaran Literary Reader*, Issue 14, Santa Cruz, CA, 2016; reissued in *The Best Travel Writing*, Volume 11, 2016

saw it parodied with a wink in graffiti spray painted on the side of an official government building as: "*Liberté,Égalité, Béyoncé.*" Simplistic though my distinction may be—and I am full well aware of the historic inconsistencies and discrepancies, of the vagaries of collaboration and resistance—in Germany my throat tightens and stomach twitches with apprehension, in France I breathe easy, eat well, and fall in love.

*

In the harried but hopeful expression of every African street peddler of counterfeit Louis Vuitton handbags, inflated plastic flying saucers, creepy crawly, sticky fingered little figurines that shimmy down windows and walls, and other innocuous knickknacks knocked off in China and hawked on the streets of Montmartre and the Parvis de Notre Dame, I see the face of my late beloved father, who, as a young man, an illegal alien struggling to make ends meet, lived off the doughnuts he whipped up illegally in his garret room on the Île Saint Louis to peddle to tourists at the *Exposition Internationale des Arts et Techniques dans la Vie Moderne* (International Exposition Dedicated to Art and Technology in Modern Life), better known as Paris Expo 1937, where the pavilions of Nazi Germany and the Soviet Union, situated within winking distance directly across from each other at the fairgrounds, represented the opposing forces of a world order soon to dissolve around him.

These greasy Viennese treats flavored with zest of lemon rind were called *Gebackene Mäuse* (Baked Mice), a name derived from the tiny tails sprouted from the globs of dough congealed in boiling oil, which name and notion sent us children into peals of laughter every time our father fried us up a batch. And so, for me, the Île Saint-Louis, that little, mouse-shaped lump of land where mimes, magicians, musicians, pickpockets and puppeteers play the crowd—a pauper's paradise in my father's day, more recently co-opted by sheikhs and erstwhile Russian apparatchiks-turned "insider traders"—and where the exclusive ice cream-confectioner Berthillon dispenses exquisite scoops, will forever be associated with sweetness.

*

I am a French irregular verb. My father sowed the insidious seeds of French syntax in me early on. It was his grown-up pleasure and my childhood chore to have me practice French pronunciation almost as soon as I learned to mouth and mimic English. My ears were receptive, but my mind was lazy. I failed to grasp why these nasally linked syllables mattered so much. French declensions wouldn't help much on the baseball mound. Rolling the lips into a hollow circle to shape a proper *Bon jour* wouldn't buy me a bubble gum or a pretzel stick at Jimmy's Luncheonette. My father lost patience and slapped me when I mispronounced. I protested. But resistance was futile.

In junior high, I was always the best in French, but when at the parents-teachers conference, my father challenged the "very good" as opposed to an "excellent" that Mr. Banks, my Junior High School French teacher, circled on my report card, Mr. Banks shrugged: "Not even Charles De Gaulle deserves an excellent in my book!"

My high school French teacher, Miss Lorenzo, a skinny, tight lipped, mouse-haired, prematurely old matron of indeterminate age who must surely have learned her French at a convent school, unwittingly took us to see the movie "Viva Maria!" directed by Louis Malle, wanting to expose us to things French, but when Brigitte Bardot proceeded to perform a striptease on the silver screen, a scandalized Miss Lorenzo promptly shuffled us ogling adolescent boys out of the cinema in disgust. That and reading "Le Dormeur du Val," a poem by Arthur Rimbaud about a soldier found lying in a field, who, only after the poet discovers a red hole in his head, we realize is dead, are my most vivid memories of French class.

But I do recall having to assume all kinds of contorted positions, the painful polar opposite of stances featured in *The Kama Sutra* (which text I would discover in college), pressed body to body on the subway in the morning rush hour, my wrist thrust into the overhanging strap, hand gripping a French grammar, memorizing my noun declensions and my irregular verbs. And once, arriving late for a first period French exam, on account of a delay on the Canarsie Line (now better known as the L-Train), I remember passing the gauntlet of pigeons positioned on the overhead ledge of the school, when one let drop its liquid payload that landed on my forehead and ran down my left cheek. I wiped myself with a handkerchief in disgust, still muttering French irregular verbs to myself, bravely marched into class, inured but able, scored a perfect one hundred on the test, and have retained a hostility to pigeons ever since.

And so, I graduated high school with the gold medal in French, a tri-color ribbon dangling from the fake gold pin, which Miss Lorenzo proudly attached to my graduation gown, kissing me on both cheeks, the closest I will surely ever come to nomination to the *Legion d'honneur*—which somehow stirred up the memory of the striptease scene in "Viva Maria!", though Miss Lorenzo was definitely no Brigitte Bardot—and which medal I recently rediscovered upon rummaging through old papers and possessions in a desk drawer. (I wonder if wearing the medal and fluttering tri-color ribbon while waiting on line to board an Air France flight might impress the ground crew and merit consideration for an upgrade.)

I started off college as a French major, the favorite of Professor Rothschild, a somewhat more erudite and intellectual, albeit equally tight-lipped and stoic replica of Miss Lorenzo, until I fell from grace. In the final exam she asked for an analysis of one of the works covered in class. I had underlined racy excerpts from *Les Fleurs du Mal* (The Flowers of Evil), by Charles Baudelaire:

> *"C'est l'Ennui! L'oeil chargé d'un pleur involontaire,*
> *Il rêve d'échafauds en fumant son houka.*
> *Tu le connais, lecteur, ce monstre délicat,*
> *—Hypocrite lecteur,—mon semblable,—mon frère!"*

> "It's BOREDOM. Tears have glued its eyes together.
> You know it well, my Reader. This obscene beast
> chain-smokes yawning for the guillotine—you—
> hypocrite Reader—my double—my brother!"[2]

And having taken the scholarly initiative, laudable I thought, of furthermore reading the poet's *Les Paradis Artificiels*, his treatise on the stimulating effects of opium and hashish, and in the undergraduate Romantic mood of the moment, taking what I thought to be his message to heart and mind, smoked a pipe of hash before class, boldly confessing to the fact in perfect French in my blue exam booklet, Professor Rothschild took my bravado as a personal affront and gave me an F. Whereupon I switched my major to English, but thought it advisable to keep my fondness for Coleridge's opium-induced dream poems to myself.

But French profoundly infiltrated my private life. My father would never, alas, live to meet my native-born French wife-to-be, Claudie, whom I met at a party in a state of total intoxication, true to Baudelaire's poetic dictum:

2 English adaption by Robert Lowell

> *"pour ne pas être les esclaves martyrisés du temps, enivrez-vous, enivrez-vous sans cesse de vin, de poésie, de vertu, à votre guise."*
> (so as not to be the martyred slaves of time, get drunk, keep getting drunk on wine, on poetry, on virtue, as you please.)

I managed to charm her in the warp and woof of my slightly slurred irregular French verbs and perfectly declined French nouns; intoxicated state notwithstanding, my sentences held together and actually made seductive sense.[3]

Nor did my father ever live to see the French seeds he planted in my thankless mind bear fruit in the form of our hybrid Franco-American, perfectly bilingual, perfectly cheeky offspring, our daughter Aurélie and son Jacques, walking, talking bundles of Gall, with a twinkle of insouciance, an ironic smile, and emulating Albert Camus, Simone de Beauvoir, Serge Gainsbourg, and countless French rebels with or without a cause, with a cigarette forever riding the lower lip, who correct my gender errors and my wife's occasional English faux pas, and in the way all children do, remind me of my many faults. *Merci, Papa!*

*

It's only *natural*! we Americans maintain to affirm those truths we hold to be self-evident. *C'est bien normal, ça*! (It's normal!) the French insist to substantiate the naked facts at the tip

---

3 Still fond of a drop of spirit on select occasions, years later I identified with a soused breed of spider that lives down under the Chateau de Cognac, in the pit of the former dungeon known as "le Paradis" (Paradise), where the oldest casks of spirit are left to age in a snow-white coat of fungus. Its state revealed in the asymmetrical weave of its web, the spider feeds on insect larvae and watches over the precious stash with a certain sloppy majesty.

of the nose. There is perhaps a certain irony that we Americans should harp on the natural in our Brave New World of artificiality, the home of artificial flavoring and coloring, plastic, MSG, Accent, processed foods, fracking, and Monsanto's genetically engineered blockbuster crops. "All natural ingredients," as per the required marketing etiquette, can be found on the box or flap of most American packaged, i.e. processed foods. Our seemingly limitless "natural resources" are there to be drained dry. *It's only natural* in a country with an elected Congress inclined to gloss over environmental protection.

As for the French *norm*, consider the following definition found on the website about.com:

> "*Normal* is a semi-false cognate. While it can mean 'normal,' it is often used in a more figurative sense, as in 'usual' or 'expected.' For example, the weather is supposed to be clear and sunny all week, but there's a freak rainstorm. One might say: *Ce n'est pas normal*—'That's not right, not what was supposed to happen.'"

French schoolteachers earn their stripes at various *Écoles Normales* (Normal Schools). The French inculcate the *norm* early on in untutored little savages, and the upper echelon of educators, like my wife, are graduated from one of a handful of *Écoles Normales Superieurs* (Superior Normal Schools), whose graduates, the elite *normaliens*, comprise a select pedagogical club of sorts (roughly equivalent to the privileged spawns of the Ivy League, only in France, they pay you to attend) who ascend to leadership positions in which they, in turn, set the new norms. An ordinary person, particularly an American, can sometimes be made to suffer a sense of abnormal ignorance in the company of *normaliens*. It is only normal, I suppose, that, as an American,

I should be held personally accountable for all artificial flavoring and coloring, plastic, MSG, Accent, processed foods, fracking, McDonald's "Happy Meals" and Monsanto's genetically engineered crops, just as I hold the French personally responsible for the dissemination of smelly cheese. Naturally, I protest my innocence. But such protestation of innocence is further proof of a shamefully abnormal ignorance of the norm.

*

Just as geography situates the French hexagon as a natural bridge between the sun-drenched Mediterranean and the chilly gray North Sea, so, too, are the French people, in custom and manner, a hybrid of Latin looseness and Teutonic rigidity. But the formidable bulwark against linguistic corruption upheld by the stiff-lipped members of the Académie Française, the solemn brotherhood of guardians of the language, who collectively comprise a veritable dictionary-dyke in a valiant, albeit vain, attempt to keep the sacred tongue from springing holes, is sabotaged by an unstoppable influx of Americanisms and a seemingly bottomless well of argot and colorful idiomatic expressions, some mentionable in good company, some not.

Loose-tongued on a drop of wine, the poetry comes pouring out. The popular French expression for twilight, for instance, "*entre chien et loup*" (literally: between dog and wolf) perfectly captures the visual drama at the tenuous border between day and night when daylight drops its muzzle of civility and darkness bares its fangs. How Chaplinesque, or rather Jacques-Tatiesque, are the Gallic takes on "to be lost": "*marcher à côté de ses pompes*" (literally, to walk beside one's clodhoppers); and "to be sleepy": "*ne pas avoir les yeux en face des trous*" (literally, not to have your eyes lined up with their slits). How perfectly bobo (Bohemian-Bourgeois) is the inverted, self-mocking snobbery of the tongue-in-cheek term for tap water, "*Château de la Pompe*" (literally: Château Water Fountain). How anti-clerical and positively blasphemous is the French equivalent expression for "not in a million years": "*à la Saint Glin Glin*" (literally, when Saint Glin Glin wills it).

But French curses, insults and idiomatic expressions really let it all hang out with true poetic license. The anodyne Anglo-Saxon nitpicker becomes a "*sodomiseur de lépidoptère*," (sodomite of Lepidoptera), or better yet, "*un enculeur de mouches*" (fly butt-fucker). The French equivalent of the English "looking for a needle in a haystack" is: "*chercher un pet dans une bain à jacuzzi*" (fishing for a fart in a Jacuzzi). More lustfully vulgar still, the French for "Step on it!" is: "*Il faux pas tortiller le cul pour chier droit!*" (Don't wriggle your ass to shit straight!) Or the ultimate scatological French standby for "really having to take a dump": "*avoir le cigarre au bou des lèvres*" (to have a cigar at the tip of your lips). And since we've metaphorically dropped our *culottes*, so to speak, what coarse Anglo-Saxon expression could possibly match the sheer lyric license of the Gallic take on "she's got the hots for you": "*Elle a la moule qui baille*," (literally: Her mussel is yawning for you).

*

And then there's the division of creation by sex. How curious for an American accustomed to a neuter world in which all else outside the "I" is a swathe of "it," to fathom that everything around you is gendered to the French eye. The logic is often perplexing. So, the perennially gray sky (*le ciel*) overhead is a moody old masculine. But the rain (*la pluie*) falls in female tears. The building (*le bâtiment*) you pass on the street is a strapping buck, but the house (*la maison*) is a sleek lady, to which only a privileged few are given the pass code, inviting or forbidding entry. The person (*la personne*) you meet, man or woman, is a female a priori, as is the conglomerate crowd (*la foule*). Bread (*le pain*), most typically in the elongated phallic shape of la baguette, is male, as is wine (*le vin*) and cheese (*le fromage*), the two other staples of the French diet. But the table (*la table*) at which you eat it is a woman. The truck (*le camion*) is a lumbering porter bearing his load. But the car (*la voiture*) is a woman that transports destinies in her metal womb. The same gender divide holds true for French states of mind. Joy (*la joie*) is a she, as is sadness (*la tristesse*). It is as if the world around us, in its stark duality, comprised infinite models or mirrors, constantly instructing us not only in how to behave, how to walk, talk and dress, but also how to think (*la pensée*), thought being female, and dream (*le rêve*), reverie being male. The gender of the French noun, furthermore, affects the adjectives that decorate and adorn it as a kind of costume jewelry and the verbs that manipulate, or rather are manipulated by it.

And what about those gender-bending homonyms, like manly liver (*le foie*) and feminine time—as in how many times —(*la fois*), or the manly mold you bake with (*le moule*) vs. the feminine mussel you buy at market and simmer in white wine (*la moule*)!

In France I walk around in a constant state of hermaphrodite grammatical confusion, my male body (*le corps*) enveloped by my female skin (*la peau*), ignorant of the distinction that every French schoolchild has categorized in the filing cabinet of a male mind (*un esprit*) lodged in the female head (*la tête*).

*

Speaking of gender, every Parisian, and particularly every *Parisienne* is a walking billboard advertising the ever-present possibility of seduction that a walk down a Paris street just might entail.

Mick Jagger may not have managed to find "satisfaction" in London, but if Serge Gainsbourg, the patron saint of '69, with his big nose, stick-out ears and droopy eyes, could bed down BB (Brigitte Bardot), surely you could too—or so the tantalizing legend would have us believe.

My attachment to French gender difference is up close and personal. At the Tuileries Gardens one memorable 14th of July I danced a dizzying *valse musette* with Claudie, the perky petite brunette who would become my wife, faking the steps, though she later convinced me to take dancing lessons for our wedding. I remember exactly the outfit she had on, the cinched yellow polka dot top beneath which her belly button peaked forth, and a short, white, tri-layered skirt that flared up in enticing cascades of cotton, baring leg well above the knee, and her perky brown ponytail that sashayed like the tail of a proud thoroughbred as we whirled about. I remember the rhythmic rippling notes of the accordion played by Aimable Pluchart, better known by his first name Aimable, the legendary French bandleader, already of advanced age back then, but no less lithe and supple, beaming and swaying as he played, hovering above the dusty dance floor on a prefab stage like a puppeteer directing our clip clop with the invisible strings of his music, unabashedly fondling his instrument, as my fingers replayed the melody down the keyboard of Claudie's spine. We swirled in an ocean of bodies, a whirlpool of humanity, when an older man, a fleet-footed hoofer, brashly reached out, plucked my fiancé out of my arms, and spun her round like he was a planet and she was the sun. Whereupon I boiled over with a cocktail of contradictory emotions, burning with jealousy, glowing with pride, seething with heretofore untapped erotic fury whipped up into a virtual frenzy by the ever-accelerating pace of the music. And when at last, after what seemed at the time like an eternity but could only have been a matter of minutes at most, he returned her to my waiting arms with a bow and a wink that betokened both gratitude and regret, my jealousy melted into boundless love leaping from my eyes (*mes yeux*), those masculine orbs, to my beating heart (*mon coeur*), that dumb male muscle, encased in my head (*ma tête*), that feminine lockbox of mind and emotion, for granting me this moment of beatitude.

Meditation in Translation
Transcending Ego and Transmitting Voice[1]

1.

My subject, I should make clear from the start, is not translation per se, but the psychic territory to which translation gives access, and only incidentally, the treasures to be retrieved from frequent forays into that territory.

Jakob Grimm, of Grimms' Fairy Tales fame, suggested the following metaphor to describe both the mundane and the mysterious aspects of this most misunderstood of pursuits. "Whoever has the talent for navigation," he wrote figuratively of the translator, "whoever is able to man a ship and lead it with full sail to the opposite shore, still has to land where the air and the soil are different." And the poet Johann Wolfgng von Goethe, who celebrated that different air and soil in his *West Östlicher Divan*, 1819, discovered a dynamic tension in the commingling of foreign and familiar evident in translation. "Inside it," wrote Goethe, "the coming together of the foreign and the native, the unknown approximation and the known, keep moving towards each other."

As a writer and translator, I am interested above all in tapping that tension, and by assimilating ostensibly alien influences, in uncovering again and again the foreign face hidden by the mask of the familiar, the wet and wormy underside beneath the flat rock of consciousness.

1 This essay was first delivered as a lecture originally delivered under the auspices of the University Professors Program, run by Rosanna Warren, at Boston University, Boston, MA, March 24, 1987, and later published in *Trans-Lit-2*, Vol. XV, No. 2, Autumn 2009

2.

Every time I translate, I take a trip. Equipped with dictionaries, a crude intuition, and the linguistic map of the original text, I forsake the safety of my native English (the glue that binds things to words), and venture out into the fog of intralingual impression, the space between languages, a no man's land much like that strip of barren earth between the borders of neighboring nations. And there I linger a while, inhaling unspoken space. It is the space surrounding words, the tenuous silence that precedes and follows meaning.

To me, an asthmatic author, a man obsessed with breathing, compelled to turn every im-pression into an ex-pression, and thereby to assuage the ever-present fear of suffocation, words are and always will be exhalations burdened with meaning. How I long for the slow and easy breathing that means nothing! The unencumbered respiration we commonly seek on mountain tops and sea sides. Paradoxically, it is this unencumbered breath, this very emptiness that clears the way for the poetic voice.

3.

In *The Problem of Anxiety*, Sigmund Freud characterizes the ego as a kind of psychic organ of resistance. "The ego," he writes, "finds it difficult to consider perceptions and fancies which it had heretofore, as a rule, done its level best to avoid, or to acknowledge impulses that constitute the very antithesis of those which it had formerly thought of as its own."

Ego then, to loosely paraphrase Freud, is the great procrastinator. It clings to consciousness, or rather to self-consciousness, relaxing its vice grip on the lid holding down the repressed strata of the self only by accident, in a joke, or in the safe confines of sleep. It covets cliché, preferring the dull repetition of prescribed patterns of thought to the perils of improvisation.

Translation, an apparently safe compromise between the psychic risks of original composition and the grip of inertia, tricks the ego into lowering its guard—all risk dispelled by the reassuring presence of the original text—just long enough to release the airy impulse of voice. To those intimidated by the prospect of creation, it offers a delimited challenge on the order of a thousand piece puzzle as opposed to the dizzying specter of a blank canvas or an empty page.

Ideally, the translator is pure medium, both in the spiritual sense, as a conduit, and in the mundane sense, as a vehicle of extraneous communication. Part ventriloquist, part dummy, we translators most completely satisfy our purpose when we cease to be, or rather, play at emptiness. Free of all intention other than to follow the prescribed current of the original text, we paddle down foreign rivers and streams in a leaky borrowed craft. Even the oars do not belong to us, and the water we bail out of the hold to stay afloat is "*non-potable,*" a foul tasting, salty brine which, by means of a psychic desalinization process, we must make sweet.

In reality, however, ego clings to the side of the craft with a thousand stubborn tentacles of Angst. And well that cowardly creature should shiver, for what we navigators seek is not smooth sailing, but a confrontation, a head-on collision with our own antithesis, our alter, the "Other" represented by the original author, though not to be confused with him. "Ahoy!" yells the translator-navigator into the fog. "Ahoy!" replies the echo of another voice.

Two processes are here superimposed: the confrontation with an ideal imagined Other, and that with the actual author, with whose reality the translator has no choice but to contend.

4.

Some translators claim it is imperative to be infatuated with an author whose work you set out to translate. This is, in my experience, a romantic fallacy akin to the obligatory starving-in-the-attic-tubercular-bleeding prerequisite for poetry. On the contrary, love tends to blur language, and generally gives rise to an imprecise and fuzzy blubbering in translation. I would go so far as to assert that it helps to feel ambivalent about the author you are translating. A certain degree of repressed animosity serves to temper too much reverence, particularly in the case of dead masters. For in the course of this confrontation with the text, the translator is compelled to attack the original as well as its maker. With Promethean guile, we must inevitably betray its Olympic grandeur, steal its fire, as it were, to render its shimmer. Without that spark—stolen, not borrowed!—without that callous violation, the glow of the original could never survive the vast distance that separates one life and language from another.

And always, living or dead, the author will glance over your shoulder and grumble, in the words of Mr. Elliot: "That is not what I meant at all./That is not it, at all." Often you must turn to that annoying, if authoritative, presence, and respectfully reply: "Shut up, you don't know English!"

For this reason, in any case, I prefer to translate the silent dead, as opposed to the jabbering living. Though even the former do, on occasion, voice posthumous protest. The late great Robert Musil, whose book, *Posthumous Papers of a Living Author* (*Nachlass zu Lebzeiten*) I translated with some success a few years back, appeared to me in a dream, rapping with his impertinent knuckles on the window pane of time. "*Schlamperte Arbeit*! ... Sloppy job!" he chided me in vitriolic Viennese, pointing out a handful of typos in the English.

On another occasion, Herr Goethe himself, whose work I had contracted to translate, "*im Traum*," rang me up very long distance, disturbing my peaceful slumber to inform me that he had known my mother as a young girl in Vienna, and to inquire if he could be of any assistance in my literary career. Unfortunately, the alarm clock rang before he could do much on my behalf—or perhaps he had a hand in arranging for this publication!

5.

In "The Old Man's Toys," remarks presented at the Conference on Literary Translation held in New York City in May 1970, and printed in a volume put out by PEN, the celebrated poet and translator Richard Howard spoke of the translator's "extreme commitment to alterity as playfulness." I cannot find or invent a better phrase to explain the playful thrust of this very serious pursuit.

Translation, I am convinced, best serves all parties concerned: the original author rooted in his linguistic and literary tradition, the target reader ensconced in his own set of cultural conceits, and the translator—if practiced in the spirit of play with all the zeal of a five year old coupled with the intellectual control and literary sensibility of an adult mind.

Consider the life and death resolve with which we all once tiptoed along the line of the sidewalk crack, lest by wavering from our prescribed path we were to jeopardize the tenuous balance of fate and will; or else leaped across each divide, avoiding contact with the crack for blocks on end—"Step on a crack, break your mother's back!" The concentration we demanded of our shaky hearts and limbs was simultaneously serious and whimsical as we plotted our precarious path across the nascent mine fields of the psyche. We were training for future reconnaissance missions. It is that same extended sidewalk crack (its role now filled by the patterned grid of the original text) that I follow religiously when I translate.

But we translators take that childhood challenge one step further. For not only must we tiptoe along the crack of the strange sentiments expressed in foreign syntax without slipping, but we must do so wearing the imagined shoes of the author, while feeling the alien leather chafe against the skin of our own feet. We must, in short, walk the psychic tightrope of split personality, being both ourselves and the imagined other.

It is a peculiar, simultaneously arousing and disturbing sensation to see the world through the eyes of another, to dive into an ocean of alterity, your wetsuit being another person's skin. Inevitably this hand-me-down garment doesn't quite fit. It sags a little, pinches at the midriff, and is frayed at the rib cage where once beat the active heart of another whose sentiments do not necessarily coincide with our own. Reluctantly at first, recalling your parents' sage counsel: "You'll grow into it!," you slip it on for size, and little by little, that strange skin becomes almost indistinguishable from your own—almost, but not quite.

For the game's immediate goal is to re-animate, not the author himself, but the track he lay down: to bring it, not him, to life. Part Orphic descent, part graverobbery, translation calls for cold-blooded precision, as opposed to reckless abandon.

For once fished out of its native pond, the text must be kept alive. We can't let it die the miserable wriggling death of poetic asphyxiation. We must coax and pamper it, tickle it to life, thrill it with the tongue of an adroit wooer, and only then will the essence of the original reveal itself, reclining naked and prone on the clean white sheet. A bad translation is one that fails to let the reader inhale even a faint trace of its seductive scent, the same scent that first lured the translator to make his or her rude advances.

6.

A further complication suggests itself here. Ought we translators to render or exclude the sense of wonderment, that luminous mingling of strangeness and familiarity that first attracted us to the foreign text, a glow not indigenous to the text itself, but inscribed in our perception of it. To render that exotic halo is to add something extraneous to the original, and so to betray the authenticity of the text. To exclude it, however, is to deny the particularity of the translator's identity as a reader, and thus to suppress the specific passion of appreciation. Good translators, prestidigitators par excellence, must combine both: we must preserve the particularity of the original, but also the tinge of that which drew us to it, as well as the infinitesimal space in between. I think of the crack Michelangelo left between the celestial forefinger of God and the shaky finger of man, a crack across which the spark of creation can fly.

I am not here implying that the translator's role is identical to that of the creator of the text, but merely that it demands a complementary reverence. Creators, strictly speaking, we are not. The creative authority, the authorization for the words and spirit of the original belong to the author, living or dead, and yet an effective translation calls for a creative re authorization of the original which only the poetically inclined translator can offer.

Translation as I see it is not an art per se, but an artfully practiced craft, whereby I embrace the ambiguous double meaning of "artful" and "craft," words that encompass both skill and guile.

It is for me a prelude to creation.

7.

The language that for me facilitates a head-on entry into a sustained state of alterity is German, it being quite literally my mother tongue, the language I spoke with my mother. English, on the other hand, the language in which I feel both grammatically and culturally more secure, it being the language of my adult coming to consciousness, affords me a safe haven. But safety has its price. Security, the realm of the right hand, knows nothing of the shaky thrill of the left. The two languages and all that they connote lie side by side in my psyche, each washing up strange debris onto the shore of the other, alternately adding to and eroding each other's territory as the tide shifts. There are other tributary currents, French, for instance, learned later in life, and thus the bearer of its own set of associations in my private geography. But the primary oceans, my Atlantic and Pacific, as it were, remain English and German.

8.

The German terms correlative to translation, "*übersetzen*" or "*übertragen*" suggest a bringing or carrying something over from an elsewhere to a here. What do we carry over when we translate? The question harkens back to the traveler's dilemma: what to bring back from a trip abroad to the folks back home. What souvenirs and trinkets will best exemplify our experience of that other place? But gifts weigh heavy and must, of necessity, be restricted to the portable minimum, a tiny, albeit optimally representative, sampling of all that had to be left behind. Additional technical problems arise. For the process of transport involved in translation likewise entails a displacement. Thus not only must the packaging be strong enough to weather the upsets of handling, but a new space, an adequate setting must be readied for its arrival. Concepts and images brought home from an exotic elsewhere tend to be fragile and demand special care.

9.

Franz Rosenzweig, the German-Jewish theologian and philosopher (known for, among other works, his poetic co-translation, with

Martin Buber, of the first five books of the Hebrew Bible into German), acknowledged the simultaneous impossibility and necessity of translation. "To translate," he wrote, "is to serve two masters. Which is why nobody can do it. Which is why it is, in practice, everybody's task, like all the other things nobody is able to do in theory." He goes on to present the universal mundane model of this impossible pursuit. "Whoever speaks, translates," said Rosenzweig,

> "from his opinion into the presupposed understanding of another, and not the understanding of a nonexistent general 'other' either, but of this very concrete other he sees in front of him and whose eyes light up or fall shut, depending on how he translates. Whoever hears, translates words that sound in his ears into his intellect, that is, practically speaking, into the language of his mouth."

The British Catholic theologian and literary thinker Walter J. Ong plumets kindred metaphysical depths in his essay "Voice as Summons for Belief," in which Father Ong contends:

> "Every human word implies not only the existence at least in the imagination of another to whom the word is uttered, but it also implies that the speaker has a kind of otherness within himself ... The human speaker can speak to the other precisely because he himself is not purely self, but is somehow also other. His own 'I' is haunted by the shadow of a 'thou' which it can never exorcize."

Here I return to a conceptual crossroads passed early on in these remarks, that point at which I pretended, for simplification sake, that the imagined 'other' and the actual other/author parted ways. In fact, a far more complex split occurs in translation.

The translator coopts the voice of an actual other/author to rouse the heretofore suppressed 'other' in himself, and in the process, breathes new life into borrowed words. A strange communion binds him to the text, and through it, to its author: for in translating, the translator becomes, not the author, but the author's 'other,' the speaking ear to his listening mouth, their interlocking souls engaged in intimate dialogue. Or, as the German Romantic poet Novalis described the "true translator must be the poet's poet."

10.

Ideally, I translate texts that speak to me directly, and of which I have the sense that, but for the constraints of time and space that separate their original matrix from my mouth, the words flow easily. Such was the case some years ago when I happened to pick up a little book by the Austrian novelist Robert Musil, flipped through the pages and came upon a short prose text entitled "*Hellhörigkeit*," which virtually translated itself in my mind as I read it—becoming "Clearhearing" in the English.

And the woman Musil addressed, listening to and recording the sounds of her undressing—"... all the walking up and down, in this corner of the room, in that..."—became my wife, though I was not married at the time. And now that I am married, and have published my translation, that woman is all the more a vision of my wife.—"Then I recognize the familiar sound of hair being undone and brushed. Then the swirls of water in the sink," wrote Musil, listening intently in a hotel room in pre War Vienna, as I have done on many a night in New York, "waiting for you."

Such a perfect commingling of the spirit is, of course, rare, and a translator is forced to tackle many texts with which at first he feels no particular affinity. But such are the limitations of life, as opposed to literature.

11.

In an interview given shortly before her death, the Belgian-born Francophone author, Marguerite Yourcenar, the first woman and first foreigner to be named a member of the Academie Francaise, who ended her days in a little cottage in the State of Maine, whose impressive opus includes novels, short stories, essays, plays, poetry, and many translations, was challenged to justify the unity of her work. "For me, it all comes down to the same thing," she said, eluding the imposition of a label.

> "Whether a decent verse has been written by me or by Cavafy makes no difference. I've often said this and it's not a paradox. In any case, when one writes one is always translating. When I try to describe a character, my description is based on an image already partly shaped by the words present in my mind. I then have to put it down on paper in a way that the reader can understand. It's a translation, it's not at all the primary image in my head. I try my best to render it as well as possible, but it's only the translation of fluid thought, black marks on white paper. As for the name at the bottom of the page, that is not important at all."

Though my own spirit is not generous enough to completely deny the demands of ego and do without a byline, I concur with the thrust of Ms. Yourcenar's words.

And whether I happen to be the author, or whether he/she serves me as a kind of understudy or standby for a submerged side of myself, makes no difference in any case to the reader. Voice is what we're all after, a rendering on paper of what Yourcenar called "fluid thought."

12.

So much for my mediation in translation. Let me dwell no more upon it. For to speak of translation is in a sense to dissect it. It is to unravel a ball of thread intricately wound, to shine a rude beam on the work of the poetic bee, a creature that prefers the darkness of the honeycomb. To speak of translation, as to speak of anything, is to destroy its aura. But we live, do we not, by the cruel axe of consciousness, which every morning of our life severs the head of our nightly reveries, translating the darkness into light.

Talking in Tongues: Translating Others and Myself[1]

The celebrated neonatologist and child development expert, Dr. T. Berry Brazelton, believes that rudimentary expressions of displeasure, the precursor of speech, begin with the first howl of the newborn—and even before that, in the preconscious state of the womb, where, as my wife would readily confirm, fetuses kick up a storm in response to various stimuli, translating their malaise—as do we ever after, restless homo sapiens struggling to communicate the existential shock of being and becoming. A recent study conducted in Germany and France found that newborns wail differently, French babies with a rising pitch, their German counterparts with a falling tone, each mimicking the speech pattern of its mother. So, in a sense, it seems that we are all translators from the start.

*

From the first whoop, we translate what's inside and wants out. Those of us, like myself, driven to keep on translating in adulthood are afflicted with a profound confusion—both psychic and linguistic—which we seek to assuage, if not relieve, by the act of translation. The translator is a two-tongued virtuoso on the vocal cords, whose tendencies toward duality are channeled and just barely kept under control.

*

1 This essay was first presented, in my capacity as Holtzbrinck Fellow at the American Academy in Berlin, Germany, on February 9, 2010

Writing and translation have been intertwined for me from the start, linked strands in the double-helix of my DNA. Translation is part of my morning ritual, a verbal splash of cold water on the sleep-soaked psyche to stimulate the synaptic sparks and bridge the shaky divide between dreaming and waking self. If properly approached, giving oneself wholly over to the Zen rigor of this selfless task, it stills the Angst, loosens the stranglehold of ego, and makes way for the transmission of voice. In preparation for which, I pull from their dusty perch on the window ledge my battered green "New" Wildhagen's German-English Dictionary (vintage 1965), my old blue Oxford Universal and faded red Roget's International Thesaurus, Third Edition. These are the tools of my trade, my compass, barometer and monkey wrench. Their spines are broken, their bindings barely held in place by yellowed packing tape. Some pages are loose, double-dog-eared, torn and taped. But I could not imagine replacing them. Security blankets are, by definition, ratty and frayed—which is not to say I never cut my tongue on their pages.

*

How is it that my dear old Wildhagen's—a gift of my late father, compiled by Drs. Wildhagen, of the University of Kiel, and Héraucourt, of the University of Königsberg—keeps falling open at the word "*Jüdeln,*" defined as "to speak like a Jew"? And that my left eye invariably wanders to the bottom of the preceding page, where I read and re-read: "*Jude:*" 1. Jew, (slang) Jid; (American slang) kike—"*der Ewige*" ~ the Wandering Jew—"*haust du meinen Juden, hau ich deinen Juden*—neutrally translated by Messrs. Wildhagen and Héraucourt as "measure for measure, tit for tat"—though literally, a bit more problematic: you beat my Jew, I'll beat yours; 2. (figurative) usurer,*—für das Gewesene gibt* *der Jude nichts*—(for the past the Jew does not care a fig) …"—surely a misnomer for the history-obsessed people of the book. These are loaded definitions, to say the least!

*

You will have gathered by now that my attachment to translation, more specifically, to German-English translation, is not a light-hearted matter.

*

At some point in the evolution of our species, the tongue, that molder and mover of edible mulch and shaper of shrieks and hollers, metamorphosed into a rudder of utterance.

The Judeo-Christian tradition postulates a garrulous godhead muttering it all into being: "And God said: 'Let there be light,' And there was light."

Next step, name giving: "And God called the light Day, and the darkness He called Night."

Then man appears on the scene, as a vain afterthought: "Let us make man in our image, after our likeness …"—and the birth of human language, the business of naming, follows as a re-creative act: "… and whatever the man would call every living creature, that was to be the name thereof."

This is Mankind's stage debut as the interpretor-translator of divine creative intent.

"And the whole earth was of one language and of one speech." the Old Testament testifies.

And thereafter, following the first documented homicide, alienation sets in, guilt being the sublimated source of culture—as Dr. Freud will later remind—mankind's restless drive ultimately coalescing into the ill-fated building and subsequent downing of the Tower of Babel, the World Trade Center of antiquity:

> "And the Lord came down to see the city and the tower, which the children of men builded. And the Lord said: 'Behold, they are one people, and they have all one language; and this is what they begin to do ... Come let us go down, and there confound their language, that they may not understand one another's speech ... Therefore was the name of it called Babel."

Translators have been doing their best to set things straight ever since. And every time we appear to get close to a consensus, linguistic chaos stirs up trouble again, Ugarit locks horns with Cuneiform, Hieroglyphs wrestle with Hebrew characters, Urdu with Bengali. More recently, Arabic and English have been having it out—no doubt, in part, on account of the conceptual head-on collision of two mindsets moving in opposite directions, reality read from right to left vs. left to right—and the tower came tumbling down again. The Western World forgets that Arabic, the language of Bin Laden, was also the tongue in which the Classical Greek and Latin learning of the Occident was sheltered and protected during Europe's Dark Ages, waiting to be reawakened from centuries of hibernation by Hebrew and Arabic linguists in Andalusia and other Arab lands.

I myself was deeply troubled at the attack—conquest or liberation, whatever you prefer to call it—of Basra, the birthplace and hometown of my childhood hero, Sinbad, whose sense of adventure and supple spirit have guided me through life:

> "I rendered thanks to Allah for rescuing me from my ordeal, and soon my past sufferings were no more than half-forgotten dreams."

It's a utopian pipedream, no doubt, but what a wonderful thing it would be if the high commands of would-be warring powers were compelled by international law to translate, read and comment on each other's literary classics before taking up arms! It might avert some misunderstandings.

I think of the French film "Joyeux Nöel!" based on an actual incident in World War I, in which battle-weary battalions of the French and German armies heard each other singing carols on a cold Christmas Eve. Each side responding in their own tongue, battling troops by day, they temporarily suspended hostilities and crawled out of the tenuous shelter of their trenches to celebrate with songs (in whose ubiquitous tunes they found commonality), and had, thereafter, to be replaced by fresh recruits, as these "tainted" conscripts refused to fire at fellow humans with whom they'd harmonized.

I think of my maternal and paternal grandfathers conscripted by the Hapsburg Austro-Hungarian Kaiser, the one as a cook, the other as a military engineer, to battle it out with the great-uncles of my French wife, men I never met who fell at Verdun and the Marne, their memory reduced to names on a provincial *Monument au Morts*. And I cannot help but wonder if it wouldn't have been better for all concerned to remain anonymous, grow old and hoarse singing together.

*

As the first-generation American-born son of Austrian immigrants of Jewish extraction, I have always felt a bit culturally off-kilter and linguistically befuddled. And though I developed early on an ear for language, and can pick up a few words and start talking wherever I go, I have forever forfeited the native speaker's confidence in the holding power of that intangible glue that binds things to words.

*

English, as I wrote in a previous essay, "was the public channel of communication at school and on the street, a peppermint tongue that stings and excites. German, all chocolaty, viscous and sweet, was our private funnel of intimacy, the dialect of our tiny city-state of five afloat in the teeming megalopolis. English meant business, sharpened Number-2 pencils, white shirt and tie; commerce: 'I'll trade you a Roger Maris for a Mickey Mantle!'; and diplomacy: 'If you don't, I won't be your best friend anymore!'

> "German coddled, cursed and cajoled. My late father fondly referred to his belly as his '*Backhändlfriedhof*' (his fried chicken cemetery), ceremoniously, properly, with knife and fork, dissecting and laying to rest in its round perimeter many a South Jersey pullet. We children were his '*Affengesindel*' (his monkey mob). On some days, depending on his mood, we were dubbed '*Affengesichter*' (monkey faces), on others '*Arschgesichter*' (ass-faces), '*Arscherln*' (little asses) for short, or, simply '*Scheisserln*' (little shitters). But none of these apparent imprecations, softened with a wink and a smile into paternal terms of endearment, were translatable in public. And I'm quite sure that my little playmates would have been horrified to fathom just what my father called us—though, no doubt, the sons and daughters of the Sicilians, Irish and Poles down the block had their own untranslatable equivalents."

*

My father qualified as "*verwortackelt*," by which he meant muddled, any dense or puffed-up pronouncements or turns of phrase. I can't find the word "*verwortackelt*" in my German dictionary and will never know for certain if it is of German, Viennese, or Yiddish derivation, or a term of his own coining. But it perfectly bespeaks my complex attachment to the German language, a "*verwortackelte*" twisted business of never-ending sentences in search of a verb.

*

For me, the big abstractions, like "Liebe" (love), "Traum" (dream) and "Tod" (death), will always resonate in German and somehow fall flat in English. The English word "remembrance" has a vaguely vulgar ring, like groping around in the flea market of the mind and subsequently reassembling the cracked and broken knickknacks; whereas the German word "Erinnerung," literally "internalization," raises the conceptual bar, lifting those haphazard knickknacks to precious antiques. Which brings to mind a lovely line of occasional verse by the poet Goethe:

> *"Was der Mensch als Gott verehrt,*
> *Ist sein eigenstes Innere herausgekehrt."*

Prosaically rendered: What man reveres as God is his own inwardness turned outward. Between mundane "remembrance" and godly "Erinnerung," avowed atheist though I be, I go for Goethe's sense of the godly. So at times, every second word I utter in English sounds like a bad translation.

*

Talk about feeling linguistically and culturally off-kilter. In a creative writing class in college, the teacher made me a laughing stock, because in that sexually liberated era, I had never uttered and could not bring myself to say the English word "penis," and still thought of and called that tingling appendage my "*Schwofferl*" (little tail), as it was euphemistically referred to in the family lingo.

*

Sometimes, indeed, I doubt my own identity. Am I myself, or a blatant case of identity theft, a ventriloquist or a ventriloquist's dummy? Are the words I utter my own or is my subconscious merely taking dictation in a secret code and automatically translating the original before I wake? It's a very American dilemma, shared by the descendants of the slaves shipped over from Africa, the Chinese coolies who came to build the railroad, the Swedes who came to cut the timber, the Chicanos still picking grapes in California, and more than likely a couple of listeners here today. To this day, I often feel like one of those plump, round, hand-painted, Russian, wooden Martryuschka dolls, with German imbedded in my English, Yiddish hidden inside the German, Hebrew pulsing in the Yiddish, and the universal cry of the newborn echoing within.

*

I am quite convinced that Dr. Brazelton is right and that it's the half-remembered sounds muttered by the mother's tongue and filtered through our burgeoning consciousness that underlie and inform our tenuous grasp on reality.

*

In Freiburg, in the Black Forest, where I spent a year, 1973-74, on a Fulbright Fellowship studying German fairy tales, reflecting on "Hansel and Gretel" and the other cruelly enticing narratives I'd been raised on, I fathomed that we all have our own witches and demons to turn tables on and toss into the oven, and had best be quick and nimble about it, since the same ovens that bake gingerbread can also be used to bake children.

And then and there in Germany, in a state of psycholinguistic inversion—my private family tongue having reverted into the tongue of public discourse, and English pressed into private status—I first began to write and translate in earnest.

*

In a bookstore in Freiburg I happened to pluck a slender volume off the shelf, *Nachlass zu Lebzeiten*, by a certain Robert Musil, of whom I hadn't heard at the time. Its narrative nuggets spoke to me as few texts had before. Here was a compact prose that combined the abstract and the concrete, the metaphysical and the mundane, the cerebral and the emotional in a delicious mix, in sentences replete with grammatical subordination and pickled in philosophical Schnapps, in which Aesop meets Nosferatu, and the physical suddenly goes meta—as if, for the edification of imagined progeny, Kant himself got trapped in the telling of a Grimm fairy tale, never getting beyond the once upon a time.

Some years later, I picked that little book up again and on a whim began to translate it.

And though it took a while to make its way into print, my English version, *Posthumous Papers of a Living Author*, became something of a literary bestseller. First published in 1988 as Volume One of the Eridanos Library, in Hygiene, Colorado; reissued in 1995 by Penguin 20th-century Classics, Penguin UK; and yet again in 2006, in a third edition, by Archipelago Books, in New York; and excerpted in 2010 in the selection *Flypaper*, by Penguin Mini-classics, my translation was, I am proud to say, referred to in one review as "a classic in its own right."

But it was not my first published translation.

*

My first foray into the ambiguous terrain of translation proved part Orphic underworld descent, part grave robbery, calling all the moral and ethical issues of the pursuit into question.

In 1974, thanks to another fellowship, this one from the Thomas J. Watson Foundation, I traveled to Vienna and Eastern Europe to revisit the unhappy history that sent my parents packing. I visited the sites of the Nazi concentration camps and contacted and interviewed survivors in several countries. A question troubled me throughout my research, and led indirectly to my first halting attempt at translation. What room if any, I wondered, was there for art on the threshold of death? Do poetry, painting and song constitute a superfluous indulgence, mere costume jewelry, or a vital component of human life essential to the survival of the species? Did the voice go on singing in the shadow of the ovens?

And then I met and interviewed the late Aleksander Kulisiewicz, himself a survivor of Sachsenhausen Concentration Camp, in the Berlin district of Oranienburg, a man who had memorized hundreds of poems and songs in the course of his incarceration—some of his own creation, others composed and sung to him for "safe keeping" by those who knew their fate was sealed. Kulisiewicz committed himself for the remainder of his life to sing those songs to audiences around the world. A few years before his death, in 1982, I helped arrange for his visit to the United States, where, together, we produced an album entitled *Songs from the Depths of Hell*, (New York: Folkways, 1979; reissued Washington D.C.: Smithsonian Folkways, 1993), including a booklet of liner notes and lyrics, with English and the original language side by side—my first published translations.

*

The interviews I conducted, mostly in German, a few in French, with aging survivors of concentration camps then living in Austria, Israel, France, Canada and Poland, now comprise the "Peter Wortsman Collection of Oral History" at the U.S. Holocaust Memorial Museum in Washington D.C. But having conducted these interviews, I did not know what to do with them. They were too hot to handle.

Some 24 years later I started having nightmares in which my respondents, most since passed away, appeared to me and asked what I'd done with their words.

And since, after various futile attempts at gainful employment I settled on interview journalism as my bread and butter job, I decided to liberate the voices on those tapes. So I transcribed and translated them, not knowing why or to what end.

As transcriber-translator-adaptor of this material assembled from tape and memory, I had the eerie experience of serving as a kind of medium and middle-aged secretary to my 23 year-old self, picking up where they and he left off. The interchange recorded on tape was painful to revisit, painful as much for my interlocutors' merciless bluntness as for the insufficiency of my response and the time it took me to make something of it. And as I pored over the translated transcripts, the voices congealed into the stuff of a play, "The Tattooed Man Tells All," a one-man show for a man and a marionette, first presented as a staged reading by the Total Theater Lab at NYU's Fales Library and published in 2000, in the literary journal *text(e)*, in Toronto.[2]

*

I would like to mention another translation-related literary project whose seed grew out of my English rendering of 16th-century German Humanist Johannes Reuchlin's landmark call for religious tolerance, *Ratschlag ob man den Juden alle ire Bücher nemmen, abthun und verbrennen soll (Recommendation Whether to Confiscate, Destroy and Burn All Jewish Books)*, which helped prevent the burning of the Talmud and other Hebrew books in Germany in 1510. The text had never before been translated into English, and its appearance as a slender volume put out by Paulist Press, in 2000, sparked a multi-disciplinary symposium which I co-organized that same year at NYU's Deutsches Haus.

But the story with its colorful cast of characters would not let go of my imagination.

A play somehow assembled itself, a kind of re-translation of history for the stage, though it took me years to shape and chisel the script into performable form. Directed by Lucinda Kidder, "Burning Words" was premiered by the Hampshire Shakespeare Company in 2006 at the Northampton Center for the Arts in Northampton, Mass. My script was subsequently translated into German by Peter Torberg under the title "*Wo man*

2 "The Tattooed Man Tells All" was first produced in its entirety by the Silverthorne Theater Company, directed by Ellen Kaplan, starring Keith Langsdale, at the Hawks and Reed Performing Arts Center, Pushkin Studio, in Greenfield, Mass., in 2018; and in a German translation as "Der Tätowierte Mann," by Dr. Karin Rausch, and directed by Kevin Barz, at the Deutsches Theater, in Göttingen, Germany, in 2021, where it ran for a record eight months. The play was published in a bilingual English-German edition by Palm Art Press, in Berlin, in 2024.

Bücher verbrennt ... Reuchlins Streit um das jüdische Schrifttum," and produced and published by the Theater Ensemble of the Kulturhaus Osterfeld, under the direction of Reinhard Kölmel, in 2014.

*

Always in advance of the writing, I cleare my throat and gargle with translations.

Among other texts, I translated Adelbert von Chamisso's black comic classic, *Peter Schlemiel,* about a man who sells his shadow to the devil. That surreal 19th-century novella (a favorite of Italo Calvino's) was, incidentally, also an inspiration for Barrie's stage pay, "Peter Pan," which begins, as you may remember, by Peter chasing his lost shadow and asking Wendy to sew it back on.

Chamisso was a French aristocrat who, as a child, escaped the Reign of Terror and ended up in a military academy in Berlin. A reluctant soldier, he preferred the pen to the sword. And one day, recuperating from a nervous breakdown brought on in part by Napoleon's declaration that any Frenchman found in the enemy forces would be shot on sight without a trial, he stumbled and stuttered onto his literary voice in German, his adopted tongue.

In my introduction to that translation, I coined the term "lingovert," to refer to those writers who discover their literary voice in another language. Lingoverts, those blessed honeybees of culture, are more widespread than one might imagine. Their ranks include the likes of Joseph Conrad, the Polish seaman-turned novelist, who wrote in his third tongue; Isaac Dinesen, the Danish baroness and planter turned English author; Samuel Becket, Fernando Arrabal, Vladimir Nabokov, et al. The subject continued to pique my imagination.

*

In the maverick film "My Dinner with André," by French film director Louis Malle, another late onset lingovert who pivoted from French to English, one of the protagonists makes reference to a monastery in Scotland in which ritual prescribes that everything be done with the left hand. Having just then, coincidentally, broken the middle finger of my right hand, I conducted a series of experiments tapping what I call "the left-handed consciousness." I started by doodling cartoons, the limiting factor of which was that they had, of necessity, to be drawn with the left hand. For some reason I found myself ascribing German captions.

*

These succinct captions later sprouted into short dark tales, the English adaptations of which found their way into my first collection of short fiction *A Modern Way To Die*, published in 1991.

*

What an unexpected thrill it was years later, when, on the urging of a German friend, Frederick Lubich, Professor of German Emeritus at Old Dominion University, in Norfolk, Virginia, I dug up the German original versions of a few of these stories—versions I had previously viewed as disposable, the way a photographer views his negative or a sculptor his slip mold, and had consigned to the bottom of a drawer—dusted them off and submitted them to the Colorado-based German literary review *Translit-2*, and proceeded, not only to publish them, but also to win a literary prize.

*

The little child does not immediately grasp the meaning of all that it blabbers. The words, not wholly formed, still half-belong to the realm of the scream; they are the component parts of a shaky bridge between the unspeakable and the spoken and, so, have more in common with whining and grumbling than with grammatically prescribed speech; and, nevertheless, for that very reason, express something otherwise unutterable. For a middle-aged writer to have reached the beginner's stage in another language, after many years of plodding in English, is a bit like having finally dug down to the bottom of the playground sand pit in New York and come out alive and kicking in Beijing.

*

In his classic work, *Major Trends in Jewish Mysticism*, Gershon Scholem makes reference to an old adage: "whoever is full of himself, has no room for God." Translating helps me to empty myself out, dump the ballast, as it were, and if the wind is right, to permit the voice to sing and my soul to soar.

The Converted Tongue[1]

Where from? The womb. Where to? The tomb.

Human life plays itself out as an infinite number of variations on the same old theme hummed to kill time on a one-way commute. If there is a true native tongue it can only be the howl and holler of the newborn and the last gasp and death rattle of the soon to be silent. No translation necessary. From Cincinnati to Siberia, from Brooklyn to Burundi, people get the picture.

Dialects do however differ along with the lay of the land, and if you want to get a good meal you have to know how to ask for it, which is why most people prefer to stay put. There's a comfort in familiar syllables, something akin to the nursling's acquired knowledge of tit lingo—his second tongue. For "Mama!" is, after all, not a primal scream, but a calculated, response-oriented clamor, and by association, the name of the tropical island with its twin volcanic peaks on and off which little darling lives. The difference between "Waawaa!" and "Mama!" is a recapitulation of the two types of language in Genesis--: the primary celestial invocation: "And God said, Let there be light;" and the secondary human denomination: "and whatever Adam called every living creature, that was the name thereof." It's that second-degree nicknaming function that got screwed up along with the blueprints of Babel.

*

Where was I? Oh yes, I was going to welcome you all to this symposium—the first of its kind, I believe—to consider the unique contribution of the "lingovert" writer to international letters.

1 This essay was first presented as introductory remarks at "The Converted Tongue: A Symposium on Literature in a Second Language," which I organized at La Maison Française, at New York University, NYC, Nov. 18, 1994.

But what, you may ask, is a "lingovert?"

I can see several of you squirming in your seat, worrying lest the term be casually dropped with a savvy wink at your very next cocktail party—"Did you know, Samuel Beckett was a 'lingovert'!?"—and not being privvy to its meaning, suspecting a reference to some abnormal sexual inclination you missed in your cursory adolescent under-the-covers flashlight reading of Havelock Ellis or Kraft-Ebbing, you are forced to fake it.—"Beckett a lingovert!—*Sans blague?!*"

A cursory list of classic and contemporary cases might help shed light on the phenomenon.

Charles D'Orléans, William Beckford, Giovanni Jacopo Casanova, Adelbert von Chamisso, Joseph Conrad, Isak Dinesen, Tristan Tzara, Vladimir Nabokov, Arthur Koestler, Fernando Arrabal, E.M. Cioran, Julian Green, Elsa Triolet, Jorge Semprun, Jerzy Kosinski, Jakov Lind, Eva Hoffmann, Billy Wilder, Chinua Achebe, Andrei Codrescu, Charles Simic, Raymond Federman, Marianne Hauser, Ursule Molinaro…

You still need a definition?

Alright. A lingovert writer is one who discovers and mines the jewels of his or her literary voice in a second language. (In Conrad's case, it was actually a third language—but who's counting?)

Again, I can sense the squirming. This time it's the nitpickers objecting to crossed categories and incongruities in the list. Nabokov, you insist, had a British nanny and grew up speaking English, along with his Russian, German and French, which ought to disqualify him. Roumanians like Tzara and Cioran come from a romanic culture, and are, therefore, predisposed to French. Achebe, I hear you argue, opted for the Colonial English he learned in school, as opposed to his native Ibo, to reach a wider audience. Wilder didn't have much of a choice if, as a refugee Viennese German-Jewish director, he wanted to make movies in Hollywood.

Alright so the category "lingovert" is bursting at the seams, its implications spilling across border turfs from comparative literature (the very core of which it constitutes) into psycholinguistics, sociology, politics and history, already making a mess of itself. But what a rich and fertile mess it is!

Let us follow then the restless hegira of that literary "foreign legion," comprising uprooted aristocrats and paupers, seafarers, soldiers of fortune, adventurers, itinerant intellectuals, and refugees of every ilk who, for reasons that run the gamut from whimsy to necessity, hip-hop across linguistic and geopolitical borders. Who are they, these cultural amphibians, these ambassadors at large, who, lacking the special parking privileges and legal immunity of the acknowledged diplomatic corp, have no choice but to blend in with the host culture and risk a violation of the rules? License plates and passports can be forged. Facelifts are all too common nowadays. But these daredevils take exile to the limit, and shed not only the outward trappings of national affiliation, but also that most intimate I.D., the very syllables of self!

"... if I had not written in English I would not have written at all," asserts Conrad.

"I don't think in any language. I think in images," claims Nabokov.

Says Triolet: "I write with my authentic accent, it's in the character of my writing, in my style, in my madness: madness also has a nationality."

Asked why he wrote in French, Beckett teases: "*Parce qu'en français c'est plus facile d'écrire sans style.*" ("Because in French it's easier to write without style.")

What effect does such a sustained literary stunt have on the stuntman and his spectators? Does it strengthen or destroy a sense of self if the self becomes another? Does it confirm or call into question our certainties and *idées fixes* if the glue that binds things to words is dissolved? How long can you cling to petty prejudice if you recognize the stranger in the mirror? Can it be that in embracing verbal alienation, Conrad, Beckett, Nabokov and company are speaking a new world language, leading the way to a truly global culture, and ultimately taking us back before the Tower of Babel came tumbling down?

As to the formulation of the concept for which I coined the term "lingovert," please permit me a personal reflection.

I am the child of wanderers, Austrian-Jewish refugees who fled their native Vienna—a city once as dear to them as New York (blessed Babylon!) is to me. My father was hexalingual, equally conversant in German, French, English, Italian, Spanish, and Portuguese, not to speak of Latin, Greek and Hebrew, and the Turkish and Arabic he was studying in his shortlived retirement before he died. In England, where my parents spent the War years, my father mastered the King's English to such an extent that when a colleague at work complained of "those damn refugees taking our jobs," he smiled and said: "I know, I'm one of them." In America, he skillfully and convincingly peppered his office English with baseball metaphors, though he had never, to my knowledge, set foot in a ballpark. These were no mere charades, but rather the verbal accoutrements of personae he could slip on and into, and which subsequently proved inseparable from himself—or should I say, him-*selves*?

Having grown up with German as my first language, I am heir to my father's benign cultural schizophrenia, a precious gift my French wife and I are taking pains to pass on in a different form (that is, in French) to our bilingual bi-cultural children. My father's son, I can land in a foreign place and rapidly appropriate a core vocabulary of 20 some odd pivotal words and start talking. To me, languages are made to be deployed, lumps, bumps and all.

I have not always been comfortable with my linguistic split, a personality divided by and between English, German and French. For the longest time, I felt as though my voice and the words I uttered were not really my own, and it may well be that the determined effort to clarify, focus, and yes, to celebrate the stereophonic nature of my thinking is at least one of the factors in my becoming a writer.

Whereas English, the language I learned in school and on the street, is undoubtedly my primary multi-purpose vernacular for calculating, cursing and cajoling; and French (the language I speak at home with my wife and children) is my domestic lingua franca for the mundane and the intimate; German, the dialect of childhood, remains my true mother tongue, the language I still speak with my mother and in which I think most emotionally.

The problem I face as a writer is how to combine these various strands of self and weave them into a single cohesive whole.

My early attempts to write in English, though syntactically correct, seemed somehow flat, omitting much, emoting little. It was during a year abroad in Freiburg, Germany, that I dusted off my German and began to play with its literary possibilities. A subsequent year in Vienna and two years of graduate study in the German Department at New York University further reinforced my sense of the German literary tradition.

And so I began to experiment.

On a whimsy, partially inspired by Louis Malle's film "My Dinner with André," in which reference is made to a monastery in Scotland where all is done with the left hand, I drew left-handed doodles and cartoons and invariably found myself writing the captions in German.

Little by little, the cartoons shrank and the captions grew in length, until one day, I wrote an odd little tale in German, "*Der Vogelmann,*" ("The Birdman"), a story so unsettling that it frightened and embarrassed me. It was too hot to handle. But when I cooly translated the words into English, it was as if I had developed the negative of an illicit snapshot of a heretofore off-limits corner of my psyche. Other texts composed in like manner followed: "*Stadtbild*" ("Cityscape"), "*Der Milchmann Kommt Nicht Mehr*" ("The Milkman Isn't Coming Anymore"), "*Der Zigarettenfresser*" ("The Cigarette Swallower"), and "*Das Haus der Fantasie*" ("The House of Phantasy")—the latter first draft of which I originally wrote in German, transformed and published in English, subsequently supervising its re-translation by the Swiss writer Jürg Laederach back into German, for publication in the German literary journal *Schreibheft.*

Is it a coincidence that my first book of fiction, *A Modern Way To Die*, was selected by Thomas Thornton, the German editor of a German-owned American publisher, Fromm Publishing International?

The experiments continue, and I have more recently ventured into French as the source language of a series of prose fragments subsequently published in English.[2]

Am I, by my own definition, a lingovert? Yes and no.

I publish primarily in English and there is little on the surface to distinguish my sentences from those of any other American-born author. Yet the syntax is ever so slightly eccentric and the inspiration distinctly transatlantic.

My private poetics might well be summed up by these lines from a prose poem I originally composed in French:

2 I published the original French version of a selection of these prose poems titled "Sélection insomniaque pour une rêve party, a dossier presented by French poet Yves-Jacques Bouin, in Décharge, revue de poésie, Auxerre, France, 2020.

> *"Le rôle de l'auteur, si dangereux à cause de l'incertitude de chaque phrase, est joué bien entendu par un cascadeur. Il se cache dans la tête du lecteur et saute par hasard, vêtu comme une fille, un virus, ou une virgule ..."* ("The author's role, so perilous because of the uncertainty of each sentence, is naturally played by a stuntman. He hides in the head of the reader and leaps haphazardly, alternately disguised as a girl, a virus or a comma ...")

*

Two conversations bear mentioning here for the light they shed on our subject.

The first, with a Japanese couple in Grenoble, both visiting scholars of French. Over lunch, while chasing away the noisome wasps hovering 'round my *gâteau au miel*, I tried to explain the theme of the symposium I was planning. We'd been talking about literary crosscultural enigmas like the American-born author, Lafcadio Hearn, whose Japanese tales in *Kwaidon*, and the Japanese film of the same name it inspired, capture the magical essence of Japan, and the Anglo-Japanese author, Kazuo Ishiguro, whose novel, *Remains of the Day*, and the film based upon it, produced by the Anglo-Indian team of Merchant-Ivory and scripted by the Polish-Jewish-Indian author, Ruth Prawer Jhabvala, so perfectly render the subtleties of British class society. Then swiping at a wasp, the Japanese professor of French quipped: "*Un pilote Kamikaze!*" Whereupon it came to me in a flash by a strange leap of associations:

> "'*Les Linguovertis*,'" I said in French, "*ce sont les abeilles de la culture qui, en cueillant des nectars exotiques, en font un miel splendide!*" ("Lingoverts are the honey

> beas of culture, who in mingling exotic nectars create a splendid honey.")

The image could not have coalesced in English, I'm quite certain. Its poetry belonged to the true multiculturalism of the moment and was immediately clear to all.

Later I happened upon the following passage addressed "To the English Reader" in a translation of Karl von Frisch's classic study, *Aus dem Leben der Bienen* (*The Dancing Bees, An Account of the Life and Senses of the Honey Bee*):

> "Suppose German and English bees were living together in the same hive, and one of the Germans found a lot of nectar: its English companions would easily understand what it had to say about the distance and direction of the find. Human language is not so perfect ..."

The second conversation took place in Paris at the home of friends, a couple from the former Yugoslavia—he, the grandson of a former Moslem Imam of Bosnia and a Serbian Orthodox mother, an itinerant diplomat freelancing human rights missions for the U.N.; she a Catholic-born Croatian Scholar of Hindu Philosophy, currently lecturing at the Collège de France, who writes and speaks Serbo-Croatian, French, German, Italian or English, depending on the context. Dinner was a delicious Peruvian cevice of cod whipped up by the diplomat. Our daughter lay sound asleep on a couch in the livingroom.

"The literary phenomenon I'm talking about," I tried to explain, "involves a cross over, a tapping of the knowledge of the left hand by the right ... *C'est la main gauche qui reste souple comme un enfant,*" I shifted to French, "*tandis que la droite, l'adulte, est devenue raide dans sa sûreté!*" ("The left hand stays as supple as a child, while the right hand, the adult, has grown stiff with certainty.")

Whereupon our hostess leapt up to pluck a volume off her shelf, *L'Hermaphrodite, Sarrasine sculpteur*, by the French thinker Michel Serres, from which she read the following passage aloud:

> *"Le gaucher vit dans un monde, physique et humain, dextrogyre, c'est à dire tournant vers la droite, comme un paralytique maladroit qui doit accepter à chaque instant le choix inverse au sien propre. Le plus souvent, il écrit même avec sa mauvaise main. D'où un corps estrangement instable, mais stable pourtant, dans cette liberté. Toujours contrarié, ou plus ou moins, s'il prend à droite, il fait le bon choix, mais s'il décide à gauche, il fait encore le bon choix. Depuis sa naissance, par sa posture et ses gestes, il acclimate la tolérance: il comprend tout et ne peut rien rejeter. Vous ne ferez jamais d'un gaucher contrarié un fanatique, un militant, un dogmatique, ni un philosophe de l'antithese."*

In English:

> The left-handed person lives dextrogyrically in a physical and human world, that is to say, veering to the right, like a clumsy paralytic compelled at every turn to accept the choice contrary to his own. More often than not he even writes with his wrong hand. Thus a body that is strangely unstable, though stable nonetheless, in this liberated state. Always confused, more or less, if he takes a right it's the right choice, but if he decides to take a left turn, it's still the right choice. Since the day

> of his birth, he has been acclimatizing himself to tolerance in posture and gestures: he comprehends everything and can reject nothing. You will never make of a thwarted lefty a fanatic, a militant, a dogmatist, or a philosopher of antithesis.

Her husband, our hostess pointed out, casting him a loving smile, happened to be left handed, though he could do every thing but brush his teeth with either hand. Just back from a special assignment supervising the first free elections in South Africa, he was beefing up on his Creole, as he would soon be headed for Haiti. "He's Bosnian, I'm Croat. The fanatics are tampering with our language back home," she sighed, "inserting differences that were never there." It's getting harder and harder for her to write in Serbo-Croatian, she said. Her latest work, a non nationalist analysis of the Yugoslav crisis, was written and published in French.

The conversation was suddenly interrupted by a piercing cry in the universal common denominator: "Mama!" shrieked our daughter, waking in the darkness of a strange room. Immediately comprehending that powerful translingual invocation—"And God said, Let there be light!"—we hastened to flick the switch—"And there was light."

No translation necessary.

II

Making Bones Sing

I have always viewed each new translation undertaken as a crash course in the work of that particular author, a privileged opportunity to commune up close, my ear to his/her whispered words, to mine the mindset of the creator. Consequently, almost all of my literary translations have been accompanied by introductions or afterwords in which I expound on my own particular take. Most of the essays in this section previously appeared as introductions or afterwords to my translations.

Don't Burn What You Don't Understand[1]

Difference is out of fashion in Europe today. Cultural exclusivity is back in. The president of France[2] tried to boost his lagging popularity last year by lashing out at a minuscule itinerant Roma minority. Switzerland banned the building of minarets. Austria, Holland, Italy, Sweden and several countries in Eastern Europe include parties with anti-immigrant platforms in their governing coalitions. And Germany found itself caught up in a media-fed public attack on multiculturalism, sparked by former Bundesbank Board member Thilo Sarrazin's insidious suggestion in print that Islamic immigrants are "dumbing down" the dominant culture.

Five hundred years ago another German war of words was waged concerning another embattled minority, and one man's words made a difference.

To the modern reader of conscience, German Humanist Johannes Reuchlin's Ratschlag *Ob Man den Juden All Irre Bücher Nemmen, Abtun und Verbrennen Soll* (*Recommendation Whether to Confiscate, Destroy and Burn All Jewish Books*) drafted in Stuttgart, in 1510, and first published in *Dr. Johannes Reuchlins Augenspiegel*, in Tübingen, in 1511, is a stirring response to a preposterous question.

A coup de grace to blind ignorance, this long forgotten text drew a fateful line in the sand. Its message is as fresh and apt today as ever: Don't burn (or scorn) what you don't understand! Conceived as a legal brief to bend the ear of an emperor, Reuchlin's *Ratschlag* still reads like a lucid bolt of lightning.

*

1 This essay marking the 500th anniversary of the publication of German Humanist Johannes Reuchlin's landmark call for religious tolerance was first published, in German translation, in *Die Zeit*, Hamburg, Germany, January 5, 2011
2 Nicolas Paul Stéphane Sarközy de Nagy-Bocsa, then president of France, 2007-2012

In the years 1507-1509, Johannes Pfefferkorn, a recent Jewish convert to Christianity, a butcher by trade, alleged in various pamphlets printed and disseminated at the Frankfurt Book Fair that the Talmud and other Jewish books contain profanities and attacks against the Christian faith. It is highly unlikely that the butcher, who was neither well-versed in Hebrew (the language of the allegedly defamatory texts) nor knowledgeable concerning the works in question, could, on his own accord, have conceived the idea of so maligning his former brethren and their most precious possession, their books. Pfefferkorn had the active support of influential members of the Dominican Order in Cologne who saw in him a willing tool. They hoped to spread to German lands the flames of the Inquisition, which, by 1492, had effectively completed the ethnic cleansing of Jewish (and Islamic) life and culture on the Iberian Peninsula.

With the help of the Dominican friars, Pfefferkorn managed in the winter of 1509-10 to bring his case before Emperor Maximilian I. The Emperor issued a decree ordering local magistrates throughout his realm to confiscate Jewish books so as to study their contents (a formidable task, considering the fact that none of the authorities so charged knew a word of Hebrew). After the Emperor's mandate had already been partially carried out, he inexplicably changed his mind and issued a second decree staying the execution of the first until such time as the allegations could be thoroughly considered.

In June of 1510, Maximilian ordered his Lord High Chancellor, the Bishop of Mainz, to solicit expert opinions from knowledgeable persons. Two of the individuals called upon to offer their views were Jacob van Hoogsträten, Papal Inquisitor, Professor of Theology, and Prior of the Dominican Cloister of Cologne (whose foregone conclusion favored Pfefferkorn's position) and Dr. Johannes Reuchlin, Professor of Law and Judge of the Swabian Bund, and a renowned classical philologist.

Why did the Emperor's Lord High Chancellor turn to a lawyer and a linguist for a theological opinion?

*

Born January 29, 1455, in Pforzheim, where he learned Latin at a monastery school, Reuchlin pursued his classical studies in Freiburg, Paris, Basel and Orléans, opting for law as a profession. He subsequently established a reputation as one of the foremost jurists of his day. But his real passion was classical philology and philosophy. At age 20, he published a Latin dictionary and later produced notable translations from Greek into Latin. Reuchlin became famous in Humanist circles with his *De Rudimentis Hebraicis* (1506), the first Hebrew grammar written by a Christian scholar in Latin.

How is it that a devout Christian, like Reuchlin, took the trouble to delve into a linguistic domain that had long been considered obsolete at best by most of his contemporaries? For just as the Jews themselves were reviled as a people who, in rejecting Christ, had missed the boat, an alien body that had long since outlived its usefulness, so, too, was their language and literary heritage, though essentially unknown, held in ill repute. Reuchlin himself, it should be noted, was no particular friend of the Jewish People, whom he, like other "enlightened" Christians of his day, hoped to convert to the "true" faith by "reasonable," i.e. non-coercive means, through debate and disputation. He was, however, an enthusiastic student of their sacred literature, for in it he saw the spiritual foundation of Christianity.

Like other Northern European Humanists drawn by the Classical cultural currents preserved and fostered to the south, Reuchlin took several trips to Italy. There a small intellectual elite lead a relatively open exchange of ideas under the patronage of enlightened lords and clerics, a discussion in which, to a limited extent, Jewish notions and Jewish scholars were also included. Italian philosophers like Marsilio Ficino and Giovanni Pico della Mirandolla (both of whom Reuchlin met and befriended) knew and read Hebrew. They developed in their thinking a curious synthesis of Christian doctrine, Neo-Platonic concepts and ideas drawn from the Jewish mystical tradition of the Kabala.

For Kabbalists (Jewish and Christian alike), the Hebrew language itself held a sacred significance. For it was with Hebrew words that the Judeo-Christian God quite literally *called* the world into being. Each word passed on to Man through the Bible, the Kabbalists believed, is a muttering echo and shimmering mirror image of "the eternal." The Hebrew language, as such, is a bridge, a lasting link between the finite and the infinite, between Man and God. Christian students of the Kabala perceived in it a confirmation of Christian mystical doctrine.

*

From the standpoint of its historical significance, Reuchlin's *Recommendation* is first and foremost a masterpiece of jurisprudence, a model of legal rigor and critical reason. In response to the question, "Should the Jews' books be legally confiscated, destroyed or burned?"—one could sum up Reuchlin's answer: Do not burn what you do not understand! He begins with an overview of the charges brought against the Jewish books: that they

> "... were written to counter the Christians; that they malign Jesus, Maria ... the Apostles ... and our Christian Order"; that they "are false;" that they induce "the Jews ... to stubbornly cling to Judaism."

In response to such claims, he argues: that "the Jews ... have a right to protection under Imperial Law;" that "according to Imperial and Royal laws, no one may by forceful means [be relieved of] his property;" that "every individual is assured the right to [retain] his ... practices, customs and property;" that "such books were never repudiated or condemned either by canonical or secular law ..." This was the first written affirmation of the rights of Jews to live alongside Christians as co-citizens of the Holy Roman Empire.

Reuchlin proceeds thereafter to enumerate the various kinds of Jewish books under consideration: "the Holy Scripture"; "the Talmud" (i.e. the commentaries); "the glosses and comments ... concerning individual books of the Bible;" "sermons, disputations and prayer books," "philosophical and scholarly works of all sorts;" and finally, "poetic works." By outlining, in brief, the nature of each of the aforementioned kinds of books he succeeds in his primary objective, which is to tear away the veil of strangeness and the pall of superstition surrounding these books in the popular consciousness.

In the last-mentioned category, "poetic works," he concedes the possibility that certain books may indeed contain scornful references to Christianity. "Of these," Reuchlin writes, "each book has its own title, just as the author conceived it" A poetic work, he reminds, is the individual expression of its author and not representative of the collective voice of his people.

Reuchlin's presentation is straightforward and his argument airtight. Paraphrasing Aristotle, he asserts that:

> "A wise man should possess two qualities, namely the following: that he not lie, and that he be able to counter that which is the stuff of lies."

Consequently:

> "He must not fly into a rage and burn the books if he has not studied enough to oppose them with reasoned arguments in sermons or debates."

And wisely citing irrefutable ecclesiastical sources in support of his premise, he quotes St. Jerome:

> "But how can anyone oppose that which he does not understand?"

And back to Aristotle, to reiterate the obvious:

> "Whoever knows not the meaning of words and of their language easily errs in his interpretation."

From which Reuchlin logically concludes: "How then can we countenance that the Christians reject the Talmud, which they do not even understand?"

Reuchlin is particularly adamant when it comes to linguistic ignorance.

"With all due respect," he prefaces a sharp counter-attack against his opponents,

> "one can find many Christian scholars who because of their ignorance of these two languages [Hebrew and Greek] cannot rightly explain [the Scripture] and in this are often made a laughing stock."

It must be reiterated here that Reuchlin was not primarily concerned with the protection of the Jewish People per se, but rather of Jewish books, which he considered the foundation of Christian culture. And yet, his innate sense of justice and truth was greater than any Anti-Jewish sentiments he himself may have harbored. In answer to the question of whether the Jewish books were essentially "false," i.e. "untrue," Reuchlin insists:

> "And even if in this regard the Jewish books may be false, according to our way of thinking, they are not false according to their [the Jews'] way of thinking and according to their faith."

Reuchlin finds fault with the very allegation of falsity and proceeds by elimination (in an attempt to establish a legal definition of the term), to peel away the layers of prejudice and ignorance that underlie the allegation. If "false" means "faulty," then:

> "... the first scribe of the Holy Gospel According to Matthew likewise erred and made mistakes in his transcription ... For if the [Jewish] books would have to be burned for that reason, namely because they were not transcribed and copied accurately, then we would have to burn many copies of the Holy Bible ... [For] they are all based on the immaculate Jewish original text."

And further, regarding the alleged "falseness" of the books in question:

> "If 'false' means a deliberate suppression or alteration of the truth with malicious intent,[...] then I know of no people on earth that takes greater pains to assure accuracy in copying the Holy Scripture than do the Jews."

"False" in the legal sense means "having false [i.e. fraudulent] intent" and that precisely is what Reuchlin demonstrates the accused Jewish books are not; and therefore, they most definitely do not deserve to be burned.

For Reuchlin, the Jews themselves were not so much a living people as the archivists of our common heritage:

> "For the Jews are in a certain sense our *Capsarii*, bookkeepers and librarians, who preserve for us those books from which we may derive proof for our faith [...]"

On the eve of the Reformation, launched seven years later by an early follower of Reuchlin's named Martin Luther, religious faith was still a fundamental tenet. But true faith, Reuchlin firmly believed, cannot be imposed; and herein lies the justice of the man: for though he viewed the Jewish faith as wrong or misguided, he nevertheless supported the right of the Jewish people to adhere to it:

> "for as to matters of faith, they [the Jews] are of the opinion that their faith is right and ours is wrong. Indeed, we find among certain Jews the view that every nation ought to be allowed to practice its own faith; and just as we are not bound by the Laws of Moses, so they are not subject to the laws of Jesus; rather, they are bound to comply with Moses' laws, for God gave them to the Jews and to no one else [...] and all that follows from those laws constitutes their faith: and in their practices, they wish to injure no one."

Jurist-linguist-Humanist-Kabbalist, Johannes Reuchlin strove for a transcendent all-encompassing concept of truth, the terrestrial as well as the eternal. We heirs to the colossal lies of the 20th century, whose ideological bonfires consumed people and books, find it hard to even entertain a notion of "eternal truth." We have been schooled in eternal doubt; such certainty is quite simply alien to our way of thinking—we lack the capacity to believe—and yet, like amputees, we continue to kick as if we had it, in the vain hope perhaps that if we kick enough it might someday grow back.

Reuchlin drafted his *Recommendation* in response to the Emperor's query, never intending it for publication. But Pfefferkorn got wind of its contents and promptly lashed out in print at the text and its author. Only thereafter did Reuchlin respond by publishing his *Recommendation* as part of the aforementioned *Dr. Johannes Reuchlins Augenspiegel*, as a public self-defense.

The fact that this heated exchange of views was transmitted via the new media of the day, the printed book, and was followed with great interest at the Frankfurt Book Fair, fanned what would otherwise have remained a local disagreement into a widespread controversy, in which the literate public took sides, causing a seismic rift in German society. The mostly pro-Reuchlin Humanists battled it out with the more conservative Scholastics, though the real underlying issue was a burgeoning German self-determination butting heads with the authority of Rome.

Reuchlin's vocal defenders, leading Humanists like Ulrich von Hutten, Crotus Rubeanus, Mutianus Rufus, weighed in with a work of their own, *Epistolae obscurorum virorum* (better known as *Die Dunkelmännerbrief*) poking fun at the ignorance and faulty Latin of the opposition.

But no one in the pro-Reuchlin camp actually cared about the Jews or their books. No one except Reuchlin, that is, who paid dearly for his defense. Dogged by the Dominicans, Reuchlin was hounded in trial after trial, his resources drained, his reputation dragged through the mud, his writings declared anathema, and he himself finally condemned by Papal edict to silence. History has largely acceded to Rome's ban of silence. Reuchlin has all but been forgotten.

The German philosopher Jürgen Habermas responded to Germany's recent outbreak of xenophobia in an op-ed piece in *The New York Times* (October 29, 2010) titled "Leadership and Leitkultur." "It doesn't make things any better," Habermas writes,

> "that today *Leitkultur* is defined not by 'German culture' but by religion. With an arrogant appropriation of Judaism—and an incredible disregard for the fate the Jews suffered in Germany—the apologists of the *Leitkultur* now appeal to the 'Judeo-Christian tradition,' which distinguishes 'us' from the foreigners."

It was Reuchlin who put the "Judeo" back in "Judeo-Christian." Perhaps it's time, in the spirit of the Humanism he espoused, given our common cultural roots and the demographic reality of Europe today, to add another dash and acknowledge our Judeo-Christian-Islamic heritage. Lest we forget, Arabic was the tongue in which some of the Classical Greek and Latin learning of the Occident was sheltered and protected during Europe's Dark Ages, waiting to be reawakened from centuries of hibernation by Hebrew and Arabic linguists.

Five hundred years following the publication of Reuchlin's eloquent defense of difference, firebrands are still at it. Just last September a fundamentalist Christian preacher in Florida fostered and fed a media-frenzy with his threat to burn the Koran. Reuchlin's words still resonate today. We still need an effective fire extinguisher.

Making Bones Sing—Tales of the German Imagination[1]

"Perhaps there are also different ways of writing, but I only know this one; at night, when fear keeps me from sleeping, I only know this one [...]," Franz Kafka wrote to his friend Max Brod in a letter from 1922. Or as Jorge Luis Borges aptly observed: "Kafka could only dream nightmares, which he knew that reality endlessly supplies."[2]

Fear has indeed proven rich fodder for fantasy in the German storytelling tradition, at least as far back as the Romantics. The very notion of Angst has been absorbed into the English language by its German name, as if we English speakers conceded the terrifying as Teutonic turf. Wielding Angst like a power drill, certain *Dichter*[3] have trepanned the German unconscious, reaming straight for the imaginative motherload. Fearless in their readiness to face fear head-on, they have mined their nightmares for precious literary ore. But if the resulting narratives succeeded in transcending the German particular and managed to tap the collective unconscious, appealing to readers across the divide of language, temperament, time and space, something more than just morbidity must be at play. Contrary to the cliché, the darkest German literary confections are such a pleasure to read because they are also spiked with humor—therein lies their enduring appeal, eliciting laughter when you least expect it and in the most unlikely places.

Perusing the offerings at a bookstore in East Berlin a few years before The Wall came down, I was amazed at the apparent

1 First published as the introduction to *Tales of the German Imagination, from the Brothers Grimm to Ingeborg Bachmann*, selected and translated by Peter Wortsman, Penguin Classics, 2012.
2 "Franz Kafka, the Vulture," in *Selected Non-Fictions: Jorge Luis Borges*, edited by Elliot Weinberger, Viking, 1999.
3 The German term "Dichter" applies not only to poets strictly speaking, but also encompasses authors of prose of acknowledged literary merit.

profusion of literature and the crowd of would-be book buyers. Not just the collected works of Karl Marx and Friedrich Engels, as I'd expected. Books were clearly still a prized commodity in the German Democratic Republic. Word spread far in advance of the appearance of new editions, and because of the price of paper and limited printing runs, books sold like hot cakes, often disappearing as quickly as they hit the shelves. It was here in East Berlin that I first happened upon a copy of *Café Klößchen, 38 Grotesken,*[4] a book rife with gallows humor from a host of irreverent authors from the Twenties and Thirties I'd never heard of, Klabund, Lichtenstein, Mynona, Kisch, et al—one of the sources of the stories in this volume.

And much to my surprise, the GDR even countenanced Kafka. I was flabbergasted to spot his name out of the corner of my eye on the spine of a book. But the irony was too good, too Kafkaesque to be true: for the title I had at first squint read as *Sämtliche Schriften* (Complete Writings) turned out on closer examination to be *Amtliche Schriften* (Administrative Writings), a compendium, not of his elusive parables, but of the official reports and letters he drafted on the job for the insurance company, the bureaucratic taskmaster to which he sacrificed his daylight hours and which he cursed in his diaries and letters to friends at night.

"Yes," an unsmiling, bespectacled clerk said, "other works by the author have been published."

"Can I buy them?" I asked.

"No," she regretted to inform me, "they are out of print."

A situation straight out of *The Trial*! Kafka himself would have gotten a kick out of it, I thought, pressing my lips together to squelch a chuckle. I remembered what my late beloved Aunt Steffie,

4 *Café Klößchen, 38 Grotesken*, Herausgegeben und mit einem Nachwort versehen von Joachim Schreck, Eulenspiegel Verlag, Berlin, DDR, 1980

my mother's sister, a native of Vienna, once said of a Kafka reading she'd attended in her youth.

"What was he like!?" I pressed her.

She paused. A rationalist to the bone, Steffi had to admit that she did not know what to make of the gawky man and his strange stories. "But one thing I do remember," she said, "he could hardly keep from laughing."

*

By a fortuitous conjoining of literary taste, popular Zeitgeist, and publishing fashion in the wake of World War II, and thanks to the tireless machinations of his friend and impassioned posthumous promoter, Max Brod, Kafka's dark premonitions broke through the bulwarks of culture, language, time and place, to make the author a catchword, a one-man symbol of our angst-ridden age, a secular saint of the Twentieth Century. In 1984, the Centre George Pompidou, in Paris, presented an unprecedented exhibition, titled "Le Siècle de Kafka" (Kafka's Century). It was perhaps the first time that a major public exhibition space devoted to the visual and plastic arts launched a show ostensibly revolving around the work of a literary artist. Kafka himself served as a curatorial clothes line on which to hang a diverse body of artworks and artifacts, including sculpture by Alberto Giacometti, drawings by Paul Klee and Alfred Kubin, and a sentimental novel by a certain Dr. Josef Goebbels, better known for his rants and ravings. The conceptual clothespin that held the exhibition together was the metamorphosis of the proper noun Kafka into the adjective *Kafkaesque*.

Yet in our justifiable adulation of the writings of the visionary German-speaking Jewish scribe from Prague we tend to overlook the fact that he was not spontaneously spawned, Athena-like, from the cranium of German letters. Kafka had his precursors among the German Romantics, as well as his contemporaries working in kindred veins, writers of talent, imagination and stylistic daring scribbling away in Berne, Berlin, Vienna and the far corners of Germany and the Austro-Hungarian Empire. He also had his heirs.

This anthology seeks to reassemble some of the threads of that tradition.

If Kafka's dark fantasies resonated with readers across The Channel and The Pond, it is not only that they spoke to the existential angst of the moment. The path had already been paved by Carroll and Wilde, Kipling, Wells and Orwell—an author whose name inspired an almost synonymic adjective, Orwellian. And the American imagination had already been primed by homegrown fabulists, Irving, Hawthorne and Poe, whose inspiration had been stoked by Hoffmann, von Eichendorff and Tieck (translations of whose works were serialized in *Blackwoods* magazine, a well-respected review in its day.) The Gothic influence later seeped into the Southern mindset of Faulkner, O'Connor, McCullers, Capote & Co., and, thereafter, thanks in part to Borges' erudition and imaginative breadth, and Cortazar's Spanish translation of Poe, took root and found fertile ground in South American Magical Realism—which, in turn, infiltrated, or rather, tapped kindred tendencies back in Britain in the likes of Roald Dahl, Angela Carter and Iain Banks.

*

Darkness is, of course, not a German prerogative. But the German imagination set an early standard, poignantly and precisely sounding the sinister with prescient insight in the flights of fancy of E.T.A. Hoffmann and the tales collected and retold by Jakob and Wilhelm Grimm.

Anyone who in childhood has ever read, or rather been read a Grimms' *Märchen*, will forever remember the effect: that terror combined with the immediate recognition that such tales tap otherwise unutterable truths. (Until the end of his short life, Kafka still savored *Märchen*, unquestionably a major influence on the form and content of his own enigmatic short prose.) The standard English translation of the German *Märchen* as fairy tale sugarcoats the raw German grit with hovering fairies and flickering lights, replacing the cannibalistic witch of "Hansel and Gretel" with the cute and kindly Tinkerbell, tapping, but ultimately quelling fledgling fears. Disney added another layer of prettification, safely encapsulating the malevolent in a shell of nicety. But German *Märchen* aren't nice. Rather than cocoon the virgin consciousness, they blurt out the unspeakable, and so, from early on, vaccinate with the ring of truth. ("A New Kind of Plaything," by Mynona and "The Experiment or the Victory of the Children," by Unica Zürn, two of the 20th-century German fables featured in this volume, are directly rooted in the Grimms' aesthetic. And Ingeborg Bachmann's "The Secrets of the Princess of Kagran" taps the same source.)

In "The Singing Bone," one of the Brothers' lesser known, albeit most telling, tales, a wandering shepherd-cum-minstrel stumbles on a little white bone, out of which he carves a mouthpiece for his horn. But the bone has its own agenda:

> "Oh, dear little shepherd boy,
> The bone you blow on knows no joy,
> My brother, he slayed me,
> Beneath the bridge he laid me,
> All for the wild boar's hide,
> To make the king's daughter his bride."[5]

5 The English translation of these lines of verse is my own.

No mere accommodating object this, no mouthpiece for an idle ditty—the bone cannot help but echo the smothered cries of the misdeed that did its *I* in. The shepherd's breath, like an archeologist's glue, a singer's voice, a listener's ear, *re*-members the dismembered. Implicated as accessories in the crime of forgetting, the shepherd who unwittingly played the song, the king who heard it, the old nursemaid who retold it, the Brothers Grimm who collected, transcribed and adapted it, and generations of little listeners and readers simultaneously revealed truths and derived meaning by recycling the song and keeping the story in circulation. (In "The Onion," an anti-*Märchen* included here, the Dadaist jack of all arts, Kurt Schwitters, best known for his visual collages, reconstitutes another kind of re-*membering.*)

The Grimms, it turns out, albeit unbeknownst to them, had a prehistoric prototype. In 2009, archeologists from the University of Tübingen digging in the Hohle Fels Cave, in southwest Germany, not far from Ulm, reported their discovery of a 35,000-years-old, 8.5-inch-long, five-holed flute carved out of the hollow bone of a griffon vulture.[6] It is only fitting that a bone flute, a singing bone of the sort immortalized by the brothers should have been discovered, not in a riverbed in broad daylight, but in the dark pit of a cave where it was surely played by its maker to tame the restless spirits and still the fears of night.

*

This anthology gathers German imaginative texts from a span of several centuries and from various literary movements born of crisis and doubt. The German Romantics (Jakob and Wilhelm Grimm, E.T.A. Hoffmann, Ludwig Tieck, Josef von

6 "Flutes Offer Clues to Stone-Age Music," Science Section, *The New York Times*, June 24, 2009

Eichendorff, Heinrich von Kleist, Adelbert von Chamisso, Heinrich Heine et al.) formulated an imaginative reaffirmation of German identity in response to the trauma of the Napoleonic occupation of German lands. Expressionists like Georg Heym, Georg Kaiser, and Alfred Lichtenstein, and Dadaists like Kurt Schwitters functioned as a visionary Avant-Garde responding to the economic and cultural decline leading up to, and collapse in the wake of World War I. And proponents of *Neue Sachlichkeit* (New Objectivity) like Wolfgang Borchert embodied a poetic attempt to put the shattered fragments of German identity back together and start over again after the cataclysm of the Holocaust and World War II. The collection also includes lone tales and texts, like those of Paul Celan and Ingeborg Bachmann, that adhere to the tenets of no movements. The narratives gathered here have been variously referred to by those inclined to categorize as allegories, fairy tales, tales of the fantastic, parables, fables, prose poems and grotesques. I prefer to think of them as enigmatic tales. The common thread that runs throughout is a feverish intensity and a predilection for the stuff of dreams.

Styles and tactics vary. Hoffmann's "The Sandman," Tieck's "Rune Mountain" and von Eichendorff's "The Marble Statue" are prime examples of a hallucinatory literature of heightened consciousness and extreme states of mind. Hoffmann employs an ecstatic prose, a hybrid blend of half-science, mystical leanings, strained sobriety, and barely controlled madness. (Freud who attempted to elucidate the mysteries of "The Sandman" in his essay "On the Uncanny" (*Über das Unheimliche*), elsewhere, in a letter to Martha Bernays, dubbed it "mad, fantastic stuff.") Tieck posits a traditional Teutonic fascination for mountains and forests against the tug of *Heimat* (homeland). Von Eichendorff ultimately resorts to religion to reign in and wrap up the chthonic anarchy of his restless imaginings. And in transcendent and totally original works, like "The Earthquake in Chile" and "St. Cecilia or the Power of Music," Heinrich von Kleist, the most and least Romantic of the lot, employs the astute tactical maneuvering of a soldier and the sometimes dispassionate, sometime plodding, prose of a Prussian civil servant to render the ineffable. (A century later we will find a kindred tendency in Kafka.)

In *Peter Schlemiel's Wondrous Tale*, Adelbert von Chamisso, a French émigré who discovered his literary voice in German, adds a twist of Gallic whimsy to the German *Märchen*, toying with its constraints, freeing up the willful possibilities of metaphor. When asked which book by another author he would most like to claim as his own, the great Italian fabulist Italo Calvino sited Chamisso's small masterpiece. This eerie black comic tale of the hapless Schlemiel who foolishly bartered his shadow for worldly stature and wealth influenced the diverse likes of Hans Christian Andersen, who borrowed the premise for a story of his own, "The Shadow"; Karl Marx, who alludes to it in his famous essay "The Eighteenth Brumaire of Louis Bonaparte;" Jacques Offenbach, who includes a likewise shadow-less character of the same name in his opera "Les contes d'Hoffmann;" J.M. Barrie, whose play "Peter Pan, or the Boy Who Wouldn't Grow Up," begins, as you may recall, with Peter in search of his lost shadow; and Ludwig Wittgenstein, who makes mention of it in his "Philosophical Investigations." Having borrowed the Yiddish word "*schlemiel,*" a hopeless bungler liable to trip on his own shadow, from his Jewish friends in Berlin, with whom he identified as fellow outsiders, Chamisso returned the favor by introducing the term into the German language. Among those with whom the displaced Frenchman crossed paths at the literary salon of Rahel Levin Varnhagen, the converted Jewish muse of the Romantics, was Heinrich Heine. Heine paid tribute to him in "The Harz Journey," where he noted his delight at discovering in the guest book of an inn at which he stopped "the much-cherished name of Adelbert von Chamisso, the biographer of the immortal *Schemiel.*"

The last Romantic and the first Modernist, Heine, himself a Jewish convert to Christianity, had a field day with idealized German Romantic notions, singing odes to nature, and giggling all the while. In his description of the life of miners in "Descent into the Mines," a passage excerpted from *The Harz Journey*, the first book of his *Travel Pictures*, with a folklorist's eye, a poet's insight and reverence and a satirist's wit, Heine sounds the depths of German *Märchen* and myth, in the process pressing the limits of German locution. The witty vitriolic Austrian critic Karl Krauss went so far as to accuse him of having "un-corseted the German language and enabled every Tom, Dick and Harry to fondle its breasts."[7]

What unites the Romantics with writers to come is a firm grasp of language, not just any language, but the German language with its syntactical complexities. Each author, in turn, bravely tackled the formidable imperatives of the German sentence, replete as it is with main and subordinate clauses, with semicolons to cling to and commas to clamber up, and the elusive promise of a predicate and a period if you persevere.

The same Kraus who reviled Heine, revered his fellow Viennese, Peter Altenberg, for cultivating the hybrid poetic-prose form Heine had launched. All three were, of course, consummate stylists, linked by their love of the German language, but also, incidentally, by their alienated stance as converted Jews straining for acceptance in a largely hostile Christian society.

7 "*Heine und die Folgen*" (Heine and the Consequences), Karl Kraus, in "Untergang der Welt durch schwarze Magie", Wien and Leipzig: Verlag Die Fackel, 1922.

Jewish authors of the German language comprise an important literary strain in the late 19th and early 20th century, particularly in the literature of angst and enigma. In grotesques like "The Magic Egg" and "A New Kind of Plaything," Mynona (aka Salomo Friedlaender), a philosopher by training and temperament, manages to lace Kant's pure reason with the absurdist logic of Chelm, the legendary Jewish village of fools. The irreverent satires of Kurt Tucholsky and Egon Erwin Kisch, likewise included in this anthology, combine an in-your-face Jewish chutzpah with an unflinching German political idealism.

Scholars have traced Kafka's inspiration back to the dark parables of the Hasidic Rabbi Nahman of Bratislav and other Jewish mystics, the influence of which cannot be doubted. Kafka's roots indeed reach all the way back to the Biblical Book of Jonah, the nightmare of a man literally engulfed and spit back out by the physical manifestation of his angst. But it would be a foolish error to try to extract Kafka's words from the language and literary tradition in which they were written. As Tucholsky detected in a glowing review of "In the Penal Colony,"[8] Kafka had a more than passing affinity with Kleist. "It is not true, as people maintain, that dreams are dreamy," Tucholsky wrote. "So mercilessly hard, so gruesomely objective and crystal clear is this dream of Franz Kafka's [...] Since [Kleist's novella] *Michael Kohlhaas* no German story has been written that with such a conscious force appears to stifle every semblance of sympathy and yet is so infused with the spirit of its author." In a letter to his sometime fiancé Felice, Kafka confirmed Tucholsky's prognosis, referring to Kleist as one of his "true blood relations."[9] Fellow misfits,

8 "*In der Strafkolonie,*" a review by Peter Panter (aka Kurt Tucholsky), *Die Weldbühne*, June 3, 1920.

9 In a letter from Franz Kafka to Felice Bauer, Kafka designated Grillparzer, Dostoyevsky, Kleist and Flaubert as "my true blood-relations." Franz Kafka, *Letters to Felice*, Schocken Books, 1967.

Kleist scorned by the Prussia Aristocratic lineage out of which he sprung, Kafka by the assimilated Jewish provincial Middle Class that spawned him, both writers harvested their trauma, and managed in the merciless prose of the military tactician and the office bureaucrat trained in the law, respectively, to capture and depict the incomprehensible. The fact that Kleist's "The Earthquake in Chile," first published in 1807, so uncannily predicts the social repercussions of natural tragedies in our own time, and that Kafka's "In the Penal Colony," written in 1914, prefigures the technocratic reasoning of Adolf Eichmann and his ilk retroactively adds a chilling prescience to the prose.

*

Whoever has spent a winter in Berlin knows the natural origin of German gloom. The climate of Vienna and Prague are hardly more temperate. Gray without respite, the sun seldom breaks through the clouds for months on end. Sun-starved, the mind is compelled to tap a tenuous inner light.

A streak of depression bordering on madness unquestionably runs through the authors and tales in this book. Hoffmann's hero Nathaniel toys with and ultimately succumbs to it, leaping to his death. Tieck's protagonist, the young hunter, likewise loses his mind. Von Eichendorff's young nobleman battles it out with his demiurges that almost get the better of him. Painstakingly depicting the contours and constraints of a hopeless world, a world from which he felt excluded, Kleist's last period on the long sentence of his short life was a bullet through the head. The great Austrian modernist master Robert Musil's "The Blackbird" is either a vivid account of the inexplicable, the precise charting of an alternate universe, a parallel ir-reality, or else of a descent into madness, which may very well be one and the same. Fellow flaneurs, the Austrian Peter Altenberg and Swiss Robert Walser, spent spells of time in asylums, Walser ultimately withdrawing to one, where he wiled away the last 20 years of his life. Georg Heym dramatized schizophrenia, a condition with which fellow Berliner Unica Zürn battled for much of her life, and to which she ultimately succumbed with a fateful leap. Kurt Tucholsky and Paul Celan were suicides. Ingeborg Bachmann a casualty of depression, alcohol and pills. And yet it would be ill-advised to label their work the literature of lunatics.

Tucholsky and Celan did have extenuating historical circumstances for their depression and their decision to do themselves in. Society itself had gone mad. The collapse of social democracy and the seemingly unstoppable rise of Adolf Hitler drove Tucholsky, first into exile, and finally to his wit's end. Born in the Bukovina, at the time the eastern-most German-speaking outpost of the Austro-Hungarian Empire, today the Ukraine, Celan saw his world collapse and lost his family and almost everything dear to him in the Holocaust—everything, that is, except for the German language. Though his was a death by drowning—he leapt into the Seine—one might well take the metaphoric liberty of suggesting that he gagged on the same syllables he had braided into verse.

It is precisely the uncanny ability of the authors in this book to hold onto lucidity, sometimes at considerable cost, often with an unsettling humor, and to share their flashes of insight into the dark recesses of the human condition, that makes their work worth reading.

Facing Fear and Furies
The Unexpurgated Brothers Grimm[1]

A 600-kilometer-long stretch from Hanau, the birthplace of the Brothers Grimm, in the German State of Hessen, to Bremen, the destination of the fabled musicians, in the State of Bremen, has been designated as the *Deutsche Märchenstrasse* (German Fairy Tale Road). The road runs past Sababurg, supposed somniferous nook of Sleeping Beauty; the Trendelburg Tower, Rapunzel's alleged lock-up; and Hameln, where the Pied Piper plied his trade. The Grimms have posthumously nurtured a veritable industry, nearly as global in its distribution network as Coca Cola. Countless selections of their tales keep pouring off the presses in every language under the sun. But most omit the more savory details and leave out the darkest of the lot, candy-coating the content and tone. Disney's 1937 animated hit "Snow White and the Seven Dwarves" set the modern standard, turning the film's theme song "Whistle While You Work" into an anthem to the Protestant Work Ethic, while judiciously deleting the evil queen's predilection for the little girl's lungs and liver.

Why then issue yet another selection and translation of these tales? Because it is this translator-editor's hope to hereby salvage these enigmatic narratives from the insipid pabulum to which they have been reduced and restore the sting and the bite of the original.

*

For English language readers, as for their German counter-parts, the term *Märchen*, or fairy tale, is practically synonymous

1 This essay was first published as the afterword to *Selected Tales of the Brothers Grimm*, illustrated with paintings by contemporary Haitian artists, selected and translated by Peter Wortsman, Archipelago Books, Brooklyn, NY, 2013

with the name Grimm, as though the genre itself spilled fully formed from the lips and pens of the celebrated brethren, the two attached in the popular consciousness like talkative Siamese twins. Inevitably, given the dark and cruel character of many of their tales, notwithstanding repeated attempts at expurgation—a process in which Brother Wilhelm himself already had a heavy hand—we likewise tend to conflate the name Grimm with its homonym *grim*, as in Grim Reaper. For the tales do indeed reveal monstrous intentions and recount cruel acts, like child abuse (Cinderella), child abandonment (Hansel and Gretel), mutilation (The Girl with No Hands), fratricide (The Singing Bone), incest (All-Kind-of-Fur), and cannibalism (The Tale of the Juniper Tree). They readily acknowledge fear (The Tale of One Who Set Out to Learn Fear), greed (The Golden Goose), and desire (Rapunzel.) They titillate like horror films and terrify like nightmares. But it is a playful, and therefore, paradoxically comforting, terror, since as with scary movies and dark dreams, we know all along that it's only the stuff of fantasy, and relish it all the more the *grimmer* it gets.

These tales captivate because, in imaginative terms, they tell it like it is, sublimating nothing, mining the tenuous realm of make-believe. Their enduring appeal, as Bruno Bettelheim reminds in his classic defense of the grim stuff in Grimm, *The Uses of Enchantment, The Meaning and Importance of Fairy Tales*, lies precisely in their bluntness:

> "'Safe' stories mention neither death nor aging, the limits to our existence, nor the wish for eternal life. The fairy tale, by contrast, confronts the child squarely with the basic human predicaments."

Bettelheim elaborates:

> "The deep inner conflicts originating in our primitive drives and our violent emotions are all denied in much of modern children's literature, and so the child is not helped in coping with them. [...] The fairy tale, by contrast, takes these existential anxieties and dilemmas very seriously and addresses itself directly to them: the need to be loved and the fear that one is thought worthless, the love of life, and the fear of death."

Let us acknowledge here and now, notwithstanding our best attempts to sugarcoat and coddle the reality, that childhood is a fearful state. Virtual victims dwarfed by powerful giants, children spend much of their time petrified of an infinite number of imagined and actual threats, and are themselves hardly innocent of violent intent. Biting, kicking and scratching take precedence over walking and talking. Even babes born with a golden, or stainless steel, spoon, as the case may be, suffer and/or inflict oodles of actual or fantasized grief, and plough back the terror as imaginative mulch to mull over again at night. What children want in the stories they like and ask to be read or told again and again—what I remember wanting, and still crave now in the literature that speaks to me—is a narrative drawn in broad elemental strokes that acknowledges the mystery, the cruelty and the terror, encompassing all the dark contradictions of life, and in so doing, defangs the threat, vaccinating the ever-vulnerable psyche with denatured venom.

*

A word about the Brothers and their background. Two of a family of nine children, six of whom survived, Jakob Ludwig Karl (1785-1863) and Wilhelm Karl (1786-1859) were born to Philipp Wilhelm Grimm, a privy counselor at court, and his wife Dorothea, née Zimmer, daughter of an apothecary, in a comfortable household in Hanau, in the principality of Hessen, at a time when Germany was still a patchwork quilt of principalities loosely linked by a common tongue. Three occurrences, two domestic, one external, shattered the protected idyll of the brothers' childhood: the death of their father in 1796, and grandfather two years later, leading to the family's financial ruin; and in 1806, Napoleon Bonaparte's invasion and occupation of the Rhineland and the formation of the Confederation of the Rhine, an amalgamation of city states, electorates and duchies under French dominion.

With a determination worthy of one of their fairy tale protagonists, and with the aid of an affluent relative, Jakob and Wilhelm, both of bookish bent and with a penchant for reflection, studied law and gravitated to philology. Jakob worked for a time as court librarian to the King of Westphalia, later joining his brother as a court librarian in Kassel. Both subsequently secured appointments, Jacob as professor and librarian, Wilhelm as professor, to the University of Göttingen, in the State of Hanover, where they lived under the same roof. Wilhelm married, Jakob remained single. Both were dismissed, along with five other colleagues on the faculty, for protesting the revocation of the state constitution by Hanover's autocratic King Ernst Augustus I, and were thereafter invited by Friedrich Wilhelm IV, King of Prussia, to join the Akademie der Wissenschaften in Berlin, where they pursued their studies until their dying days. Their adjoining graves in the St. Matthäus Kirchhof in Schöneberg, Berlin, are still a place of pilgrimage.

While engaged in various scholarly projects over the years—Jakob wrote extensively on the history and structure of Germanic languages, publishing a four-volume *Deutsche Grammatik* (German Grammar), and later authoring a three-volume *Deutsche Mythologie* (German Mythology); together they worked on a *Deutsches Wörterbuch* (German Dictionary), reaching the letter F, and a two-volume book of *Deutsche Sagen* (German Legends)—the Brothers are, of course, best known for their collection of *Kinder und Haus Märchen* (Children's and Household Fairy Tales), a project they began as young students and continued to tinker with well into old age. Notwithstanding sluggish sales of the first and second editions, the work was reissued in seven large editions and ten small editions during the Brothers' lifetimes, bringing them a modicum of celebrity, if not material comfort. But it was only in the late 19th and the 20th century that the book, commonly known as *Grimms Märchen,* flooded the market in countless editions, and came to achieve a popularity in Germany and abroad second only to *The Bible.*

Solicited by their friends, the writers Ludwig Achim von Arnim and Clemens Brentano, who compiled a German folksong collection, *Des Knaben Wunderhorn* (The Boys' Magic Horn), Jakob and Wilhelm began gathering folk fairy tales for a planned sequel. The sequel never materialized, but the Grimms took the task to heart and ran with it. Culture and politics mingled in their motivation; sharing the burgeoning German nationalism of the moment stirred in response to the French occupation, the Brothers found a scholarly outlet for their patriotic zeal. They set out to collect, and thereby preserve, what they believed to be an endangered store of popular German lore. As they put it in the foreword to the second edition:

> "This is how it seemed to us, when we saw that of all that blossomed in former times nothing survived—

> even the memory thereof was almost erased—nothing, that is, but a few folksongs, a handful of books, some legends and these innocent household tales. [...] It was perhaps high time to collect these fairy tales, for those who ought to safeguard them are fewer and fewer in number."

Or as Jakob would reflect, in retrospect, in 1841, they sought "in the history of German literature and language, consolation and refreshment ... from the enemy's high spirits." By collecting and publishing these texts, they felt that they were "fostering national self-reflection." The first volume of what would become the first edition, published in 1812, was, in fact, intended strictly for scholars. It was only later that Wilhelm, the worldlier of the two, fathomed the work's appeal for a younger readership, and modified its tone and content accordingly, elaborating on the spare folk descriptions and adding moral lessons to please and appease parents and educators. Still, scholars continued to take note. The second edition was proofread by the philosopher Friedrich Schleiermacher.

From the start, the collection was, in fact, as much a work of fine-tuned fiction as of popular folklore. Pretending to have tapped peasant lore, the Brothers enjoined friends to transcribe narratives from old books and sought their respondents among the neighboring gentry, notably in families of noble origin, like the Haxthausens, who, in turn, sounded out their servants. And as for the purported Germanic folk purity of their sources, their favorite informant, the *Märchenfrau* Dorothea Viehmann, touted in the aforementioned foreword as "a peasant woman," was, in fact, the wife of a tailor, and herself of French Huguenot origin. The provenance of many of her tales proved to lead back across the Rhine to Perrault and other Gallic sources. Nationalism was one of those nifty 19th-century fictions whipped up in the frenzy of political self-affirmation, but geographic borders are infinitely porous, and stories slipped between the cracks.

The Grimms have been accused of tampering with the narratives entrusted to them. But as Maria Tatar makes clear in her balanced book of reckoning, *The Hard Facts of the Grimms' Fairy Tales*: "It is an error to see in the Grimms' collection printed transcriptions of oral folktales. The tales are simply too far removed from oral source material to deserve the title." Scholars have shown to what extent the brothers, and Wilhelm, in particular, raked through the material, deleting here, amending there, censoring, moralizing, and bowdlerizing. "But what name do they then merit?" Tatar asks.

> "Clearly one cannot call them literary fairy tales, for notwithstanding Wilhelm Grimm's unending editorial intervention, they are a far cry from the kind of narratives penned by E.T.A. Hoffmann, Hans Christian Andersen or Oscar Wilde. The texts in the *Nursery and Household Tales* seem to lead an uneasy double life."

The fact remains that their original source, that of a folk narrative tradition passed on from generation to generation, still breaks through and speaks out, no matter how tinkered and tampered with the tales may be.

Their appeal spread rapidly. No doubt exaggerating a bit, the tall tale teller Baron von Münchhausen declared that: "In an old-fashioned German household, Grimms' fairy tales occupied a position approximately midway between the cookbook and the hymnal." And across the English Channel, in London, Karl Marx kept his little daughter Eleanor's German alive with daily doses of Grimm. In an 1819 review in *The Quarterly Review*, an English journal, a certain Francis Cohen, aka Sir Francis Palgrave, wrote appreciatively:

> "The most important addition to nursery literature has been effected in Germany, by the diligence of John and William Grimm, two antiquarian brethren of the highest reputation. Under the title *Kinder und Haus-Märchen*, they have published a collection of German popular stories, singular of its kind, both for extent and variety, and from which we have acquired much information."

The first English translation, titled *German Popular Stories*, penned by Edgar Taylor, with illustrations by George Cruikshank, appeared in 1823, and proved an immediate smashing success. Three more English translations followed. Charles Dickens called Little Red Riding Hood "my first love," declaring that "if I could have married [her] I should have known perfect bliss." Charles Dodgson (aka Lewis Carroll) hailed "the love-gift of a fairy-tale" in *Through the Looking Glass*. A generation later, in the midst of World War II, in his 1944 review of the Margaret Hunt translation, W.H. Auden wrote: "It is hardly too much to say that these tales rank next to the Bible in importance." He furthermore declared them "among the few indispensable common-property books upon which Western culture can be founded."

Meanwhile, back in the German Fatherland, National Socialist theorists praised Grimm's' fairy tales as epitomes and models of the character of Nordic peoples, offering "a rare insight into the soul of peoples of German blood," and clues to the "primary principle of German character." It is true that the Grimms favored golden haired princesses and heroes of solid peasant stock, and included popular anti-Semitic motifs that make the modern reader wince. In "The Jew in the Thorns," a Jew who tried to trick a fiddler is made to dance himself bloody among the thorn bushes as a prelude to his hanging, presumably to the giggling delight of little readers and listeners. But the questionable role of the Jew as whipping boy in the German imagination was not invented or cultivated by The Brothers Grimm, nor are nationalist fervor and racist tinges any more marked in their work than in that of other 19th century *Dichter* and *Denker*, like Kleist and Nietzsche, both likewise posthumously conscripted to the Aryan cause. Still, Nazi theorists had a field day interpreting the material and extracting narrative elements in support of their theories. The scholarship was sometimes questionable. A certain Georg Schott saw the protagonist of "The Brave Little Tailor" as "an altogether crafty character," divining definite Jewish traits. He furthermore viewed the giants in the tale as "fine specimens of German manhood" taken in and victimized by the tailor's lies. "All this is truly Jewish," claimed Herr Schott. "We need only think of the brash publicity: 'Seven in one stroke.'"

But according to the post-war German scholar Ruth B. Bottigheimer:

> "It was not that the *Kinder und Haus-Märchen* themselves conspired to produce warlike behavior, but that decades of nationalistically steered propaganda had hallowed their 'authors' as quintessentially German or Germanic, and therefore, as worthy standard-bearers for Germany at war. Wartime editions of the *Kinder und Haus-Märchen* poured off German presses."

For the British and American occupation forces in the immediate wake of World War II, Grimms' Fairy Tales were considered taboo, akin to *Mein Kampf*, and consequently removed from circulation in libraries and schools. But the German fondness for the fairy tale could not be expunged and the books were soon reissued, with some of the grimmer bits removed. Yet while it may not be too farfetched to perceive an imaginative link between the oven of the cannibalistic witch in "Hansel and Gretel" and the human ovens of Auschwitz and Treblinka, party officials and functionaries and the German engineers who helped realize their murderous schemes can well be credited for the mechanization and assembly-line efficiency of genocide, but the Grimms bear no blame for the blueprint. The healthy individual, then and now, knows the difference between make-believe and reality. (Or does the right to bear arms, assured by the Second Amendment to the U.S. Constitution, reveal an innate violence in the American psyche that makes us more bellicose than others?) Any attempt to excise the cruelty of these tales, the very element that endears them to so many of their little readers, is to my mind as ill-advised and foolish as the ban on toy guns in a country where the real thing is readily available. As W. H. Auden reminded: "No fairy tale ever claimed to be a description of the external world and no sane child ever believed that it was." To make believe is all about playfully working through the aggressive and violent tendencies innate to the human species, rather than unleashing them on one's little playmates.

The sexuality in these tales is another prickly point of contention. Ever since Freud's *The Interpretation of Dreams*, psychoanalytic theorists have kept busy finding phallic symbols and oedipal complexes hidden at every turn. There is indeed an undeniable erotic subtext to many fairy tales, sometimes readily apparent on the surface, sometimes at the metaphoric level. It is not too farfetched to recognize that Rapunzel's door-less tower recapitulates her virginal body, to which her sorceress-chaperone permits no point of access for the prince. Nor need one be sex-obsessed to surmise a figurative allusion to something else in "Hans My Hedgehog" in the princess' fear of the prick of the protagonist's quills on their wedding night. And when the young protagonist in "The Blue Light" first steals the clothes of his invisible bride-to-be, and later lays his head in her lap, am I the only reader to respond with a libidinal rise?

The Grimms' tales have likewise been lambasted for their alleged sexism. To which novelist Margaret Atwood offers a ready reply:

> "I'm always a little astonished when I hear Grimms' Fairy Tales denounced as sexist. [...] It seems to me that traits were evenly spread. There were wicked wizards as well as wicked witches, stupid women as well as stupid men [...] When people say 'sexist fairy tales', they probably mean the anthologies that concentrate on 'The Sleeping Beauty,' 'Cinderella,' and 'Little Riding Hood' and leave out everything else. But in 'my' version, there are a good many forgetful or imprisoned princes who have to be rescued by the clever, brave and resourceful princess [...] And where else could I have gotten the idea, so early in life, that words can change you?"

And as for accusations of these tales being wellsprings of authoritarian attitudes, there is far more revolutionary fervor and standing up for the little man here than any fondness for authority. In "The Master Thief," an ingenious thief of peasant origin repeatedly hoodwinks and outwits a gullible lord, and gets away with it. In "The Devil's Three Golden Hairs," a good-luck child of humble birth tricks the treacherous and greedy king, who had intended to send him to his death, turning tables on him and sending the king into eternal servitude as a doomed ferryman on the German tributary of the River Styx. The tasks the heroes of fairy tales set out to accomplish are humble takes on knightly quests, no search for the Holy Grail and the like, but stacking a forest full of logs, fishing a pond dry, and sorting lentils from ashes. But the humble character of the task makes its accomplishment no less noble.

Some have perceived in fairy tales the residue of ancient myth. There is indeed a certain similarity between Hercules' trials and all the impossible chores of fairy tale protagonists, and a kindred theme in Danae's father's attempt to keep her childless in a bronze chamber open to the sky and Rapunzel's imprisonment in a tower with no point of entry. Might the marvelous minstrel in the tale of the same name, who charms wild beasts in the forest with his fiddle, be a distant cousin or an heir to Orpheus? And when the servant Faithful Johannes, in the tale of the same name, is turned to stone on account of his loyalty and his master's folly, would it be too farfetched to read into the prescribed remedy, that the king kill his sons, an echo of Jehovah's test of Abraham's faith on Mount Moriah in the command to sacrifice his son?

Like Sigmund Freud a century later, the Brothers Grimm were first elevated to saintly status and thereafter dragged in the mud, their tales accused of fostering every sin under the sun. These stories tap the unfiltered fundament of the collective unconscious as few others have before or since, dredging up ugliness along with beauty, bravery with cowardice, kindness with cunning. In uttering the unutterable, fairy tales retain the ring of truth. Which is why they have weathered the whimsies of successive social theories and political ideologies, and the passing fads and fashions of childrearing, and why they are likely to stand the test of time for years to come. As the Grimms' tales remind, life is full of pitfalls and traps with ogres at every turn. We are forever getting bottled up in the infinite manifestations of our fears and our furies. But if we face them, instead of shying away, we might stand a chance of cutting through the thicket of thorns, and come away all the stronger for it. As the long-suffering protagonists of "All-Kind-of-Hide" and "Hans My Hedgehog" remind, redemption is sometimes a matter of shedding our old skin and discovering another.

The Displaced Person's Guide to Nowhere
The Forked Tongue and Divided Loyalties of Adelbert von Chamisso[1]

It is an overstated truism perhaps—though like most truisms, for the most part true—that the two key prerequisites of the literary pursuit are a sense of place and a command of the native idiom. Like the Faulkner of Yoknapatawpha County or the Marquez of Macondo, writers worth their salt are generally supposed to be astute homeboys, local yokels with a canny ear for backyard palaver and a keen eye for the contour of the land. Certain notable exceptions, however, wreak havoc with the rule. A formidable literary "foreign legion" comprising uprooted aristocrats and paupers, seafarers, adventurers, itinerant intellectuals, and refugees of every ilk have hip-hopped 'cross linguistic and geopolitical borders, and in the process, created a parallel tradition to the literature of place—call it the literature of displacement!

For reasons that run the gamut from personal to political, these "lingoverts"—a term I am herewith coining to connote the internal psychic and emotional transformations that accompany linguistic conversion—took exile to the limit, shedding not only the outward trappings of national affiliation but also that most intimate i.d.: the very syllables of self.

English literature has been immeasurably enriched by the vision and voice of such great lingoverts as the Polish Count-turned-seafarer, Jozef Korzeniowski (aka Joseph Conrad); the Danish Baroness-turned coffee planter, Karen Blixen (aka Isaak Dinesen), and the uprooted Russian butterfly collector,

1 This essay was first published as the introduction to *Peter Schlemiel, The Man Who Sold His Shadow*, by Adelbert von Chamisso, translated by Peter Wortsman, Fromm International Publishing Co., New York, 1993.

Vladimir Nabakov. The French have profited from the political and social upheavals of modern times and the lure of a nation in love with its language by welcoming the diverse talents of: Dutchman, J. K. Huysmans; Irishman, Samuel Beckett; Roumanian, Eugene Ionesco; Catalonian, Fernando Arrabal; and American, Julian Green, to mention only the most famous cases.

German literature, too, has garnered its share of the spoils. Within the confines of the two great modern German empires, Prussia and Austro-Hungary, shifting borders and political alliances fostered a state of linguistic flux and a tendency on the part of threatened minorities seeking at least an illusion of security to huddle under the protective umbrella of German language and culture. So the Jews of Czechoslovakia scorned the Hebrew of their scholars, the Yiddish of their grandparents and the Czech of their immediate neighbors, opting for the imperial lingua franca. (Franz Kafka, though not a lingovert, strictly speaking, is nonetheless a product of the process.) German letters forfeited the quatrilingual Nobel Laureate, S.Y. Agnon (born in Galicia, then part of Austro-Hungary) to modern Hebrew. Ironically though, one of the great German poets of modern time, Paul Celan, a border Jew from Bukovina, who spoke Roumanian, Russian, Hebrew or Yiddish, depending on the context, composed his harrowing lyric lament to the victims of nazi atrocities in the language of Goethe and Goebbels.

It should come as little surprise then, among the many enigmas of literary history, that one of the most haunting expressions of the German Romantic spirit, perhaps the ultimate poetic portrayal of displacement, *Peter Schlemihl*, drew its name and inspiration from a Jewish notion and was written by a Frenchman.

*

Louis Charles Adelaide de Chamisso de Boncourt (better known as Adelbert von Chamisso), born in 1781 on his family's estate, Chateau Boncourt in the Champagne, fled the French Reign of Terror with his aristocrat parents in 1790, and following a circuitous escape route, eventually ended up in Berlin. There he attended the Französisches Gymnasium and proceeded under the patronage of the Emperor Friedrich Wilhelm II (whose wife he served as a page) to enter a military academy, and thereafter to join the Prussian army. When in 1801, then First Consul Napoleon Bonoparte declared an amnesty, calling on all exiled aristocrats to come home, Chamisso's parents followed the call, leaving their young son, now a Prussian officer, behind to hold the fort in the eventuality of a possible retreat. A series of unfortunate events, including the untimely death of his parents and the declaration of war between France and Prussia made Chamisso's situation all the more precarious, particularly following a decree issued by Napoleon in 1806, whereby any Frenchman found in foreign military service was to be executed within 24 hours of his capture.

Caught between two countries and two cultures, inhabiting a kind of psychic no man's land, Chamisso was faced with a terrible conflict that grew to encompass every aspect of his young life, a conflict which, moreover, led to an early suicide attempt. He put it this way in a letter he wrote in German to a friend:

> "I just don't know how to braid the wreath,— I can and cannot whip the disparate strands into any semblance of peace and harmony ... Religion; honor; the great duel; laws; the ideal and the reality; fatherland; solitary wrestling with my fate; faith as if in a fable; the spirit of God does not waft over the waters; America and Europe; Asia the cradle; blacks and whites; French

> Revolution the prelude, a new dawning; Germanness; Frenchness; Luther; Pope; Catholic; humanity; fate …"

He expressed similar sentiments in French in a letter to the illustrious Madame de Staël (the one-woman cultural bridge and clearing house between Germany and France), whose acquaintance he made as a result of his collaboration in the French translation of several lectures by the German philosopher, Friedrich Schlegel:

> "I am a Frenchman in Germany and a German in France; a Catholic among the Protestants, Protestant among the Catholics; a philosopher among the religious …, a mondain among the savants, and a pedant to the mundane; Jacobin among the aristocrats, and to the democrats a nobleman, a man of the Ancien Regime … Nowhere am I at home …!"

The pressures of such psychic turmoil and the painful reality of his status as an enemy alien proved untenable—particularly for a Prussian officer. Something had to give. Though a soldier by training, Chamisso was a scholar and poet at heart and loathed the crude rituals and rigours of the military life. His sense of awkwardness continued to express itself for years in nightmares in which he appeared on parade having forgotten his sword. (What would Freud have made of this?) One day, as he recalled in a letter, he "shot up out of sleep and wiped away the tears rolling down my cheeks … For me in this century," he realized, "no sword will do, the quill is my only refuge."

Aside from a flourishing correspondence, his literary output up until that point had been promising, if unremarkable. He was still in the process of what he described as a "tireless wrestling with the language"—that language being German. "*Il faudra que j'écrive quelque chose en allemand; car au fait il faudra bien apprendre cette coquine de langue.*" ("I really ought to write something in German, since after all, I do have to learn this minx of a language."), he had confessed to a friend at the Französisches Gymnasium in Berlin some years before. Now as a lieutenant in the Prussian army, a mastry of German became an absolute imperative. His painstakingly acquired German, however inspired, would forever be marked by mistakes (corrected for publication by his friend and publisher, Julius Eduard Hitzig) and curious turns of phrase that lent his syntax a special charm. And though he continued to count in French and, it is said, muttered French on his deathbed, with a fierce determination Chamisso adopted German as his adult literary and scholarly tongue.

*

Later in life, in the introduction to his popular *Journey Around the World*, (an account of a Russian-led expedition to Antarctica in which, as a naturalist of note, he participated), Chamisso reflected back on the circumstances surrounding the creation of the tale that was to make his name a household word:

> "The world events of the year 1813, in which I was not able to take an active part—for I had forfeited a fatherland, or rather had not yet adopted one—tore me apart repeatedly without deflecting me from my chosen path. That summer, to distract myself and to amuse the children of a friend, I wrote the fairy tale, *Peter Schlemihl*."

The "world events" of which he speaks followed the fall of Hameln (where his regiment was based) to the French, the

Prussian capitulation, his own long-awaited discharge from the army, several ill-fated trips to France and finally, an attempt to reestablish a semblance of normalcy for himself in Germany, as an enemy alien in his adoptive home.

As an outsider and the butt of considerable xenophobic sentiment, Chamisso gravitated naturally to the orbit of that other popular target of public displeasure: the Jews. In Berlin, he frequented the famous literary salons of Henriette Herz and Rahel Levin (who would later marry one of his closest friends, Karl August Varnhagen von Ense, and take his family name, by which she is known to posterity). His publisher and friend, Julius Eduard Hitzig was a converted Jew, as were many of Chamisso's friends and associates. It was, as Hannah Arendt points out in her book, *Rahel Varnhagen: The Life of a Jewish Woman*, a period of great social ferment, marked by the rise of the bourgeoisie and the waning of aristocratic power; and outcasts, intellectuals and oddballs from all quarters assembled in the living rooms of the outcast of them all. Here Chamisso found a safe haven, and came ineluctably to identify with the Christian medieval archetype of the "Wandering Jew" and the Jewish notion of the hapless "schlemiel."

In a letter to his brother, who proposed a French translation of *Peter Schlemihl*, Chamisso specified that the hero's name must under no circumstances be changed.

> "Schlemihl, or rather Schlemiel, is a Hebrew name," he wrote, "and means Gottlieb, Theophil or Beloved of God. This in the everyday parlance of the Jews is their designation for clumsy or unlucky souls who succeed at nothing in this world. A Schlemihl breaks his finger in his vest pocket or falls on his back and breaks his nose."

With a touch of the self-deprecating humor inherited from his friends, the young Chamisso undoubtedly saw himself as a blundering schlemihl.

When in 1813, war once again broke out between Prussia and France, the author's friend and later publisher, Julius Hitzig, counseled Chamisso to lay low for a while and arranged for him to apply his botanical skills tending the gardens of the Count von Itzenplitz in Kunersdorf. It was here in the summer months of 1813 that he composed *Peter Schlemihl* to pass the time and entertain Hitzig's children.

*

Certain texts erupt as naked emanations of the soul, bursts of pain transmuted straight into poetry. Such is the case with Kafka's *Metamorphosis*, the ultimate black comedy of bugging-out: — "As Gregor Samsa awoke one morning from uneasy dreams he found himself transformed in his bed into a gigantic insect." And such is the case with Samsa's spiritual precursor, *Peter Schlemihl*, the marginal man with literally no place under the sun. Though German classics both, it is clearly no coincidence that the former was written in 1912 (virtually on the eve of World War I) by a Czech Jew caught in the culture shock of a crumbling Austro-Hungarian Empire, and the latter almost a century before by a French nobleman eluding the clashing furies of his former compatriots and his adoptive countrymen.

Both tales struck their creators as bolts of literary lightning hurled by the thunderstorm of history and filtered through the imagistic firmament of the unconscious. Both elicit in the reader an embarrassed burst of Bergsonian laughter, a socially corrective chortle all too cognizant of the subliminal implications of being reduced to a bug and of forfeiting the virile bulge of a shadow. Kafka howled out hilariously in the precise bureaucratic German of his social circumstance. Chamisso, hiding out from a world in which one facet of his identity was at war with the other, might well have opted for suicide. Fortunately for himself and for posterity, he reached for the pen instead. Having turned himself inside-out and tapped the very core of his terror, he proceeded with German syntax and French esprit to tell the consummate Jewish joke.

Did you hear the one about the man who sold his shadow to enhance his social standing? No? Well then, read on!

All Fall Down: The Collapsing House of Cards of Heinrich von Kleist[1]

In a letter to his fiancé, Wilhelmine von Zenge, dated November 16-18, 1800, Heinrich von Kleist, a 23-year-old ex-army officer at the time who had not yet published a single word and would soon break off the engagement to take up a passionate romance with pen and ink, described his state of mind:

> "On that evening of the most important day of my life I went walking through Würzberg. As the sun set, it seemed to me as if my happiness were sinking. I shuddered at the thought that I might perhaps have to abandon *everything*, everything dear to me. So, there I went, walking through that vaulted doorway, my mind turned in upon myself, thinking back on the city. Why, I thought, does this arch not come crashing down since it has no support? It holds, I replied, because all the stones want to cave in at once—and from this thought I drew an indescribably comforting consolation that has stood by me until this decisive moment, always giving me hope that I, too, would manage to hold on if life were to let me fall."

In the mad tumble that ended 11 years later with a fatal bullet through the head, one of Germany's most enigmatic authors embraced his fall heart and soul, suspending the laws of gravity long enough to document the descent in a body of plays, stories

1 This essay was first published as the afterword to *Selected Short Prose of Heinrich von Kleist*, selected and translated by Peter Wortsman, Archipelago Books, Brooklyn, NY, 2010

and essays that have held up over time. It would be hard to imagine a personality of greater contradiction than that of their creator, a man at once more brilliantly adept at the practice of his art and more painfully inept at the business of living.

*

Born October 18, 1777, in the market town of Frankfurt-an-der-Oder, in the Margraviate of Brandenburg, into a family of proud Prussian Junkers, a lineage that produced 18 generals in its genetic pool, Bernd Heinrich Wilhelm von Kleist (aka Heinrich von Kleist) was predestined to bear arms and constitutionally disinclined to do so. After entering the army and rising to the rank of second lieutenant in the elite King's Guards Regiment in Potsdam he proceeded to resign his commission to pursue liberal studies, thereby vexing his next of kin and courting the disfavor of the Prussian King Friedrich Wilhelm II. Returning to Frankfurt to attend the university, after reading Kant he suffered a crisis of confidence and a paralyzing bout of existential doubt that shook his faith in pure reason and dispelled any prospect of an academic path, further rankling the already sorely disapproving clan. And when, thanks to family connections, he managed to get his foot in the door of the Prussian state bureaucracy, the last refuge of the prodigal aristocrat, and landed an entry level position in the Royal Chamber of Crown Lands in Königsberg, he promptly lost interest and proceeded to squander all goodwill, once again seeking his discharge to pursue a free life of letters. Fed up, the family broke off ties.

Kleist left for Dresden, a cultural capital at the time, but on the way an unlucky misunderstanding with Napoleon's provisional military government, then occupying the region, landed him in lock-up on suspicion of espionage. He was marched off to the

Fort de Joux, the forbidding prison in which the Haitian rebel leader Toussaint l'Ouverture had met his end. But grim as the conditions were, the period of incarceration proved a welcome respite from responsibility. Later transferred to considerably more hospitable quarters in Châlons-sur-Marne, Kleist put the time to good use, writing "The Marquise of O." and "The Earthquake in Chile." While still a prisoner, he learned that a friend had managed to get the latter story published in a respected magazine, the *Morgenblatt für gebildete Stände* (Morning Journal for Cultivated Classes). Shortly thereafter, by the terms of the Peace of Tilsit, Prussia capitulated to France and its prisoners, including Kleist, were released.

Kleist continued on his way to Dresden, where he had high hopes of launching a successful literary career. Yet he proved remarkably clumsy at maneuvering the social niceties, alienating with immoderate words and rash behavior many of his would-be patrons and benefactors, including the aged poet Christoph Martin Wieland and the *éminence grise* of German letters, Johann Wolfgang Goethe in Weimar. Lacking financial backing and adequate readership, his shaky business venture, a literary review, *Phöbus*, soon went under, as did a subsequent venture launched in Berlin, a newspaper, *Berliner Abendblätter*, though both served as the venues for his work.

But even his literary *succès d'estime*, such as it was, proved a Pyrrhic victory. With a few notable exceptions, Kleist's contemporaries missed the point and dismissed the result. His published plays were ridiculed. His stories were condemned by scandalized critics as: "hack jobs," "sheer nonsense," "senseless frivolities," "the work of a deranged mind," "un-German, stiff, twisted, and coarse." As to the assessment of his next of kin, the author complained in a letter of 1811 to Marie von Kleist, a cousin by marriage and confidant, that his siblings viewed him as "a good-for-nothing link in the social chain no longer worthy of any attachment."

"The truth is," Kleist confided to a friend, "that I find what I imagine to be beautiful, not what I actually produce. Were I able to pursue any other useful pursuit, I would gladly do so: I only write because I can't do otherwise."

His own verdict, communicated to his half-sister Ulrike, was as witty as it was merciless: "Hell gave me my half-talents, Heaven grants a man a complete talent or none."

On November 21, 1811, the illusive vaulted doorway came tumbling down. Acting as judge, jury, executioner and the condemned, in a suicide pact with Henriette Vogel, the wife of an acquaintance, a pact of convenience, rather than romance—she was dying of cancer and he had had enough—he put them both out of their misery with two pistol shots.

Yet till the end, Kleist managed to press his Prussian discipline and bellicose breeding to the service of his writing, sublimating tactical maneuvers into intricate syntax, waging a one-man war with society and himself, and in the process hammering the German language into a powerful weapon of expression. His plays, "The Broken Jug," "Penthesilea," the fragment "Robert Guiskard," and "Prinz Friedrich von Homburg," would become classics of the German theater, remarkable for their mingling of the idiomatic and the poetic, the impossible and the matter-of fact, though he never saw them staged.

The present volume is devoted to his prose. It includes two startlingly lucid and insightful meditations on the nature of thought and art, "On the Gradual Formulation of Thoughts While Speaking" and "On the Theater of Marionettes," and his most powerful narratives, "The Earthquake in Chile," "The Marquise of O.," "Michael Kohlhaas," and "St. Cecilia or the Power of Music," in which Kleist forged peerless prototypes of

German fiction that would influence writers for generations to come.

No less a master than Thomas Mann recalled discovering "the work of Heinrich von Kleist early on; it made a powerful impression on me then and this impression was always confirmed and renewed in the course of my life." Mann paid tribute in an essay published as the preface to an English language edition of Kleist's tales issued in America by Criterion Books:[2]

> "Kleist's narrative language is something completely unique. It is not enough to read it as 'historical'—even in his day nobody wrote as he did. [...] An impetus squeezed out with iron, absolutely un-lyrical detachment, brings forth tangled, knotted, overloaded sentences [...] painstakingly soldered together [...] and driven by a breathless tempo."

Another ardent literary admirer of note, Franz Kafka, found inspiration for his style and stance in that of the disaffected Prussian Junker, treasuring, in particular, "Michael Kohlhaas"—"a story I read with true reverence." There are indeed striking similarities in narrative technique in the work of the two authors, a shared use of bureaucratic precision and dispassionate language to evoke the ineffable. Kafka extolled Kleist in a letter to his own briefly betrothed, and subsequently forsaken, fiancé, Felice Bauer, as "one of the four men I consider to be my true blood-relations?"[3]The German-Jewish critic, Kurt Tucholsky,

2 *The Marquise of O, and other stories*, Criterion Books, 1960
3 In two letters from Franz Kafka to Felice Bauer, dated February 9-10, 1913, and September 2, 1913, Kafka praised *Michael Kohlhaas* and designated Grillparzer, Dostoevski, Kleist and Flaubert as "my true blood-relations." *Franz Kafka Letters to Felice*, Schocken Books, edited by Erich Heller and Jürgen Born, translated by James Stern and Elisabeth Duckworth, New York, 1967.

recognized this elective affinity, calling Kafka "the grandson of Kleist."

Kleist formulated his fate in words that prefigure the Kafkaesque: "Oh, it is my inborn misshapen tendency always to live elsewhere than where I am, and in a time gone by or not yet come."

The future confirmed Kleist's assessment. In another time and place his Marquise inspired the spare aesthetic of the French *Nouvel Vague* in Eric Roehmer's faithful screen adaptation (in which the young Bruno Ganz pulls off a tour de force performance, channeling the soul of the author). And in an artistic tribute on the far side of the Atlantic, E.L. Doctorov effectively reset Kleist's Kohlhaas in blackface, conjoining injustice and racism, in his novel *Ragtime.*

*

Kleist's prose may give pause to the contemporary English language reader, accustomed, since Hemmingway, to the simple and the succinct. Like Van Gogh in painting and Mahler in music, Kleist left no empty space, no room for silence or doubt. The effect can be a bit disconcerting. The paragraphs often stretch for pages without a break. The sentences—which this translator decided, wherever possible, to leave largely intact—are complex syntactical puzzles, claustrophobic labyrinths of pronominally linked subordinate clauses joined by semicolons that confound any prospect of foreseeable closure.

The plots defy reason, driven more by single-minded obsession carried to the bitter end than by any novelistic norms—and in this, read eerily modern.

As to character development, such as it is, Kleist's protagonists resemble the mercilessly pummeled dummies in car crash tests and the anatomical figures in medical atlases, in which the outline of the digestive tract is visible under the musculo-skeletal system and the skin. You can practically hear the heart thumping and see the words congeal in a vapor of raw emotion, but try and identify with them and you'll be confounded. For this is neither a literature of relationships nor of confession, nor is it the instructive stuff of a *Bildungsroman*. As in classical Greek drama and Biblical narrative, the die has been cast from the start, and all the reader/spectator can do is watch in stunned amazement as destinies spin out to their ineluctable end. Readers of "The Marquise of O.," an unlikely account of a highborn Virgin Mary minus the halo impregnated in her sleep, were shocked, as much by the author's detached telling, as by its socially unacceptable subject. Her mind is made up from the start. The only development the marquise undergoes is in her womb. Ticked off by injustice, Michael Kohlhaas rages with a mechanical fury: all we can do is wait for his psychic batteries to drain. Josephe and Jeronimo, the ill-starred lovers in "The Earthquake in Chile," make out, break out and march to their doom just as certainly as the social norms and the walls of Santiago come tumbling down around them. Kleist's tactic is to systematically cut off all avenues of escape.

Depending on how you view them, from the outside in or the inside out, Kleist's narrative structures, engineered to harness and channel the demiurges that drove him to the brink, are either emotional arches about to collapse overhead, or pressure cookers about to explode, that hold somehow, while the pressure gage whirrs out of control.

What then is the pleasure of reading Kleist?

His words overwhelm. His stories suck you into a visceral virtual reality. Surrendering, you stagger through the telling like a sleepwalker, gasping, unable to catch your breath or find your footing, trapped and rattled to the core, until finally Kleist lets you drop with a merciful period and an inkling of the human condition.

Facing the Music, the Melodious Imagining of E.T.A. Hoffmann[1]

On weekdays I'm a jurist, and a bit of a musician, my Sundays are devoted to drawing, and come evening I'm a quick-witted author until late at night.

– E.T.A. Hoffmann

Not far from his perch at the corner window overlooking Gendarmenmarkt, the central market place in Berlin, where he last surveyed life, paralyzed, in the painful end stage of syphilis, the epitaph inscribed on his tombstone in Cemetery III of the congregations of the adjacent Jerusalem Church and New Church reads like an abridged resumé: "E.T.W. Hoffmann, Counselor of the Court of Appeal, outstanding in accomplishment, as author, composer and painter." The man better known to posterity as E.T.A. Hoffmann plied diverse talents and packed multiple parallel careers into a mad dash life of a mere 46 years duration.

Born on January 24, 1776, in Königsberg in East Prussia, Ernst Theodor Wilhelm Hoffmann later opted to change his second middle name to Amadeus in homage to Mozart. Alongside the wildly imaginative tales for which he is justifiably famous, Hoffmann also composed eight operas and light operas, 23 musical themes for plays, ballets and melodramas, multiple masses, a miserere,[2] a symphony, 30 vocal works, and 16 piano sonatas and chamber music pieces, most of which have either been lost or forgotten. He also wrote landmark music criticism notable for, among other insights, a keen appreciation of the felicitous marriage of words and notes in operas and other vocal compositions.

1 This essay was first published as the afterword to *The Golden Pot, tales of the uncanny*, by E.T.A. Hoffmann, selected and translated by Peter Wortsman, Archipelago Books, Brooklyn, NY, 2024
2 A form of religious music

Speaking through his fictional alter ego, Kapellmeister Johannes Kreisler, in tongue-in-cheek writings published in various literary journals of the day, Hoffmann burst into print, fording the divide between tune and text.

But while his own richly evocative fictions inspired the memorable melodic creations of others, notably Jacques Offenbach's opera *The Tales of Hoffmann*, Pyotr Ilyich Tchaikovsky's ballet *The Nutcracker*, and Robert Schumann's *Kreisleriana* (Opus 16), Hoffmann himself never achieved the success he sought on the concert stage. Yet like few other authors before or sense, music informed every fiber of his being, seeping into the very marrow of his writing, not only inspiring narratives directly relating to musical themes, but also infusing his phrasing with a rich mellifluence that leaves the reader with the sense of stories sung.

Consider the following passage from "Ritter Gluck," Hoffmann's first published narrative, drafted in 1809 and issued in the *Allgemeine musikalische Zeitung*, in Leipzig, a respected musical newspaper at a time when music really mattered in cultivated German society; Hoffmann subsequently included it in his first collection *Fantasiestücke in Callots Manier* (Fantasy Pieces Conceived in Callot's Manner), published in 1814. An account of the narrator's meeting with a mysterious stranger who may either be the eponymous composer Christoph Willibald Gluck or else a brilliant lunatic, the tale is an attempt to compose with words a virtual tone poem evoking the psychic state of musical inspiration:

> "Hah, how in heaven's name is it possible to even intimate the thousand some odd paths to musical composition!—It is a broad thoroughfare, along which all romp along, whooping it up and crying: 'We are the anointed

> ones! We've made our mark!'—Passing through the ivory gate, you reach the realm of dreams; there are precious few who see the gate even once, and far fewer who ever pass through it! [...] Madcap figures pass back and forth, but they have character—some more so than others. They keep a low profile on the high road, you can only catch sight of them on the far side of the ivory gate. [...] many are entrapped by their reverie in the realm of dreams—they dissolve in their dreams [...]; but only a handful, awakened from their dream, [...] arrive at the truth—the supreme moment has come: contact with the eternal, an unspeakable experience!—The sun looks on, it is the tonic triad, from which chords shoot down, star-like, and spin around you with flaming filaments.—Enmeshed with fire, you lie there, until Psyche swings herself up to the sun."

Music constituted for Hoffmann a kind of sacred spell, and as such may have proved too holy, too precious to toy and tinker with. But words bore no such aura, and were consequently unencumbered with self-imposed restrictions and free to fiddle with.

"Ritter Gluck" can also be read as a kind of confessional. In the persona of the narrator, Hoffmann acknowledges his own failed attempts at musical composition. His interlocutor is clearly an embodiment of the author's own musical musings and longings. The fact that Hoffmann was best able to evoke such mellifluent euphoria in words, rather than notes, must have proved both immensely gratifying and infinitely frustrating to him.

In any case, music continued throughout the author's life to embody for him both an artistic and a spiritual ideal after which he strove, and as such, not only to inspire fiction directly relating to music, but also to spark in the echo chamber of his imagination such fulminous outbursts as "The Sandman" and "The Golden Pot," the two enigmatic tales for which he is best known. In these and other phantasmagorical narratives, Hoffmann allowed himself to take prodigious artistic liberties, wildly leaping back and forth across the border between the physical and the metaphysical, the perceived and the imagined, the accessible and the unattainable, hazarding with language the daring leaps of his musical idols, Mozart and Beethoven. The astute reader can sense the notes pulsing inside his words and recognize his narratives as the quasi-musical compositions that they are.

*

The opposition between the accessible and the ideal also plays itself out in his plots. In both "The Sandman" and "The Golden Pot," Hoffmann's male protagonists waver between their attraction for actual flesh-and-blood women and the seemingly irresistible lure of ideal objects of desire, an automaton in the former narrative and a sultry, green snake in the latter, invariably opting for the unattainable ideal over the actual, and consequently descending into madness. One cannot help but wonder if his characters' unflinching preference for the impossible was a consequence of the "grass is always greener" syndrome, or rather, contingent on some unresolved childhood trauma in the author's own life.

Fascinated by the man and his imaginings as a potential minefield for psychoanalysis, Sigmund Freud repeatedly sought to posthumously stretch him out on the virtual analytic couch and dig into his dreams. In Freud's late work, *Der Mann Moses und die monotheistische Religion (Moses and Monotheism)*, completed in 1939, he included the following aside:

> "E.T.A. Hoffmann liked to trace back the source of the wealth of characters that fed his fictions to the play of images and impressions he gleaned as a suckling babe at his mother's breast on a weeklong journey by postal coach."

Much as the author might have fostered this farfetched fiction about himself, it is impossible to confirm, albeit unlikely, that such a rife imagination could have been stoked by even the most precocious infant's photographic memory.

What is certain is that Hoffmann mythologized his childhood and his mother. He was the son of an unhappy union; his parents separated in 1778, when he was only two years old, whereupon he lost contact with his father and moved back with his emotionally cold and unresponsive mother to her maternal home. That reconstituted household was headed by a strict, unforgiving grandmother, two batty maiden aunts, and a repressed, albeit musically inclined, bachelor uncle, whose sole saving grace from the boy's perspective was that he encouraged him to take up music. A virtual automaton, his mother often spent the whole day motionless, staring into the void, and died in despair a year later. His uncle had studied law, but abandoned the profession after losing his first court case, withdrawing into premature and permanent retirement. Except for a kindly childlike aunt, the adults remained essentially aloof to the child in their midst. Hoffmann came of age in this emotionally arid environment, taking refuge in his reveries, embroidering his longings with imagined memories of intimacy with an idealized and loving mother.

Freud had already delved into Hoffmann's rife imagination in a famous early essay, entitled *Das Unheimliche* (The Uncanny), written in 1919, in which he hailed the author as "the unsurpassed master of the uncanny in literature." In the essay, Freud focuses his attention on "The Sandman," a tale of a student's descent into madness, dated on the original manuscript, "One o'clock in the morning, November 16, 1815," and first published in his short story collection *Die Nachtstücke* (The Night Pieces), in 1817.

Traumatized in childhood by an ominous, sometime associate of his father who half-jokingly threatened to tear out the inquisitive boy's eyes, Hoffmann's protagonist, Nathaniel, later conflates a traveling oculist with his childhood bugbear; through the lens of a looking glass he buys from the latter he glimpses and immediately falls head over heels for Olympia, the dazzling, albeit a bit stiff, daughter of his professor, and promptly drops his old flame Clara. Olympia, alas, turns out to be an automaton. Upon witnessing the comely robot have her eyes torn out and thereafter be literally torn apart in the course of a quarrel between the professor and the oculist, Nathaniel suffers a nervous breakdown. He returns to his native town, where Clara, with whom he has since reconciled, cares for him in his convalescence. All appears to be going well between them, until Nathaniel goes off the deep end again, believing he has spotted his old demon in the crowd, and in a psychotic fit, attempts to toss Clara from a tower window, from which he ultimately leaps to his death.

Freud traces a fondness for mechanical automata back to a common childhood fixation, reminding with considerable insight "that at a very early age of make believe, the child does not distinguish sharply between the living and the lifeless and is particularly fond of treating its doll as a living being."

Freud furthermore conflates the eyes with the genitals, and concludes that "the uncanny element in 'The Sandman' can be traced back to fear of the child's castration complex"—a somewhat far-fetched contention perhaps more linked to Freud's own fixations than those of Hoffmann.

Whatever childhood trauma it does or does not tap, the terrifying tale and its author had a profound literary influence, particularly abroad, nourishing the eerie narratives of Edgar Allen Poe, Nathaniel Hawthorne, Nikolai Gogol, and Oscar Wilde, among countless other authors of note. "The Sandman" also inspired a novel by German novelist and screenwriter Thea von Harbou, that in turn, inspired her husband, film director Fritz Lang, to collaborate with her on the silent film classic *Metropolis*. French Surrealist André Breton viewed E.T.A. Hoffmann as a pivotal forerunner and pathfinder and included the story in his *Anthology of Black Humor*, published in 1940. The tale later primed the American science fiction writer Philipp K. Dick to pen his tour-de-force novel, *Do Androids Dream of Electric Sheep*, upon which Ridley Scott based his 1982 cult film classic, *Bladerunner*.

However we choose to interpret such enigmatic tales as "The Sandman" and another likewise included in this collection, titled "The Automaton," Hoffman's interest in and concern about the early 19th century mechanized figurines featured at fairs in his day, particularly those that also play music and nowadays still decorate Christmas show windows, as one biographer, Peter Braun, points out, "constitutes one of the earliest condemnations of the burgeoning industrial omnipresence of machines. He saw in them, not only a threat to human beings, but also, and in particular, a menace to music," excising the vital human element of variability and reducing it to a stiff, mechanical motor of music.

"The Golden Pot," first published in 1814 in the third volume of his *Fantasiestücke in Callots Manier* (*Fantasy Pieces in the*

Manner of Caillot), likewise traces a student's descent into folly. The love object here is an imaginary green talking snake, named Serpentina, first glimpsed by the delirious protagonist, Anselmus, wriggling around the trunk and branches of an elderberry tree. The shape of the snake evokes phallic phantasies, but we had best leave it to future Freudians and biographers to delve into Hoffmann's complex libido.

Hoffmann's fascination with madness was informed by his acquaintance with the physician, Adalbert Friedrich Marcus, who in 1789 founded the Bamberger Allgemeine Krankenhaus, in which he treated emotionally disturbed patients with hypnotic methods based on Franz Anton Mesmer's theory of animal magnetism.

*

What matters to posterity is not so much the root of his intuition in this regard, as how Hoffmann the writer transformed such infantile traumatic flashes into unforgettable fiction. A thin, little man with deep-set eyes, sharp features, and porcupine-like, spiked hair, with a fiery temperament and wit enough for multiple personalities, Hoffmann apparently penned the tales bubbling up from his unconscious at lightning speed. According to his diary, he wrote "The Sandman" over a period of eight days, while simultaneously attending to the responsibilities of his day job as a jurist.

This is how his friend, Julius Eduard Hitzig, described him in the first biography devoted to the author:

> "Hoffmann was very short in stature, had a yellowish skin color, very dark, almost black hair that sprouted from low down on his forehead, gray eyes that did not

> express much when he was still and peering forward, but which sparkled and took on an uncommonly crafty look when he winked, as he often liked to do. His nose was fine and bent, his mouth tightly closed. [...] He particularly prized his muttonchop whiskers, and combed them carefully close to the corners of his mouth. [...] In his entire outward appearance, one was particularly struck by an extraordinary sprightliness."

Hoffmann peppered his texts with revelatory clues concerning his character, as, for instance, in the comic description of his fictional alter ego Kapellmeister Johannes Kreisler:

> "His friends maintained that nature tried a new recipe when cooking up his character traits, and that the experiment failed, in that too little of the phlegmatic had been added to his over-excitable disposition, his imaginative faculty all too often fired up to a dangerous degree, so as to tip the balance of his equilibrium, a quality absolutely essential to the artist, enabling him to get along with the world, and to compose works of the sort that the world really needs to a higher degree than they even know."

There is another hardly veiled self-portrait in "The Golden Pot":

> "... such an individual need be of a childlike poetic disposition. This disposition is often found in youths scorned by the crowd on account of the great simplicity of their manner and because they are totally lacking in worldly sophistication."

In yet another passage, this one from "Counselor Krespel," Hoffmann's tale of a maniacally over-protective father who inexplicably prevents his daughter from singing, first published in 1818 in his friend, the Baron de la Motte Fouqué's, popular literary journal *Frauentaschenbuch*, the author once again appears to be describing a character with definite parallels to himself:

> "'There are people,' he said, 'from whom nature or some calamity tears away the veil behind which the rest of us engage in our mad doings unnoticed. They resemble thin-skinned insects that appear misshapen in the buoyant, visible squirming of their minuscule muscles, though they soon reassume their proper shape. All that in us remains merely imagined, in Krespel turns into action.—The bitter irony that our well-behaved spirit ordinarily keeps under control in our conduct and actions drives Krespel to mad gesticulations, twists and turns. But that is his lightning rod. What emanates from the earth he gives back to the earth, but he retains a flicker of the divine spark; and so, I believe, his mind is perfectly in order, notwithstanding the seeming madness of his antics.'"

Krespel, it turns out, had a perfectly rational reason for preventing his daughter from singing. (The story was inspired by the actual case of the sickly 17-year-old singer Minna Brandes, whom Hoffmann had heard sing in Königsberg; having been forbidden to sing on doctor's orders as a strain on her fragile health, she declined to follow the medical advice and died of consumption six years later.)

*

Like Krespel, Hoffmann, too, had a rational, pragmatic side counterbalancing the erratic bent of his wild emotional swings and imaginative frenzies. He summed up his attitude and aesthetic in a line from *The Serapion Brethren*,[3] the epistolary narrative frame of a collection of his tales:

> "I believe that the bottom of the heavenly ladder, upon which we seek to clamber to reach the higher regions of consciousness, must be grounded in real life, so that our readers can clamber up after us. If the reader who climbs higher and higher finds himself in a fantastic magical realm, he will be more likely to believe that this realm still belongs as an integral part of his life, and is, in fact, the most wondrous and splendid part of that life."

Another notable German-speaking author likewise trained in the law, Franz Kafka, who also juggled the responsibilities of a mundane day job with nightly reverie, and is in many ways a kindred spirit with Hoffmann, took up the same ladder metaphor, albeit with a Kafkaesque twist, in a diary notation:

> "[...] all things that occur to me to describe don't strike me from the root, but rather from somewhere in the middle. Just try to grab it, try to embrace a blade of grass that grows out from the middle of the stalk. A select few can do it, so for instance, Japanese jugglers balanced on a ladder not resting on firm ground, but rather on the uplifted soles of a half-reclining partner, a ladder not propped up against any wall either, but rather just rising in the air."

---

3 The Serapion Brethren was also the name of a Berlin literary and social circle to which Hoffmann belonged.

It might not be all that far-fetched to perceive a link of influence between Hoffmann's automaton, the cause of the protagonist's violent demise in "The Sandman," and the insidious device in Kafka's dark phantasy "In the Penal Colony" that incises the fate of the condemned in his body and immediately thereafter implodes.

Like Kafka, Hoffmann, too, kept a firm foothold in the sober reality of the law.

Having studied law, he pursued a professional career as a mid-level bureaucrat in the judicial administration of the Prussian state bureaucracy. Prussia at the time extended well beyond the borders of the present-day German state of Brandenburg, encompassing large swathes of present-day Poland, including the aforementioned Posen (Poznań) and the cosmopolitan metropolis of Warsaw. Hoffmann started out as a probationary court judge in Posen and rose to the rank of judge in Berlin's prestigious court of appeal. By most accounts, he faithfully and diligently carried out his legal responsibilities, oftentimes going out of his way to promote justice and freedom of expression in an absolutist state.

In Posen, he met and married Maria Thekla Michaline Rohrer-Trzcińska and lived happily, if not ever after, then at least for a while. But time and again, the disparate strands of his character unraveled and his pen and his penchant for mischief got him into trouble. An accomplished draughtsman, among his many creative talents, Hoffmann was fond of drawing caricatures of individuals of his acquaintance. In 1802, his caricatures of major-generals and other high-ranking officers in the Prussian military and local landed gentry found their way onto satirical masks at a carnival celebration. Discovered as the artistic trickster behind the lark, Hoffmann, who had been anticipating promotion to state councilor and transfer to the capital city of Berlin, was indeed promoted, but as a sanction for his insubordinate antics was shunted off to the onomatopoeic sounding backwater hamlet of Płock.

Two years later, Hoffmann managed to get himself transferred to Warsaw, where he reveled in the cosmopolitan atmosphere and the plenitude of cultural activities. His family life was also enriched by the birth of a daughter whom he named Cäcilia, after St. Cecilia, the patron saint of musicians. In Warsaw he met and befriended a fellow jurist, Julius Eduard Hitzig, who would become a lifelong ally and his first biographer. Né Isaac Elias Itzig, the cultivated scion of a well-to-do Jewish family, expedience led Hitzig to add an H to camouflage his Semitic ancestry, and to later convert to Christianity. Neighbors as well as professional colleagues, on warm summer nights the two men flung open their windows, and Hitzig was fond of leaning out to listen to the music Hoffmann played. Well-read and well-connected in literary circles, Hitzig introduced his friend to the Romantic literature of the day, and later to many of the leading German Romantics writers.

His friendship with Hitzig notwithstanding, Hoffmann's attitude to Jews has been studied by scholars, some going so far as to suspect a Jewish caricature in his portrayal of the villainous character who threatened to pluck out the child's eyes in "The Sandman." Certain insidious antisemitic clichés crept into such tales as "The Selection of a Bride." It should be noted, however, that in harboring such prejudices, Hoffmann was no different from most of his contemporaries.

Among his administrative duties in Warsaw, the man who had changed his own middle name from Theodor to Amadeus, was tasked with the assignment of surnames to Warsaw's Jewish community, who as per Jewish tradition, had heretofore gone by patronymics. According to Norman Davies, in his *Heart of Europe: The Past in Poland's Present* (Oxford University Press, 2001), Hoffmann undertook the task with a capricious whimsy: "Before dinner, or on an empty stomach, he issues serious or melancholy surnames, after dinner more amusing ones." On one occasion, apparently following a prolonged bout of drinking with a military man of his acquaintance, Hoffmann hastily dubbed unsuspecting individuals of Jewish provenance with military names, such as Festung (Fortress), Pistolet (Pistol), Szyspulver (gunpowder), Trommel (drum), etc.

*

Like so many other creative artists with quirky character traits, Hoffmann was surely a bundle of contradictions. His prickly personality did not always sit well with those who knew him. Contemporary assessments by his fellow German Romantics vary. Unfailingly defending him, Hitzig remained a devoted friend, lauding Hoffmann in the biography he wrote after his death. Wilhelm Grimm, on the other hand, considered Hoffmann brilliant, "but unsavory." Jean Paul held him to be an out and out madman. A friend and frequent dinner partner in Berlin, author Adelbert von Chamisso dubbed him "the king of tomfoolery." Poet Clemens Brentano deemed him "an eccentric, but honest chum." Writer and journalist August Varnhagen von Ense held him to be "an honest friend, without guile and malice, whose sense of humor nevertheless proved brash and disquieting, and could be equally insightful and fatuous."

Hoffmann offers a veiled fictionalized self-appraisal in his novel *The Devil's Elixir,* written in 1814:

> "I am what I appear to be, and don't appear to be what I am, an inexplicable riddle to myself, I am a divided self."

Whether out of restless temperament or necessity, he changed locales with some frequency, from Posen to Płock, to Warsaw, to Berlin, to Bamberg, where he landed a position as theater director, from which he was fired soon thereafter, compelling him for a time to eke out his existence as a piano teacher.

In one profoundly embarrassing and socially devastating instance, Hoffmann's libido got the better of him. His infatuation with an underage piano student, Julia Mark, in Bamberg led to a scene, compelling him to skip town. Next stops Leipzig and Dresden. Marriage did not keep his excesses in check. Always a heavy drinker and carouser, back in Posen he is rumored to have been the author of an anonymous sado-masochistic novel, *Sister Monica*, issued by a book dealer-publisher of his acquaintance. In one of his many extra-marital involvements he contracted the syphilis that would first cripple him, then do him in.

And when it was not his own shenanigans that got him into trouble, history played a hand. Prussia's provisional military alliance with Russia against France led Napoleon to occupy Warsaw. Refusing to swear allegiance to the Gallic Emperor and the newly installed French puppet administration, Hoffmann was again obliged to decamp.

*

Hoffmann's allegiance to his native Prussia did not, however, keep him from speaking and reading French, and admiring French culture and literature. French influence found its way into his work, notably in one of his most accomplished and successful works, "Mademoiselle de Scudéry" inspired by Voltaire's *Le Siècle de Louis XIV*, and other books which he borrowed from a Berlin lending library in 1818. In Voltaire's text, Hoffmann found the historic inspiration for one of his only female protagonists, Madeleine de Scudéry (1607-1701), aka Mademoiselle de Scudéry, a poet and writer of popular novels, a favorite of Louis XIV and his mistress and later wife, Madame de Maintenon. From historic strands Hoffmann wove an intricate murder mystery, published in the fall of 1819 in the popular almanac *Taschenbuch für das Jahr 1820*. The narrative, in which Hoffmann combined his legal expertise with his imaginative prowess, proved an immediate sensation, stirring interest in all of Hoffmann's writing. The publisher was so pleased, to foster future contributions he gifted the author 50 bottles of wine.

According to literary scholar Richard Alewyn, "Mademoiselle de Scudéry" is the earliest prototype of the detective genre, a clear influence on Edgar Allan Poe's "The Murders in the Rue Morgue." Against the backdrop of a series of unsolved murders plaguing Paris, the plot revolves around the inexplicable actions of a young journeyman goldsmith in love with his master's daughter, wrongfully accused of murdering the master, and who refuses to defend himself. After the young man has already been found guilty and condemned to death, Mlle. de Scudéry manages, against all odds, to ascertain and prove his innocence and gain clemency from the king. Unlike the uncanny tales for which Hoffmann is most famous, this story is an astounding intertwining of irrational actions and clear-headed, rational thinking. De Scudéry may well be the first, and surely one of the most astute female sleuths, a model for Agatha Christie's Miss Marple, among others. And in his characterization of the master goldsmith, a certain René Cardillac, at once an artist and a madman, Hoffmann gives us one of the great criminal masterminds in world literature, whose heirs must surely include Stevenson's Mr. Hyde, Sir Arthur Conan Doyle's Dr. Moriarty, and Ian Fleming's Goldfinger.

Whereas historical sources provided the seed, and rational thought is adroitly employed to tie loose knots, the twists of the imagination are always Hoffmann's primary compass. A character named Theodor (coincidentally also the author's original second middle name) in the story "The Automaton," espouses Hoffmann's literary aesthetic:

> "Nothing is more distasteful to me in a story, in a novel on the floor of which the fantastic world has wiggled its way, than that it be swept so clean with an historic broom so that not a kernel, not a grain of dust remains, when you return home, so resigned that you feel no more longing to look behind the curtains. In contrast to which, many a fragment of a spirited story sinks deep into my soul and affords me a lasting pleasure, since fantasy stirs its own vibrations."

*

The defeat of Napoleon permitted a penniless Hoffmann to return to the Prussian civil service. He moved back to Berlin in 1814 to accept an initially non-paying stint, and then a permanent appointment as judge in the court of appeal. Yet again, he got himself into trouble by parodying a sometime superior and mocking the court system in his satirical novel *Master Flea*. But Hoffmann agreed to make cuts and weathered the crisis.

It was here in Berlin, from 1814 until his death in 1822, juggling administrative responsibilities with creative drive, that he finally achieved success and celebrity. In Berlin, he reconnected with Hitzig, who had also been transferred there. Hitzig introduced Hoffmann to the Romantic writers, Adelbert von Chamisso, Ludwig Tieck, und Friedrich Baron de la Motte Fouqué, the latter also a publisher.

Throughout his life, despite all the ups and downs, personal scandals and professional pitfalls, Hoffmann kept creating.

His greatest musical triumph, the opera, *Undine*, for which he composed the music based on a libretto by Friedrich de la Motte Fouqué, with a set designed by the noted architect, city planner and painter, Karl Friedrich Schinkel, premiered at the Königliches Schauspielhaus in Berlin in 1817, and proved a critical and popular hit talked about all over town. In retrospect, viewed by some musicologists as the first Romantic opera, the combined effect of the music, text, set and costumes, was among the influences on Richard Wagner's notion of the Gesamtkunstwerk. But, alas, after 14 packed-house performances, a fire burnt the theater to the ground, also destroying the set and costumes. Hoffmann himself witnessed the fire from his window across the way, at his last place of residence, at Taubenstrasse 31. The flames threatened to leap across the way and consume his building. He later described the scene in a letter to a friend:

> "I was seated at my desk, when my wife came rushing in from the room next door, her face pale as a sheet, and said: 'My God, the theater is burning!'—Neither she nor I for a moment lost our heads. When firemen, including some whom I counted among my friends, knocked on the door, we had already with the aid of our cook, transported curtains, bed and other furniture to safety in a room to the rear, thus diminishing the risk of their catching fire. [...] In the front rooms, all the window panes shattered and the oil paint on the window frames and doors melted and dripped down in the heat."

*

It was here at this same window overlooking the marketplace, between the months of February and April 1822, in between acute spasms of pain, and almost completely paralyzed in the late stage of syphilis, that Hoffmann dictated his last completed narrative, "My Cousin's Corner Window." It appeared shortly thereafter in several installments in the journal, *Der Zuschauer*, weeks before the author's death.

The aforementioned text is included in this collection, not because it is among the author's best, or most representative pieces of writing, far from it—Walter Benjamin derided its descriptions as "backward-looking Biedermeier," in contrast to Baudelaire's and Poe's progressive modes of presentation—but precisely because it is his last published account, and because it reveals the wheels of his keen faculty for observation still turning, albeit without plot, with no other narrative end than to take in the world around him until his last conscious blink.

Translating that last completed story into English felt to me at times like eavesdropping on the privacy of a fading mind. But Hoffmann put the words out there, so he must have welcomed the prospect of a stranger from the future looking in. Celebrating seeing and telling till the end, this text reads like his last will and testament, bequeathing his disintegrating consciousness and its last fruits to posterity. Perched at his corner window overlooking the marketplace, scanning the open book of the crowd, harvesting impressions, Hoffmann kept compulsively secreting a narrative thread, spinning fiction out of life, forever enticing posterity in the web of his imaginings. According to his friend and biographer, Julius Eduard Hitzig, he was still spinning a yarn, dictating another unfinished tale, "The Enemy" with his dying breath—before finally facing the music.

Return to Sender:
The Letters of Rahel Levin Varnhagen[1]

A letter always seemed to me like immortality, because it is the mind alone without corporeal friend.

– Emily Dickinson

Now that the terse text message with its streamlined syntax and abbreviated spelling has all but supplanted the email, the handwritten pen-and-ink letter seems as anachronistic to the contemporary mindset as prehistoric handprints on cave walls. Like a prayer, the personal letter is a passionate declaration directed from an I to a thou, replete with pathos and longing, albeit minus all the holy hyperbole. In parts poetic, but not a poem, in parts prosaic, but not an essay, a letter is pure writing for writing's sake. Scholars peruse the letters of prominent people to better understand their actions and accomplishments, and in the case of poets and writers, for the insights their letters offer into the matrix of their more formal works. Only very rarely is the letter prized as a literary form in its own right.

Women have been among the most adept and prolific correspondents, at least in part because they have long been relegated to the domestic sphere and largely excluded from writing and publishing anything else. One of the most illustrious among female letter writers in the Western canon is Madame de Sévigné, AKA Marie de Rabutin-Chantal, the Marquise de Sévigné (1626-1696). Her evocative missives to her daughter, Françoise-Marguerite de Sévigné, Comtesse de Grignan (1646-1705), are considered classics of French 17th-century literature.

1 This essay was first published as the introduction to *I Just Let Life Rain down on Me, Selected Letters and Reflections of Rahel Levin Varnhagen*, selected and translated by Peter Wortsman, Seagull Books, Kolkata, India, 2024

In the German-speaking world, Rahel Varnhagen von Ense, née Levin, the illustrious German-Jewish Berlin literary salon hostess (1771-1833), is likewise renowned for her letters, over 10,000 of which she penned in the course of her life to more than 300 recipients, including princes, philosophers, poets, family members, and the family cook; some 6,000 of her letters are still extant today. Written with a wink at posterity, clearly conceived as compositions worth preserving, collected and published after her passing by her husband, Karl August Varnhagen von Ense (1785-1858), they constitute a singular contribution to German literature.

The poignant lyricism of Rahel's letters is all the more remarkable when we take into account that German was not her first language. The precocious oldest daughter of Levin Markus Cohen (1723-1790), a jeweler, banker and businessman, and Chaie, née Moses (1742-1809), Rahel grew up speaking and writing primarily Yiddish, a German dialect written in Hebrew letters, derogatively referred to in her day as "*Juden-Deutsch*" (Jews' German). The Levins were one of a little more than 300 prosperous Jewish families permitted to reside in Berlin, which at around 1800, comprised a mere one to two percent of the total Jewish population of Prussia. The homes of Berlin's so-called "*Schutzjuden*" (protected Jews), their number strictly regulated by the king, were a kind of neutral ground outside the grid of social constraints, where cultivated Christians and Jews engaged in a relatively free and open exchange of ideas.

Yet whereas her brothers were formally educated—the oldest, Markus Theodor (formerly Mordechai, 1772–1826) in business affairs, her younger brother, Ludwig Robert (AKA Liepmann Levin, 1778-1832), a poet and playwright, at the Französiches Gymnasium, a prestigious institution in Berlin founded by exiled French Huguenots—Rahel was home-schooled in German,

French, piano and dance, disciplines deemed suitable to make women more marriageable. But from early on, Rahel bucked the cliché of the accommodating female whose sole raison d'être is to make a good match, bear children, and manage a household. An autodidact in literature and philosophy, among other areas of interest, she became an avid reader of and commentator on the works of her contemporaries, with a particular appreciation for the poetry of Johann Wolfgang Goethe (1749-1832). Among the only texts of hers published in her lifetime was a commentary on Goethe excerpted from her correspondence with her husband and selected by him. But the best of her letters are more than mere commentary, they are declarations concerning every aspect of life formulated in a voice as fresh and original as that of any of the poets and thinkers of her day.

"Her letters are not really written," declared a friend, the German writer and political thinker, Friedrich von Gentz (1764-1832), "they are living people. They read as if they were spoken aloud." Another friend with whom she carried on an extensive correspondence, the German-Jewish physician and thinker David Veit (1771-1814) opined: "In her letters ... every word always reads as if she had just now invented it."

Rahel herself put it this way:

> "... our language is our lived life; I invented mine for my own purposes, I was less able than many others to make use of preconceived turns of phrase, which is why mine are often clumsy, and in all respects faulty, but always true."

Idiosyncratic in her orthography, punctuation, grammar and phrasing, she took considerable liberties with sentence structure, teased out and toyed with the meaning of familiar terms, coined new words, and spun run-on sentences that hone close to the erratic contour of consciousness—all of which often makes her writing difficult to fathom and a formidable challenge to translate. With tongue-in-cheek humor, for instance, she coined the word "*Witzschlag*," a composite of the German words "*Witz*" (wit) and "*Blitzschlag*" (flash of lightning), thus "a bolt of wit." And with a self-deprecatory irony, she invented another word, "*Scheinschreiben*," (pseudo-writing) to refer to her own "clumsy, and in all respects faulty, but always true" prose.

It is as if the nib of her pen were linked directly to her tongue.

The spoken word was Rahel's real forte, and her real passion was socializing with a select coterie of like-minded souls who gathered at her digs to indulge in a lively exchange of ideas. She hosted literary salons during two distinct periods in her life, the first begun as a precocious teen, starting when she was 19, in her parents' house, from 1790 to 1806, the year Napoleon defeated the Prussians and invaded Berlin; the second, together with her husband, Karl August Varnhagen, from 1819 until her death in 1833.

As she put it in a letter to a sometime friend, the German Romantic poet and writer Clemens Brentano[2] (1778-1842):

> "As far back as I can remember, I have always had a boundless love for socializing with friends, and am quite certain that I was so conceived and so equipped by nature. My presence of mind and quick-wittedness permit me to grasp, respond, and discuss. Endowed

2 Some of the very same German Romantic poets, including Clemens Brentano, whom she welcomed into her salon as young, up-and-coming talents, would later betray her trust, expressly excluding Jews and women, among other undesirables, from their own old boys' club, the Christlich-Deutsche Tischgesellschaft (The Christian-German Table Society), founded in 1811.

> with a keen sense of human nature and the nature of all relationships, a sense of wit and seriousness [...], humble as I am, I let down my guard by speaking; I can keep quiet for a very long time, love all manifestations of humanity, and can suffer almost all people."

While most Jewish men of means, like her father, were solely associated with and essentially reduced to their pecuniary worth, their wives and daughters functioned as relatively free agents, rare caged birds with an exotic appeal. Rahel's brilliant repartee made her a prized intellectual catalytic agent for those who flocked to her salon. Held in the highest esteem by her contemporaries—"the most quick-witted woman in the world," according to German-Jewish poet Heinrich Heine (1797-1856); "the brightest woman in Europe," according to German historian Leopold von Ranke (1795-1886)—"she had a way with words, like no other person," according to the German author Jean Paul (1763-1825).

Those who met her for the first time were oftentimes flabbergasted at the apparent dichotomy between her plain appearance and her sparkling wit. "Then the aging, perhaps never beautiful, stooped, fairy-like, not to say witch-like, woman started speaking, and I was bewitched," recalled Austrian writer and playwright Franz Grillparzer (1791-1872). "My fatigue dissipated, or rather gave way to intoxication. She spoke and spoke until round about Midnight, [...] Never in my life have I heard a person speak better and in a more interesting manner."

"The beautiful thing about Rahel's spirit was her original take on things, according to which she shaped her opinions," wrote another friend, writer, publisher, composer, and social activist, Bettina von Arnim, the sister of Clemens Brentano and wife of Achim von Arnim. "She was tolerant where others were quick to condemn, and she tasted the salt in that which others dismissed as the burnt ash of a consumed life. To be just is a godly art."

Small of stature, ill-proportioned, ungainly, lacking the physical allure and charm by which women have long been and are still judged, all the while abjuring any false modesty, she was nevertheless convinced of her own intellectual prowess: – "I am as singular as the greatest soul on earth. The greatest artist, philosopher or poet has nothing on me. They and I are made of the self-same element."

Well aware of the worth of her words, as early as 1794 she wrote to remind her brother Markus, who as the oldest male heir, was anointed head of the family following her father's death: "Save my letters, for they are my journals; I cannot write it twice, I do everything on the spur of the moment. No impression must be lost." As the lightning bolt is to the lightbulb, her letters burst the constraints of ordinary communication, flooding the recipient with insight.

Or as she phrased her intent in a letter dated July 1, 1800, to Wilhelmine von Boye,[3] in Stralsund:

> "Adieu!—and when I die—I will gather up all my letters—by devious means—hoping to retrieve them from all my friends and acquaintances [...] It will make for an original story and very poetic. [...] This, Boye, I demand of you as a duty. [...] It is not, I think, too much to ask of a friend."

3 Wihelmine von Boye, AKA Johanna Hedwig Wilhelmine Countess von Sparre, née Hitzel Bernhard (1772-1839), close friend since childhood and lifelong correspondent of Rahel's

In her letters, Rahel played language riffs as others play musical instruments.

Here she is expounding on the nature of the poet:

> "A poet is a person in whom all strings on which experience plays are plucked, whereupon they vibrate; but what of those in whom such strings are absent!"

Here she is extoling dance:

> "Yes, I waltz. For the past five Mondays we've established a dance hour at home—ever since the third session I kicked up my legs and started waltzing, and not half badly; and do you think a girl can keep a steady head with all that unwholesome twisting and turning?—though I can't quite take the sensual pleasure in it that most people do, half of them picturing it as perilous to their health, the other half as sheer heavenly delight [...]"

Here she is assessing her linguistic failings:

> "Much as I resolve to pay heed to orthography while reading, I almost never manage, and if I do so at the very start of reading something, I don't really read, but just see the way the words are written; but I soon grow tired of it and return to reading; this makes me feel terribly sad for myself, and the simplest soul can learn more than me, and it would be insufferable if I did not find some small consolation in not blaming the faulty side of my brain, but rather acknowledging that it is the good side that ill serves me. [...]"

And here she is figuratively dissecting the self:

> "A person can, like a book, be torn to shreds."

*

The author whose extensive correspondence immediately comes to mind when considering Rahel's letters is Franz Kafka (1883-1924). Though Kafka mastered German and wrote in the clear, bureaucratic manner of a doctor or lawyer, both treat language as a malleable material to express a mindset hors norm, a consciousness rooted in a uniquely Jewish mix of intellectual acuity and profound emotional insecurity.

> "But I myself cannot keep on living," Kafka wrote to a friend, "since I have never really lived, I remained mud, never managed to make the spark of life in me ignite into a flame, but only managed to use it to shed a little light on my cadaver. It will make for a funny kind of funeral, in that the writer, that insubstantial something, passed on his old cadaver, a cadaver since day one, to the grave."

Rahel, who died a half century before Kafka was born, could just as well have written the above words. And as Kafka famously vented his spleen in a letter to his father, so did Rahel, too, spill her guts in a tell-all letter to her mother, with whom she maintained strained relations:

> "Having leveled against me the easily refuted admonishment that I simply don't know what I want, you will, I trust, be so kind as to permit me to present my situation

> one last time! You know my age; but my profound distress will forever remain a mystery to you. I am dependent on you: you alone could protect me and as an expression of goodwill could assure me a refuge for my injured heart. This is how things stand for me now."

Like Kafka, Rahel likewise drew on her dreams and tapped her unconscious as a source of literary inspiration. "I am much more wide-awake in sleep," she wrote.

And just as posterity owes a debt of gratitude to Kafka's friend, Max Brod, for disobeying his express wishes to burn all his unpublished papers after his death, opting instead, not only to preserve, but also to tirelessly promote his opus, so too are we beholden to Rahel's husband, Karl August Varnhagen von Ense (1785-1858), a German archivist, biographer, diplomat and soldier, who devoted the better part of his adult life as a quasi-prophet to building her reputation. Varnhagen's admiration for Rahel bordered on adulation. "I should like to live as your apostle, […]" he wrote in a letter to her.

> "I spoke of you at Steffens'[4] house, as the third glory of the Jewish nation, the first and second chronologically being Christ and Spinoza; […] they accused me of idolatry, but Steffens was nevertheless delighted with my fervor."

In her brilliant, albeit quirky, biography, *Rahel Varnhagen, Lebensgeschichte einer deutschen Jüdin* (*Rahel Varnhagen, The Life of a Jewish Woman, 1957*), the German-Jewish philosopher Hannah Arendt (1906-1975) takes Rahel's doting husband to task, unfairly I believe, for turning his wife into a marketable

4 Henrik Steffens, Norwegian-German philosopher, scientist and poet (1773-1845)

commodity, making her more palatable to the literate German-speaking public of his day by diluting the Jewish element, to that end often obscuring the Jewish ancestry of a number of her correspondents. He did what he believed to be in her best interest, to spread the word to as wide a readership as possible, leaving it to future generations to flesh out a more complex picture.

*

Posterity is hard pressed to balance Rahel's prickly mix of pride and prejudice as to her own cultural identity. In his book *The Pity of It All: A History of the Jews in Germany, 1743-1933*, Israeli journalist, Amos Elon, glossed over Rahel's brilliance, and reduced her to a simpering product of Jewish self-loathing:

> "She hated her Jewish background and was convinced it had poisoned her life. For much of her adult life she was what would later be called self-hating. Her overriding desire was to free herself from the shackles of her birth; since, as she thought, she had been 'pushed out of the world' by her origins, she was determined to escape them. [...] She considered her origins 'a curse, a slow bleeding to death.' The idea that as a Jew she was always required to be exceptional—and go on proving it all the time—was repugnant to her. 'How wretched it is always to have to legitimize myself! That is why it is so disgusting to be a Jew.'"

But dare we condemn her in hindsight? Dare we judge what it meant to maneuver the tides of endemic prejudice and fleeting tolerance as a Jew in late eighteenth and early nineteenth century Prussia? She was hardly the only Jew in her day to feel a certain ambivalence about her ancestry and to resort to baptism as a survival tactic in an essentially hostile environment. The German-

Jewish philosopher Moses Mendelssohn (1729-1786), a friend of the philosopher Immanuel Kant (1724-1804) and the playwright Gotthold Ephraim Lessing (1729-1781), among the first Jews to emerge from the isolation of the ghetto and make his mark as more than a money-lender in German culture, sought in his social stance a viable compromise between Jewish orthodoxy and German assimilation. Of Mendelssohn's six children, however, only two retained the Jewish faith. His oldest daughter, Brendel, better known to posterity as Dorothea von Schlegel (1764-1839), a childhood friend of Rahel's, left her husband Simon Veit and her father's faith to run off, convert, and marry the Christian poet and philosopher Friedrich von Schlegel (1772-1829). Moses' grandson, the composer Felix Mendelssohn (1809-1847), was baptized by his parents at age seven. The poet Heinrich Heine, another friend of Rahel's, referred to his own baptismal certificate as his "ticket of admission into European culture." Political writer and satirist Ludwig Börne, born Loeb Baruch (1786-1837), likewise opted for baptism as a passport to acceptance.

Despite the at best tenuous accord between Germans and Jews over the more than 1,700 years of their cohabitation in German lands, a relationship disrupted time and again by outbreaks of violence, Germans and Jews established a certain entente that allowed for a cultural cross-fertilization. "The German-speaking Jews and their history are an altogether unique phenomenon," affirms Arendt, herself a product and case in point of that phenomenon, "nothing comparable is to be found even in the other areas of Jewish assimilation." Though himself hardly a friend of the Jews, Martin Luther's translation of the Bible, completed in 1534, the first full translation of the Old and New Testaments into German to reference not only the Latin Vulgate, but also the original Hebrew and Greek texts, is deemed by many to be the first work of modern German literature. So, in a sense, the modern

German mindset was reconfigured, through Luther's lens, in the mirror image of the ancient Semitic. Systemic prejudice, ongoing persecution and reoccurring violence against the Jews in German lands notwithstanding, Germans and Jews have been simultaneously harmonizing and hammering out their differences ever since. The late 19th and early 20th centuries saw the pinnacle and the nadir of that cultural dynamic. It would be impossible to conceive of a Karl Marx, a Sigmund Freud, a Franz Kafka, a Ludwig Wittgenstein or an Albert Einstein without the melding of Semitic Messianism and Teutonic idealism, Jewish savvy and "*sechel,*" (common sense), and strict German syntax. Depending on the tenor of the times and the wavering attitude of local ecclesiastic and secular authorities, tolerated and even feted by a tiny intellectual elite in periods of calm, reassuming their insidious role of scapegoat and reviled in periods of crisis, Jews remained by and large spurned pariahs in German society until their total exclusion, isolation and extermination in the 20th century. Small wonder that a brilliant and ambitious woman of Rahel's ilk, who communed with the German intellectual elite of her day without ever being fully accepted by them, wanted out of her assigned role. Catalyst and quasi-saint though she may have been to others, she suffered greatly from her dual outsider status as Jew and woman.

"I wish nothing more ardently now than to change myself outwardly and inwardly," she wrote at age 21 in a heart-wrenching letter to her friend, the German-Jewish physician and thinker, David Veit (1771-1814). "I am sick of myself; but I can do nothing about it, and will remain the way I am, just as my face will; we can both grow older, but nothing more …"

"Can us women folk help it if we also happen to be human?" she added, putting her position even more bluntly in another letter to Veit:

> "If my mother had been kind-hearted and hard enough, and she could only have anticipated what I would become, she would have let me suffocate in the dust at my first cry. [...] I have such a vivid imagination; it sometimes seems to me as if an extraterrestrial being incised these words with a dagger in my heart upon my entry into this world: 'Yes, you may be endowed with a special sensibility, you may see the world as few others see it, be great and noble, nor can I deny you a thoughtful nature. But we forgot one thing: You are doomed to be a Jewess!' And thus, my entire life is a bleeding to death! [...] I can trace every mishap, every calamity in life, every chagrin back to that!"

Or as she phrased it in a letter to her younger sister Rose:

> "I am a Jewess, not beautiful, ignorant, without grace, without talents and instruction. Oh, my sister, it's all over; it's finished before the real finale. I could not have done anything differently. [...] Meanwhile, we grow old and life falls away like old dreams."

Paradoxically, this very ambivalence to herself and her Jewish heritage and to her female gender role fueled a fierce sense of self-affirmation and self-preservation:

> "I shall never be convinced that I am a schlemiel and a Jewess; since in all these years and after so much thinking about it, it has not dawned upon me, I shall never really grasp it. That is why 'the clang of the murderous axe does not nibble at my root'; that is why I am still living."

Perceiving clearly the bind the Jews were in, Rahel's pronounced ambivalence to her roots did not preclude a sympathy for and identification with her oppressed people:

> "People say that Jews are funny; and people often laugh at them. This comes [...] from their terrible situation in the contemporary European world, to be contrasted with their ancient image."

In the wake of the so-called Hep-Hep Uprising, a wave of persecution and violent attacks against Jews that broke out in various German cities in 1819, following Napoleon's ultimate defeat, Rahel wrote with an astounding perspicacity and a poignant poetic irony to her beloved brother, Ludwig:

> "I am abysmally sad; and in a way that I have never been. On account of the Jews. What is this host of eternal exiles to do? They want to keep them around; but just to torment and despise; to vilify them for their Jewish wangling; to restrict them to meager, miserable haggling for a living; to retain them to be trodden on, and kicked down stairs. Is it the common attitude to Jews as reprehensible, corrupt through and through, that so pains me, chilling my heart? Horror of horrors! I know my country. Alas. I am a deplorable Cassandra! For three years I've been saying: they will attack the Jews ... That is how the Germans display their pluck of indignation. And why? Because they are the most law-abiding, goodhearted, freedom-loving, authority-honoring people."

But it was only on her deathbed, as per the account of her last words given by her husband, that she took a semblance of pride in and made some degree of peace with her Jewish heritage:

> "What a history!—A fugitive from Egypt and Palestine, here I am and find help, love, fostering in you people. With real rapture I think of these origins of mine and this whole nexus of destiny, through which the oldest memories of the human race stand side by side with the latest developments. [...] The thing, which all my life seemed to me the greatest shame, which was the misery and misfortune of my life—having been born a Jewess—this I should on no account now wish to have missed. [...]"

*

Whereas Elon challenged the veracity of her husband's account of Rahel's ultimate acceptance of her Jewish identity, an unquestionable proto-feminist stance marked her sense of womanhood. "This is the reason for the many frivolities to be found, and thought to be found, among women," she wrote in a letter to her younger sister Rose.

> "They have no place to put their feet, must always set them down where a man is already standing, and wants to stand; and they see with their own eyes the whole wide world like a body metamorphosed into a tree with its roots firmly planted in the ground, their every attempt, their every desire to free themselves from that unnatural state is deemed a frivolity; or worse, condemned as aberrant behavior for which they merit punishment."

*

Excluded as a Jew and a woman from playing an active role in the wheeling and dealing of high society, her salon of assembled like-minded souls served as a safe haven of her own making, a utopia of sorts, in which she and her friends, noble and bourgeois, Christians and Jews, men and women, government bureaucrats and artists, officers and scholars, and skeptics of every ilk, could, if but for a few hours, shed the burden of their strictly prescribed social roles and feign complete freedom. For much of her life Rahel reinvented herself. In this sense she succeeded in bursting out of the straitjacket of assigned social identity, transcending the limitations of a stultifying Judaism crushed into submission by the prejudices of an oppressive Christian society, and the debilitating subservient role of a woman as prescribed by men, to find a fleeting happiness in the company of others.

*

Among other qualities, Rahel had a rare gift for friendship, which she prized above all else. As she put it in a letter to her friend from childhood, Friederike Liman:[5]

> What is friendship? It is what we make of it: the gift of another personality to penetrate; the virtue to respect it and appreciate it as you do your own; the joy at having found one whose being and mere existence pleases us, in every remark, in conceding a point well made as in admitting defeat, a personality that possesses the quality to interact with ours, and in so doing, to permit

5 Friederike Auguste Liman, formerly Fradchen Liepmann, née Marcuse (1770-1844), a childhood friend of Rahel's and one of the very few people she addressed in German with the informal "du."

> itself and ours to evolve freely, i.e. based on its innate capacities. So, you permit me silence when I find it difficult to speak—with tongue or pen—you condone my writing a short letter that only says what I want to say at that precise moment, and what I ask of you! [...]

In April, 1831, the ailing, bed-ridden Rahel expressed in writing a last wish to her husband in a burst of words we have no cause to doubt: "I just thought of a fitting epitaph. Let it read: Good people, if in future times anything good should happen to humanity, in your rejoicing I ask you to kindly think also of me." Incised with these words, her tombstone in the *Dreifaltigkeits* (Holy Trinity) Cemetery in Berlin calls out in friendship to all passersby with a hopeful nod at the future.

Hiking Through Heaven and Hell: Reflections on Heinrich Heine's *Travel Pictures*[1]

The Harz Mountains, the rugged range that runs between the Elbe and Leine rivers, a walking tour of which inspired one of German literature's most famous poetic paeans to Wanderlust, is better known to the English language reader as the brand name of a popular pet supply company.[2] The association would surely have made Heinrich Heine laugh out loud—and he would, no doubt, have slipped this ironic detail into a future edition.

From the hilarious tongue lashing of Göttingen's philistine students and pedantic professors at the start of *The Harz Journey* to the send-up of fashionable bathers and ignorant islanders in *The North Sea*, from the poetic potshots at the proto-Jet Set in *The Baths of Lucca* to the quote from *Don Quixote* misconstrued as lewdness by an eavesdropping illiterate old biddy at the end of *The City of Lucca*, all four parts of *Travel Pictures* are so generously peppered with word plays, wisecracks, puns and witticisms, so primed with merriment, that one could well mistake the whole on first reading as one long literary lark (as long as we take our literary larks as seriously as a Cervantes). But to reduce *Travel Pictures* to a string of titters would be like trying to siphon the whale oil out of *Moby Dick* or the Mississippi mud out of *Huckleberry Finn*.

Nor is it a classic literary travelogue. The reader expecting to find the precise geographical descriptions and telling anecdotes of the kind that abound in Goethe's *Italian Journey* will be sorely disappointed. For Heine, travel remained a poetic pretext, nature a mottled mirror to reflect human foibles, and humor a poignant ploy

1 This essay was first published as the afterword to *Travel Pictures*, by Heinrich Heine, translated by Peter Wortsman, Archipelago Books, Brooklyn, NY, 2008
2 Founded in 1926, The Harz Mountain Corporation, a leading American pet supply company, started out importing canaries from the Harz Mountains.

behind which to sneak a scurrilous reflection or two. While rooted in the genre of Romantic travel writing, *Travel Pictures* pushes the limits and freely derides the form with a self-reflexive license:

> "There's nothing more boring on this earth than to have to read the description of an Italian journey, except maybe to have to write one—and the writer can only make it halfway bearable by speaking as little as possible of Italy." [*The Baths of Lucca*, Chap. 9]

In *Travel Pictures*, Heine fashioned a form of his own, equal parts poetic, politic, and prophetic; and in the process, shook up the German language. Strewn with conceptual landmines, his freewheeling prose made the contorted Teutonic tongue of courtiers, barristers and bureaucrats explode laughing into a modern medium.[3] Strumming wildly on the German sentence, a never-ending braid of thought homespun by Hegel, Schlegel, & Co., Heine primed its supple strings for Freud's future forays into the unconscious, Rilke's ripe poetic prose, Kafka's dark parables and paradoxes, and Brecht's biting staccato.

Readers of *The Joke and its Relation to the Unconscious* may recall Freud's psycho-linguistic analysis of a pun in *The Baths of Lucca*, in which a Mr. Hyacinth, aka Hirsch, a Jewish lottery collector-cum-podiatrist moonlighting as gentleman's gentleman to the Marquis Gumpelino (a baptized Jewish banker on vacation in Tuscany) boasts to the narrator, a certain Dr. Heine, of his close relations with the Baron Rothschild:

---

3 This freedom with the language famously displeased Fin-de-Siecle Viennese critic Karl Kraus, who, with some justification and considerable wit, lashed out at Heine for having "uncorseted the German language and enabled every Tom, Dick and Harry to fondle its breasts." No doubt Kraus, the acid-tongued suitor of the German language, faulted Heine for getting their first.

> "And by the grace of God, Doctor, I sat next to Salomon Rothschild at table, and he treated me just like his equal, altogether familionaire."

Heine's in-your-face "familionairity" with his medium and his reader, paradoxically spiked with a bitter sense of alienation, is precisely what made *Travel Pictures* a bestseller in his day and what makes it read, in parts, so utterly modern (at times even downright post-modern) to this day. But like Buster Keaton's seemingly stoic deadpan look, it was a hard stance to hold for a thin-skinned psyche. Underlying and intertwined with all this intimate knee-pulling and tongue-in-cheek kidding lurks Heine's own complex relationship to German, Germany and the Germans, a love-hate relationship fraught with all the keenly suffered and savored contradictions of the tenuous Semitic-Teutonic entente.

*

Born and raised in an assimilated Jewish merchant family in Düsseldorf in 1797, when the Rhineland was under French dominion, Harry Heine—who later officially changed his name to Christian Johann Heinrich on his baptismal certificate—became a reluctant Prussian subject upon Napoleon's defeat and a prickly Protestant. Intense ambivalence, while generally contraindicative of happiness, can be a fertile emotional state for a poet.

Though Heine idolized Napoleon, the People's Emperor, as a great liberator, and revered the French for their revolutionary bravado, he also reviled them for their alleged lack of imagination. Though he converted to Protestantism for largely pragmatic reasons (to make it in a society hostile to Jews) he lauded

Christ as a freedom-loving Jewish beggar, scorned Christianity as a suffering faith, and stubbornly clung to an Old Testament identity, while reserving his thorniest barbs for the Jewish bourgeoisie from which he sprung. Longing for Germany, he lived much of his adult life across the Rhine. Cultivated to a T, he married an illiterate Parisian shop girl who wouldn't have understood a word of what he wrote even had she felt inclined to read it, which, fortunately, she did not. A self-styled revolutionary with monarchist leanings, he loathed aristocrats of the hereditary kind and dreamed of his own poetic aristocracy. His fluctuating circle of friends at some point included fellow German émigrés Karl Marx and Friedrich Engels, even though he himself distrusted democracy and reviled the coarse manners of the people. An international celebrity, he was perennially lonely and short of funds.

To this knot of contradictions, the contemporary reader cannot help but add the ironic twist of historical hindsight. In a prescient passage from a forgotten verse drama, "Almansor," set during the Spanish Inquisition, Heine famously forewarned: "There where they burn books, they'll end up burning people too." The augur, of course, came tragically true in his homeland in the bonfires of Dr. Goebbels (himself a failed novelist) and the crematoria of Auschwitz and Treblinka. But Heine's words so infiltrated the German psyche that not even the Nazis could pry their lore and language free of his influence.

This book being a veritable grid of digressions held together by the metaphor of travel, a translator's brief digression in the spirit of the text may be permitted here. Many years ago, my mother, who had fled Hitler's henchmen and schlepped a tattered, Gothic-scripted tome of Heine's selected works with her across various borders and bodies of water, led her progeny on a poetic pilgrimage of sorts to the Rhineland. The family took a slow boat down river, skirting romantic castles and picturesque villages and sailing past the rocky perch of the Loreley, the lovely mermaid immortalized by Heine in his most famous poem of the same name. We stepped ashore at Worms, where German princes and clerics once famously dieted on ideas, to see the stone seat upon which Rashi (aka Shlomo Yitzchaki, aka Salomon ben Isaac), the illustrious Jewish theologian, allegedly held spiritual court. A concerned citizen, we were told, had preserved the seat from the mallets of the thugs. I don't remember much of what hung on the walls of the municipal museum, but I do recall the felt slippers we children were obliged to don so as not to scratch the polished parquet floor with our sneakers. The only tableau that caught my eye was a kitschy depiction of the long-haired blonde Loreley pining on her rock, a Romantic pin-up girl with barely sublimated erotic connotations.

"What does this painting represent?" my mother asked the guard, feigning ignorance.

"It's a legend based on a popular ballad," the doddering old man replied.

"Who wrote it?" she pressed, knowing Heine's name had been erased from German memory.

"Nobody, it's folklore," the guard shrugged, intent above all on preserving the parquet and retrieving the slippers.

*

Heine's Jewish roots, pulled up, pickled in Prussian Protestant brine and Gallic vinegar, ambivalently wriggling though they might have been, suffused his consciousness with a lifelong sympathy for the nobodies of this world. So, for instance, in *The North Sea*, a seemingly casual reflection on the then-popular practice of hunting on the beach sparks the following chilling remark:

> "If one's ancestors since time immemorial already shot roe-buck then the descendent is inclined to derive a pleasure from this legitimate pursuit. But my ancestors did not belong to the hunters, but rather to the hunted, and were I to pull a trigger at the descendants of their former colleagues my blood would curdle in disgust. Indeed, I know from experience that when removed at a proper distance I find it much easier to fire at a hunter who is himself inclined to dream back to the days when hunting people was fair game and good sport."

Which prompts one of those pivotal epiphanies that gnaw at the conscience and comprise the dark moral kernels of this seemingly lighthearted travelogue:

> "Should such hunters nowadays have a hankering to hunt a human again they are required to pay him for his troubles, say, for instance, like the long-distance runner I passed in Göttingen two years ago. The poor soul had already run himself ragged in the sultry Sunday heat, when several young Junkers from Hannover studying ethnography in Göttingen offered him a few Talers if he ran back again the way he'd come; and the man ran, and he was deathly pale and wore a red Jersey, and hot on his heels in a cloud of dust the well-endowed noble young gentlemen galloped on their high steeds, whose hooves sometimes struck that hunted panting person—and that was a human being."

The identification is clear. With horses' hooves hot on his heels, Heine, the footloose heir to the hunted, offers up a nightmare image of persecution worthy of a Joseph K, a character born a century later in the black comic psyche of another deeply divided and profoundly ambivalent German-speaking Jewish student of the law.

*

In the fall of 1824, following a single semester of legal studies at the University of Göttingen, Harry Heine, age 27, took three weeks off to hike some 280 miles of mountainous terrain in the neighboring Harz. His enthusiasm for the trek and the reflections it inspired far outweighed any fondness he might have harbored for law and the locus of his legal studies.

Having previously failed in the textile business, a popular Jewish pursuit at the time to which his poetic temperament was ill-suited, and with no other apparent marketable aptitude, young Harry was dispatched to study law, first at Bonn, then at Göttingen, by an ambitious mother, and with the financial support and concomitant needling of a rich banker uncle, Salomon Heine. His feelings for Uncle Salomon were encapsulated in the pithy put-down, which the ingrate nephew once, allegedly, muttered to his face, "You know, dear uncle, the best thing about you is that you bear my name." His feelings for Göttingen, the good old college town with the good old boys on its faculty and in its student body, are summed up in a pithy passage from The *Harz Journey*:

> "The residents of Göttingen are commonly divided into students, professors, philistines, and livestock, which four classes are at the very least kept strictly separated. The class of livestock is the most consequential."

Heine's run-ins with junior scions of old established aristocratic clans, themselves ill-disposed to his Semitic ancestry, eventually lead to a planned duel. Found out and headed off by university authorities, the incident led to the would-be duelists' suspension. With his newly acquired leisure time, Heine took a happy hiatus in Berlin, where he wrote poetry, frequented the literary salons, visited the theater, and, on occasion, attended lectures by intellectual luminaries like the philosopher Friedrich Hegel. But Uncle Soloman held the purse-strings and pulled in the reins, whereupon Harry reluctantly returned to Göttingen to get on with his legal studies. After a single semester, he had once again had enough. A hike was just what the doctor ordered. "Last fall, I took a walking tour of the Harz," he wrote to a friend,

> "crisscrossed the country, visited the Brocken, and Goethe too on my return trip through Weimar. I traveled via Eisleben, Halle, Jena, Weimar, Erfurt, Gotha, Eisenach and Cassel, back here [to Göttingen] again. I have seen many beautiful things on this trip, and the valleys of the Bode and Selke Rivers remain unforgettable. If I husband my memories, I ought to be able to plant my poems with Harz trees for the rest of my life."

The seeds of the journey indeed served him well.

Laurence Sterne had fled a barrister's responsibilities and harvested digressions on an escape across the Channel encapsulated in his *Sentimental Journey through France and Italy* (though he never made it to Italy). Goethe famously chronicled his run from Weimar to Rome in his *Italian Journey.* Heine likewise found release on the run, stumbling and grumbling all the way, each step powering the imaginative dynamo inside, milling alternate bouts of ecstasy and malaise into pithy, sometimes profound, and often unforgettable prose.

Reflecting, for instance, on the home-life of miners, he perceives the spiritual mine of the German imagination:

> "As static and quiet as the life of these people might appear, it is still a truly animated existence. The trembling ancient crone seated in the cozy nook between the big cupboard and the warm oven, herself as old as the hills, may have already been seated there for a quarter century, and her thinking and feeling were intertwined with every corner of this oven and every hand-carved notch and crevice of this cupboard. And cupboard and oven are alive, for a human being imbued them with a piece of her soul."

Back in Göttingen again, he reluctantly resumed his studies and managed to squeak through his final exams, earning a Doctorate of Law. Hoping to land himself some administrative sinecure, an option barred to Jews, he underwent the formality of a baptism—"my entrance ticket to European culture," he called it—but the holy water failed to work wonders on the job market. In truth, a pronounced aversion to the drudgery of steady employment was at least as much to blame as his ethnic lineage for any difficulties in landing a long-term job.

Writing proved a more profitable pursuit. *The Harz Journey*, part one of *Travel Pictures*, published by Hoffmann and Campe, in Hamburg, his lifelong publisher, was an instant literary success, as was his ever-popular book of poetry, *Buch der Lieder*, though the former was promptly banned by the scandalized burghers of Göttingen.

While milling over future prospects, or the lack thereof, he once again indulged a craving for travel. No sooner did the newly matriculated Doctor of Law pocket and promptly shelve his degree than he took off (with Uncle Salomon's grudging approval and financial assistance) on another leave of absence, this time to the Island of Norderney on the North Sea. This and subsequent visits inspired the famous North Sea cycle of poems and *The North Sea*, part two of *Travel Pictures*, comprising observations (on the culture clash between the posh vacationers and the primitive locals) and pronouncements (on Goethe and Napoleon), intermingled with loving laments and passionate evocations to the ficklest lover of them all, the sea itself.

But it was *The Baths of Lucca*, loosely based on a subsequent escape to Tuscany, that caused the greatest stir.

Ever since the 16th century, when German Humanists crossed the Alps ostensibly to drink at the well of classical learning, young bucks had managed to slip out of their tight-fitting Teutonic skin, get a tan, and let it all hang loose in Italy. Following in Goethe's footsteps, Heine reveled in the sun-drenched vineyards and orange groves and admired the art. But whereas Goethe left Weimar behind and maintained a certain objectivity in the journal notes and letters artfully whittled into his *Italian Journey*, Heine left home in body but not in spirit. Unabashedly subjective and burdened with a heavy baggage of prejudices and grudges, through which he filtered his vision of Italy, *The Baths of Lucca*, an account of the interactions between a few summer guests and members of the Italian demimonde, reveals some of his greatest literary strengths as well as his most lamentable personal failings.

Cognizant of Goethe's lengthy and at times laborious commentaries on artworks in his take on Italy, Heine cuts to the quick in a forthright assessment of the limitations of art coupled with a bold stab at its essence in his description of Francesca, a dancing girl-cum courtesan:

> "I would like to have Francesca etched on a copper plate and supplement the print. But oh! What's the use of a dead copy of the external outline of a shapely figure whose godly charm is evident in live motion! Even the finest painter cannot make us perceive this, for painting is, after all, nothing but a flat lie...But it was the sound of that voice that tendered each of her words the loveliest and most profound meaning, and if I related her words it would only give you a dry herbarium of dead flowers whose priceless value is limited to their scent. Indeed, she often leapt into the air and danced as she spoke, and perhaps the dance itself was her real language."

A ballerina to the bone, the lovely Francesca tells the tale of her lost love, not with her words, but with her slipper-clad feet:

> "As she spoke she performed the most delicate pantomimes, kept pressing time and again her fingertips to her heart, appeared then with the hollow of her palm to draw out the most delicate feelings, finally flung herself with a heartfelt light elastic leap onto the sofa, hid her face in the pillow, raised her feet in the air behind her and let them act like wooden dolls."

And when, at last, Francesca allows the breathless poet to kiss her left foot, "whereupon, in jesting earnest, she removed the red shoe as well as the stocking," Heine's account reads straight out of the unexpurgated *A Thousand and One Arabian Nights*:

> "Today you kissed my left foot, tomorrow I will proffer my right. The day after tomorrow you may kiss my left hand and the day after that my right. Conduct yourself

with dignity and I will one day offer you my mouth … As you can see, I'm inclined to let you advance, and since you're young you may well go far in this world."

The rapturous evocation of the erotic that follows shocked and thrilled his contemporaries, and still offers up a lyrical kick:

> "And I did indeed go far in this world! To that you were witness, oh Tuscan nights, with your light blue sky studded with great silver stars, and you wild laurel bushes and sheltering myrtle, and you, oh nymphs of the Apennines, who swirled around us in your bridal dances and dreamed yourselves back to the sweeter days of the gods, before the advance of the Gothic lie that only tolerates blind, groping pleasures in the dark and slaps its hypocritical fig leaf on every frank and open feeling.
>
> No additional fig leaves were needed, for a rustling full-grown fig tree with leafy outstretched branches crowned the head of the blissful below."

But *The Baths of Lucca* is best known for a comic tour-de-force segment performed by two of German literature's most memorable clowns, the aforementioned Marquis Gumpelino, and his valet Hyacinth-Hirsch. In a rip-roaring parody of the poisoning scene in "Romeo and Juliet," a miracle salt which Hyacinth prescribes and administers to his master to lift his spirits proves instead to be a potent laxative that keeps poor Gumpelino running to the can and compels him to forego a secret tryst with Lady Maxfield:

> "'Woe is me, unlucky lunatic!' Gumpelino yammered—'love holds forth its goblet of nectar, and I, dear God! a fool for love, just downed the cup of miracle salts! Who

will help me pump this wretched brew out of my gut? Help! Help!'

'No earthly mortal can help you now,' sighed Hyacinth.

'I feel for your condition from the bottom of my heart', I likewise conveyed my condolences. 'T'is a bitter fate to forfeit the chalice of nectar for the glass of miracle salts! To trade in the throne of love for the *chaise percé*!"

Though we can't keep from laughing at the ludicrous posturing of the master and the preposterous wise cracks of the servant, the humor leans so heavily on Jewish stereotypes that the laughter hurts a little. Indeed, the pair appear to represent for Heine the sum total of his take on everything Jewish. The fact that a converted Jew of genius tapped his own insider's knowledge and plied a sometimes self-deprecatory wit to paint this less than flattering portrait of Jewish parvenus for a German readership hardly attenuates the sting—but it's still funny.

Hirsch-Hyacinth may be a classic Jewish schlemiel, and yet there's more than a little wisdom in his wise cracks and more than a little love in the poet's portrayal:

"'What is Man! Blissfully you amble past the Altona Gate, strolling up the Hamburg Hill, and there you savor the sights, lions, goldfinches and goldbergs galore, papagoyim, monkeys and misters, you ride the carousel or rattle electric, and you think to yourself, boy, would I ever have a ball in a faraway place two hundred miles from Hamburg, in the land of lemons and oranges, Italy! What is Man! Put him in front of the Altona Gate and he dreams of distant Italy, send him to Italy and he'd rather be back at the Altona Gate! [...] So here I am in Italy, where the

> lemons and oranges bloom; but when I see lemons and oranges growing, I think back to the Hamburg market where cartfuls of them lie neatly stacked [...] and where you can quietly savor them without having to clamber up so many perilous hilltops and so much sweaty heat."

Hyacinth is also Heine's comic foil to express outrageous opinions:

> 'I must confess that the Catholic faith is no fun, and as a reasonable man, you must agree. I see no pleasure in a religion in which our dear God, God help us, is dead, and it smells of incense just like at a funeral [...]'
>
> 'But what do you think of the Protestant religion, Mr. Hyacinth?'
>
> 'That one, on the other hand, doctor, is altogether too sensible for me, and if they didn't play an organ in the Protestant church it wouldn't be a religion at all. Between you and me, it's a harmless religion, as clean as a glass of water, but it doesn't do you any good either.'

And as for Judaism:

> 'You can keep your old Jewish faith, Doctor. I wouldn't wish it on my worst enemy. Gives you nothing but scorn and shame. I tell you, it's no religion at all, just a lot of hard luck.'

Heine himself seems to step out from behind the mask in Hyacinth's nostalgic evocation of traditional Jewish life:

> "An old Jew like that with his long beard and torn robe who can't utter a single orthographically correct word,

> and is even a bit scabby, may very well be at greater peace with himself than me with all my cultivation."

But there is nothing endearing or redeeming about the Marquis Gumpelino. Modeled, at least in part, on a Hamburg banker of Heine's passing acquaintance named Lazarus Gumpel, Gumpelino embodies everything Heine loathed about the moneyed world of his Uncle Soloman, a world he rejected and from which he felt permanently excluded. Though it must have amused his contemporaries, the stereotypic description of the Jewish banker, who "waddled in with his well-to-do smile and blessed belly," might make today's reader wince:

> "After his glimmering fat lips had sufficiently slathered Milady's hand and spat out the usual string of questions as to her good health, he recognized me too ..."

It would be bad enough if the text were merely marred by such seedy descriptions, but *The Baths of Lucca* also reveals Heine at his literary and moral nadir, in the crude, drawn-out, personal attack on the sexual proclivity of the poet August Count von Platen.

The history of this vendetta goes back to the satirical epigrams deriding the state of German poetry by his friend Karl Immermann, with which Heine padded the slender volume of *The North Sea*. Here we find the following couplet, concerning which Count von Platen took justifiable umbrage, for it was indeed directed at him:

> "Of the fruits that furtively from the garden grove of Shiraz they thieve,
> They eat too much, poor fools, and vomit ghazals without reprieve."

Platen, who had published a book of ghazals, an intricate Persian poetic form that begins with a rhymed couplet and alternates the same rhyme throughout, avenged the slight with a tasteless comedy entitled "The Romantic Oedipus," in which he, in turn, derided Immermann and Heine, whom he satirized in the guise of two slapstick characters, the one called Nimmermann (never man) and the other "The Baptized Heine."

Stung by Platen's cheap anti-Semitic smear, Heine hit back below the belt, devoting page after page of drawn-out diatribe to Platen's homosexuality:

> "For the Count sometimes disguises himself in pious sentiments, he avoids more precise designation of sex … he imagines that he has sufficiently hidden his true intentions from the hoi polloi by leaving out the word friend from time to time, and at such times he does like the ostrich, who believes himself hidden when he's stuck his head in the sand, so that only the bum remains visible … In truth, he's more of a man of bum than a man of mind … he's pathetic in his poems, he's a woman, and what's more, a woman who delights in the womanly, he is, so to speak, a manly tribade [lesbian]."

It seems sad in retrospect (and a bit ridiculous) that two poets, guardians of the national conscience, should go at it tooth and nail in print. Platen's play has fortunately been forgotten. Heine's rant, alas, survives to mar a masterpiece of prose. With humor more juvenile than jovial, sentiments more small-minded than subtle, and philosophy more philistine than lofty, the passage reads like the drivel of a precocious schoolboy hurling coarse insults at a rival. But poets, as we know, are not immune to petty prejudice—think of Pound!—and, thin-skinned as they are, perhaps more rancorous than the rest. Though Heine later expressed regrets at the offense caused by this passage, he never removed it.

In *The City of Lucca*, Heine once again finds his stride. On a stroll through the hills outside the city, he speaks to his surroundings with that endearing mix of arrogance and intimacy that marks his poetic voice:

> "Oh Nature! You silent virgin! How well I grasp your sheets of lightning, those futile attempts to speak that flash across your lovely face, I pity you so profoundly that I weep. Whereupon you understand me too, and you cheer yourself up and laugh at me with your golden eyes. Lovely virgin, I understand your stars, and you understand my tears!"

But, as always, he is far more interested in the foibles of his fellow man than the splendors of nature. His path and his prose soon lead him back into the city, where he is several days late for a tryst with Francesca, the lovely dancer we encountered in the previous part.

Stumbling past a religious procession, which he describes in vivid detail as a march of the living dead, he happens upon her prostrate form lying, more ghostlike than real, on the altar of a church. But she has gone through a religious reawakening and will not accept his carnal caresses. The pining poet contemplates a temporary conversion:

> "Francesca!' I cried, "Star of my thoughts! Thought of my soul! *Vita della mia vita!* My lovely, kiss-covered, sleek, Catholic Francesca! For this one night, if you grant me it, I'll become a Catholic myself—but just for one night!"

*

Which brings us to a conversion of another kind. While parts one and two of *Travel Pictures* are sprinkled with rhymed Romantic poetry, and part three is blotted by a kind of anti-poetry in scornful citations from Count Platen, *The City of Lucca* is totally devoid of verse. It is as if, ever more averse to constriction in life, Heine had finally broken free of the law, so to speak, and renounced meter and rhyme.

Though he went on to write some of his most powerful verse, while sinking into physical paralysis, shrinking into a ghost of himself, the victim of an undiagnosed condition that kept him in its grip until his final release in 1856, his prose voice seemed to take precedence.

"For some time now," he wrote in 1837 in the foreword to the second edition of *Buch der Lieder* (Book of Songs),

> "something in me has bristled against all forms of corseted speech, and as I hear, some of my contemporaries feel a similar aversion. It seems to me as if too many lies lurk in pretty verses, and the truth is reticent to appear in metrical garb."

Some commentators have dubbed *Travel Pictures* a poem in prose, though the form as such had not yet been invented. Whatever we call it, a poem in prose, a modern-day book of hours, or a poetic travelogue, this little text ploughed a new path, beckoning us to follow, and if we dare, to break free and climb our own Harz Mountains wherever they may rise up out of the mundane flatland of our lives.

To Make a Long Story Short: The Prose of Peter Altenberg[1]

His walrus mustache was emblematic, like Walt Whitman's wild wooly beard: no mere untrimmed tuft growing wild, but a Zeitgeist gage, a canny alley cat's whiskers tailor-made to fit through tight fixes. And like the bewhiskered Brooklyn bard, to whom he has been compared—in stance, not in style—Peter Altenberg (1859-1919), the turn of the century Viennese raconteur-scribe, was a walker and a talker and an inveterate loll-about. Both had a penchant for lyrical digression and irregular punctuation, but the similarity stops there. For while Whitman went on at length in epic outbursts of freewheeling verse, Altenberg choked back the flow.

His own avowed paradigm for the pearls he spit out, most while propped up in bed in bouts of chronic insomnia, was Charles Baudelaire's *Spleen de Paris* (1869). Yet whereas Baudelaire's pioneering work comprises texts that tease and test, but never forsake the playing field of poetry, Altenberg extracted the poetic essence of impressions and spat them out in spare narratives situated to the prose side of the divide.

Other formal influences include the "*Correspondenzkarte*," the world's first postcard launched and disseminated in Austria in 1869, which subsequently sparked a vogue; and the Feuilleton, a lyrical form of first-person journalistic prose often of a decidedly purple slant produced by, among other Viennese wordsmiths of the day, the young Theodor Herzl before the latter forsook *belles lettres* for the nation-building business.

1 This essay first appeared as the afterword to *Telegrams of the Soul, Selected Prose of Peter Altenberg*, selected and translated by Peter Wortsman, Archipelago Books, NY, 2005, and was excerpted in *The New England Review*, Middlebury College, Middlebury, VT, Spring 2005

The artfully crafted fairy tales of the great Dane, Hans Christian Andersen, have been noted as yet another influence. And Altenberg's writings can indeed be read as pruned *Märchen* minus the "once upon a time" and without any pretense of a "happily ever after." "We relegated fairytales to the realm of childhood, that exceptional, wondrous, stirring, remarkable time of life!" he wrote (in a text entitled "Retrospective Introduction to My Book," in his book *Märchen des Lebens*, (The Fairy Tale of Life, 1908)

> "But why rig out childhood with it, when childhood is already sufficiently romantic and fairytale-like in and of itself?!? The disenchanted adult had best seek out the fairytale-like elements, the romanticism of each day and each hour right here and now in the hard, stern, cold fundament of life!"

Disenchanted adult or overgrown child, Altenberg never quite managed to break out of his self-constructed cocoon, except on the butterfly wings of his writing and the charmed cadences of his café conversation. Like his English contemporary, Lewis Carroll (1832-1898), Altenberg idealized childhood as the indigenous province of poetry and adulated children as its natural priests and purveyors. Like Carroll, he also flirted with a photographic (though to my knowledge, never practiced) pedophilia, prizing above all his possessions a collection of suggestive postcards, many of pre-pubescent girls. Like Carroll, he too managed to metamorphose (or sublimate) his worship of young girls into the stuff of literature. Did not Dante do the same with his Beatrice fixation and Petrarch with his predilection for Laura?!

The fact that Altenberg clung psychologically to the province of childhood, reticent to forsake its cozy confines for the constant compromise and abject spiritual poverty of adulthood, can either be viewed—depending on your point of view—as indisputable proof of imaginative fortitude or a telltale sign of the emotional frailty that landed him in a mental asylum and ultimately led to his psychological and physical collapse. His Viennese contemporary, Sigmund Freud, would have had a field day analyzing a rife knot of neuroses, but analysis was not Altenberg's inclination or forte and his neuroses proved nourishing. Thirteen books and a copious posthumous opus, including reams of letters and inscribed postcards, attest to a prodigious and prescient verbal fortitude that outlived his own collapse and that of the world that produced him.

*

Born into a prosperous assimilated Jewish family in Vienna in 1859, the young Richard Engländer (who later took the pen name Peter Altenberg) was labeled by a grade school teacher as a "genius without abilities." The characterization bears a striking parallel to the title of the great Viennese novel, *The Man Without Qualities*, by Robert Musil (an ardent Altenberg fan), the first part of which appeared in print in 1931. Altenberg described himself as "the man without compromises," in a concise five-and-a-quarter page long "Autobiography," in his third book, *Was der Tag mir zuträgt* (*What the Day Brings*), 1901.

He flunked the writing segment of his high school graduation exam, as self-promulgated apocryphal legend has it, responding tersely to the theme: "The Influence of the New World (America)," with a single word: "Potatoes." Passing the test a year later, he took up and promptly abandoned the study of medicine, botany and the law, respectively, and halfheartedly explored the business of selling books, before finally concluding that he preferred to write them.

In 1883, a psychiatrist hired by his concerned father diagnosed "over-excitation of the nervous system" and concluded an "incapacity for employment." Altenberg took it as a one-way ticket to Literary Bohemia and the life of the coffeehouse poet, of which he became the epitome, and never looked back. His befuddled, albeit tolerant, father provided a modest living allowance until the family business (subsequently bequeathed to a brother) went bust, leaving the down at the heels Bohemian henceforth beholden to the fickle kindness of strangers. The grateful son wrote of his father in the aforementioned "Autobiography:"

> "He [the father] was once asked: 'Aren't you proud of your son?!'
> "He replied: 'I was not overly vexed that he remained an idler for 30 years. So, I'm not overly honored that he's a poet now! I gave him his freedom. I knew that it was a long shot. I counted on his soul.'"

Long before his words found their way into newspapers and periodicals, Altenberg was well known as a vetted Viennese eccentric who lodged in various hotels and traipsed around town in baggy clothes of his own conception (he was a pioneer in leisure wear), curious walking sticks and open sandals whatever the weather, favoring the companionship of young girls and loose women. He gave out as his official address the Café Central—also the sometime haunt of Russian emigrés Leon Trotsky and his chess partner Vladimir Ilyich Lenin—where Altenberg presided over his own table of garrulous caffeine-primed regulars.

How and when he first broke into print is the stuff of another homespun legend. One day, the author recalls, the members of

Vienna's ascendant literary avant-garde, Jung Wien, caught him scribbling away at his café table and immediately recognized his talent. The poet Richard Beer-Hoffmann is said to have first appreciated his writing, but it was the brilliantly sardonic critic Karl Kraus who sent Altenberg's fledgling selection of prose to S. Fischer Verlag, the foremost German publisher of the day, which promptly published his first book, *Wie Ich Es Sehe* (*How I See It*) in 1896. The book was a popular sensation and immediately put its author on the map.

"If it be permitted to speak of 'love at first syllable,' then that's what I experienced in my first encounter with this poet of prose," wrote Thomas Mann. Other impassioned literary partisans included the playwright Arthur Schnitzler, the poet and librettist Hugo von Hofmannsthahl, and Felix Salten, the versatile author of, among other works, the children's book classic, *Bambi*, and the underground pornographic classic, *The Adventures of Josephine Munzenbacher.*

Salten's incisive description of Altenberg's prose bears mention:

> "Some [of his pieces] are like steel projectiles, so tightly enclosed in themselves, so complete and precise in their form; and like projectiles, they pierce the breast; you are struck and you bleed. Some are like crystals and diamonds, sparkling in the multicolored reflections of the light of life, gleaming with captured rays of sunlight and glittering with a hidden inner fire. Some are like ripe fruits, warm with the waft of summer, swollen and sweat ..."

And just next door in Prague, the young Franz Kafka took Altenberg's terse writing style to heart and mind as a literary model for his own work. "In his small stories," Kafka observed, "his whole life is mirrored. And every step, every movement he makes confirms the truth of his words. Peter Altenberg is a genius of nullifications, a singular idealist who discovers the splendors of this world like cigarette butts in the ashtrays of coffeehouses."

Coffeehouse poet par excellence, Altenberg claimed to toss off his texts in a cavalier fashion for the throw-away pages of weekly and daily newspapers. "I view writing as a natural organic spilling out of a full, overripe person," he wrote in a letter to Schnitzler. "I hate any revision. Toss it off and that's good–! Or bad! What's the difference?!"

But tossed off, carefully crafted or both, there is nothing sloppy about his spare aesthetic. The extreme economy of his sketches sometimes reads more Japanese than Viennese—an elective affinity borne out by the caption he inscribed for a lady friend on a postcard of Japanese women posing under blossoming cherry trees:

"The Japanese paint a blossoming branch—and it is spring in its entirety! We paint all of spring—and it's hardly a blossoming branch!"

His Japanophile propensity is reiterated in the sketch "In Munich," in which he presses his stuffy fellow Europeans to "Learn from the Japanese!," lauding the latter as "an artistic people."

Altenberg's first direct exposure to the Japanese sensibility occurred at the Sixth Exhibition of the Wiener Sezession in 1900, a show exclusively devoted to the art of Japan. Though chronologically too late to have influenced his style, which appears to have sprouted Athena-like out of his brain and remained more or less unchanged throughout the two decades of his active writing career, this encounter with an alien world view must have felt strangely affirmative, more homecoming than departure, more mirror than window.

It was not his first flirtation with the exotic. Altenberg's second book, *Ashantee*, published in 1897, recounts his dealings with and vivid impressions of the inhabitants of an African show-village on display for a year as a live exhibit in Vienna's zoological garden. The grotesquery of the very premise of such an exhibition is lampooned in a short reflection entitled "Philosophy:"

> "Visitors to the Ashanti Village knock in the evening on the wooden walls of the huts for a lark.
>
> The goldsmith Nôthëi: 'Sir, if you came to us in Accra as objects on exhibit, we wouldn't knock on the walls of your huts in the evening!'"

Yet rather than stand above it all and wag a virtuous finger at the crude voyeurism of Viennese visitors, for whom the Africans on display were little more than talking animals, Altenberg de-constructs the spectacle by stepping inside it. He falls in love and loses his heart to various black girls and ladies "on display" and peels off their shell of otherness—an otherness he knew all too well under his own white skin, as a baptized Jew trying to pass in an often-hostile world given to Catholic piety and Teutonic cult.

*

But while Altenberg the author let his imagination wander to exotic climes and loved to wax eloquent about Nature, à la Ralph

Waldo Emerson, Altenberg the man was a hopeless homebody, a die-hard city slicker who dared not venture outside his beloved Vienna, except to revisit nearby Austrian spas and resorts cherished in childhood, and on a few occasions, to soak up the sun and surf on the Lido outside Venice. A piece entitled "Traveling" is, in fact, devoted to the "dirt-cheap pleasure altogether free of disappointments, to study the train schedule from mid-May on and pick out the very train with which you would, if only ..."–in short, the pleasure of staying put.

Perils lurked outside the safe periphery of the urban grid. Altenberg's Nature is at once an idealized locale and a metaphor for an unleashed sexuality which he both craved and feared. Consider the unabashed phallic fantasy that underlies the following paean to the great outdoors from the aforementioned "Autobiography":

> "As a boy I had an indescribable love for mountain meadows. The mountain meadow steaming under the blazing sun, fragrantly wafting, alive with bugs and butterflies, made me downright drunk. So, too, did clearings in the woods. On swampy sunny patches sit butterflies, blue silken small ones and black and red admirals and you can see the hoof print of deer. But for mountain meadows I had a fanatical love, I longed for them. Under all the white-hot stones I imagined there lurked poison adders, and this creature was the very incarnation of the fairy tale mystery of my boyhood years. It replaced the man-eating ogre, the giant and the witch. All the bites and their consequences, the terribly slow and torturous pain, I knew it all by heart, how to treat a wound and so on. The wondrously delicate gray-black body of the adder seemed to me to be

> the loveliest, most elegant creature, and when I loved a little girl, I always pictured again and again only one thing happening: an adder bit her in the foot on a hike and I sucked out the venom to save her!"

Enamored as he was of Nature's lure, he preferred to take it in limited doses. In the same text, he admits to never actually having seen an adder. "It remained for me a bad but sweetly disturbing dream."

Readers disinclined to the short form may indeed find Altenberg's sketches a bit claustrophobic and his attachment to his native stomping ground positively suffocating. It may seem at times as if he managed to stretch the city itself into a giant nursery navigated on a hopscotch grid. And though Altenberg's Vienna is peopled with pimps and prostitutes, cabbies and call girls, florists and floozies, there is a certain childlike innocence about them all. The hookers may not all wear their hearts on their sleeve, but they won't give you the Clap. And some of them, like the hired subject of "Poem," even write verse. His cast of characters comprise a collection of more or less accommodating playmates in an elaborate game with rules of his own devising. Even the most venomous types have been defanged. In the text "My Gmunden," a mysterious stranger with paranoid delusions encountered, notably not in Vienna but in the resort town of Gmunden, pulls out a Browning revolver and bids the narrator enjoy his supper—"Because it's your last!" In the story, the threatening stranger becomes an odd sort of Doppelgänger, a troubled comrade in arms, a fellow *Meshuganeh.*

In the short form, Altenberg isolated and delineated pleasures and pitfalls, savoring the former and attenuating the sting of the latter, compressing life into tiny parcels of manageable experience and prescribing them like pills to his reader.

He played his own heart strings like a harp, plucking and letting go, teasing himself into a never-ending state of excitation, and in the process eliciting a flurry of charged preludes. Whether taken as crystallized spasms of a crippled libido or as grains of irritation compounded into pearls, these texts transcend the moment of their creation and cry out with a remarkable modernity.

While such celebrated Fin-de-Siècle literati as Arthur Schnitzler and Hugo von Hofmannsthal sometimes read dated and bit dowdy today, the sputtering sparks of a fire gone cold, Altenberg's clipped "telegram style" resonates like bolts of prescient lightning leaping from one turn of the century to the next. "Only in the era of telegraphy, lightning-fast trains and automobile-cabs," wrote his friend and promoter, Egon Friedell, "could there emerge such a poet whose passionate desire it is to always stick to the essential."

*

Western Union has since given way to email and text messaging, and the trains and cars have accelerated considerably. The angst-ridden rapid-fire era of the telegram and the tommy-gun has spawned the frenetic age of email and e-war, with love and death on demand at the press of a button. Raised on the knowledge that an atom of matter is all it takes to make a pretty big bang, we've refined our taste for the essential. E=MC2, the concise epic of the 20th century, is, after all, only three letters long. Now that we've turned the corner into the 21st century, Altenberg's telegrams of the soul read right up to date.

In the Caves of the Unconscious: K is for Kafka[1]

In 1984, the Centre Georges Pompidou, in Paris, presented a memorable exhibition titled "Le Siècle de Kafka" (Kafka's Century), juxtaposing a loosely-linked display of visual enigmas by Alberto Giacometti, Raoul Hausmann, Paul Klee, Alfred Kubin, Henri Michaux, Germaine Richier, Louise Nevelson, Jean Tinguely, et al., with reflections on Kafka's lasting significance by Georges Bataille, Walter Benjamin, Jorge Luis Borges, André Breton, Albert Camus, Elias Canetti, Jean-Paul Sartre, and other 20th century literary luminaries, along with the unlikely cameo appearance of a forgotten novel by the master propagandist, Dr. Joseph Goebbels. (Though Dr. K never lived to encounter Dr. G, *The Trial* and "In the Penal Colony" offer prescient forewarnings of what a tête-à-tête between the two might have been like.) Depicting a disjointed modernity that has lost its moorings, the exhibition hypothesized how: "The name Kafka had imposed itself in less than a century on the literary, artistic and everyday sensibility to the point of becoming one of the most striking symbols of our time." The exhibition poster and catalogue cover featured a blown-up stick figure from Kafka's journals superimposed on a greatly enlarged photocopy of his passport with the rubberstamped red-letter K leaping out like a final verdict.

K still resonates in the 21st century, carrying faint echoes of the 19th—K&K Monarchy—and a reverberation of the nightmare of the 20th–KZ. The name itself was consecrated as a proper adjective, *Kafkaesque*, synonymous with the nightmarish, the ominous,

1 This essay first appeared as the afterword to *Konundrum, Selected Prose of Franz Kafka*, a new selection and translation by Peter Wortsman, Archipelago Books, Brooklyn, NY, 2016

and the bureaucratically bizarre, kindred to that other adjective born of a proper noun: *Orwellian. 1984* has come and gone, but *The Trial* is still in session.

*

Kafka's stark narratives and furtive fragments continue to strike our contemporary eardrums with the timber of truth precisely because they are atemporal and take place anywhere and nowhere, which is to say, inside the portable bucket we carry around delicately balanced between our shoulders to put out imaginary fires.

It would be a fallacy to insist that his fables and parables, or whatever literary label we may apply, are really about anything, i.e. that they correspond to states of reality extant outside the tenuous confines of a solitary psyche, or that they carry a clearly decipherable moral. Aesop and La Fontaine coupled irony and wit with recognizable allusions to the social order of their day. But narratives like "The Metamorphosis," "Josephine, Our Meistersinger, or the Music of Mice," "Report to an Academy," "The Burrow," and "Investigations of a Dog" are more than mere morality tales dressed up with animal masks. Nor are they bedtime stories intended to lull the restless into a somnolent state. They rather comprise the fragmented anthem of the insomniac, mining a parallel reality at the tenuous divide between waking and sleeping logic.

In much of his opus there is no plot to speak of. There's not much in the way of local color, only a flimsy sense of place, and even where, in the case of diary notations, a place is noted, he manages to blur the specificity of the locale. No character studies, no pithy dialogue or easily identifiable dialectic of good and evil. His heroes are hardly heroic, his heroines are not hot.

The best of his texts are distilled externalizations of interior states, strange hybrids of meditation, daydream, nightmare and doubt, realistic only in so far as they correspond to a vivid internal landscape, the universal landscape of dreams, and therefore recognizable to all.

There are subtexts and winked allusions here, of course.

It is hardly a stretch of the imagination to fathom in the dancing "*Lufthunde*" (air dogs) mentioned in "Investigations of a Dog" a tongue-in-cheek allusion to the Jewish "*Luftmensch,*" the ultimate outsider, which the online Merriam Webster dictionary defines as "an impractical contemplative person having no definite business or income." Perhaps a self-portrait of the author himself as a young dog.

Art Spiegelman's graphic novel *Maus*, in which incarcerated Jews and their Nazi tormenters are depicted in a deadly endgame of cat and mouse, clearly hearkens back to Kafka's last completed story, "Josephine, Our Meistersinger, or the Music of Mice," written with a last burst of transcendent wit, according to biographer Reiner Stach, at a time when Kafka's tubercular larynx were so far gone that speech was impossible and he could only bring forth mouse-like squeaks.

One would be equally hard-pressed not to see in Kafka's ironic "Report to an Academy," in which an ape recounts his decision to mimic humanity as his sole means of escape from captivity, an allusion to the attempts of assimilated Jews to imitate Aryan ways, so as to pass in a hostile and often perilous society.

And is there not something in the grudging relationship between the private artist who thrives on physical and psychic self-restraint and his brash impresario in "The Hunger Artist" that might remind of the tight, but sometimes strained, relationship between Kafka and his friend and promoter Max Brod?

But these are mere asides of incidental interest, hardly essential to an appreciation of the prose.

*

We can likewise dispense with biographical keys to the meaning, though texts like his parable on Poseidon's bureaucratic gripe might well be interpreted as an allusion to his own impatience with the interminable tasks of an accident insurance lawyer. But the experience he taps is strictly internal. The facts of his short life have been dug up and amply ruminated on by Max Brod (*Franz Kafka a Biography*), Ernst Pawel (*The Nightmare of Reason*), Frederick Karl (*Franz Kafka, Representative Man*), and most recently in a copiously researched, three-volume biography by Reiner Stach, two volumes of which (*Kafka, the Early Years*, and *Kafka, the Years of Realization*) have appeared in English to date, ably translated by Shelley Frisch, so that we need only here reiterate a few essential details to set the stage.

Born July 3, 1883, into a German-speaking, middle class Jewish family, in Prague, Bohemia, then still a provincial capital of the Austro-Hungarian Empire, Franz Kafka (his Hebrew name was Anschel), studied law, spent much of his adult life working for the Worker's Accident Institute for the Kingdom of Bohemia, and died of laryngeal tuberculosis on June 3, 1924. Between birth and death he handled the intertwined demands of family, in particular an overbearing father, a fraught sexuality and often frustrated longing and love life, conflicted ethnic identity, juggled languages (German, Czech, a sprinkle of Yiddish and fledgling knowledge of Hebrew), and the tense interface between a professional and a private self by funneling and filtering his fears through a volcanic imagination that burst forth in periodic verbal eruptions.

*

Kafka knocks directly at the gate of the unconscious. Like bluesman James Brown, he plays it on the one beat. His first sentence often says it all.

> "As Gregor Samsa awakened one morning from troubled dreams, he found himself in his bed transformed into a monstrous bug." (*The Metamorphosis*)

> "Someone must have maligned Joseph K. behind his back, for without having done anything wrong, he was arrested one fine morning." (*The Trial*)

> "'It is a curious piece of equipment,' said the officer to the traveling investigator, casting a somewhat admiring look at the apparatus, with which he was, after all, well acquainted." (*In the Penal Colony*)

Structurally harmonious like the tightly woven fiber scaffolding of a spider's web, his sentences capture the buzzing dissonance, employing a precise, officious language to evoke the ineffable. Herein lies their essential paradox and their essential strength: spun with a studied calm, there is something so unsettling, so *Kafkaesque* in the skeletal structure of each sentence, that every reader is compelled to invent his own set of criteria to get at the marrow.

What, for instance, is one to make of this simple pronouncement?

"I was stiff and cold, I was a bridge, I lay over an abyss."

Or this seemingly inconsequential diary reflection on clothing that suddenly sprouts twisted tentacles of existential malaise?

> "Consequently my posture conceded to shabby clothes, I walked around with my back bent, shoulders stooped, awkwardly dangling arms and hands: feared mirrors since, in my view, they merely revealed my ineluctable ugliness, which, moreover, could not have been reflected all that accurately, for if I really looked like that I would necessarily have caused a greater stir, while suffering on Sunday strolls my mother's gentle pokes in the back and her far too abstract admonitions and prophecies, vague reprimands which I could not correlate with my concerns of the moment."

*

Reviewing *In the Penal Colony,* Kafka's terrifying premonition of German penal colonies to come, written in 1914 and first published in 1919, the insightful Berlin-based, German-Jewish journalist and critic Kurt Tucholsky hit the stylistic nail on the head. "It is not true, as people maintain, that dreams are dreamy. So mercilessly hard, so gruesomely objective and crystal clear is this dream of Franz Kafka's [...]" Tucholsky wrote, detecting a kinship with the merciless syntax of Heinrich von Kleist, a bond Kafka himself confirmed in a letter to his sometime fiancé Felice Bauer, in which he referred to the tormented German Romantic writer as one of his "true blood relations." The torture instrument here described is a writing machine, a proto-word processor—never has the torment of writing been more nakedly portrayed. And though we never get to read it, the juridical and syntactical sentence incised in the condemned man's skin was, we may assume, dictated and transcribed in perfect German.

But consummately German as it is, there is another language hidden between the lines: something in the tilt and twist of Kafka's native tongue that sabotages the tight grid of Teutonic syntax, or to radically shift metaphors, interweaves the confident woof of ineluctable German logic with the wispy warp of eternal Semitic doubt.

To his last lover, Dora Diamant, a young woman with whom he enjoyed a brief period of domestic bliss toward the end of his life—who herself had fled the tight grip of the Gerer Rebbe (Yehudah Aryeh Leib), one of the autocratic Eastern European Jewish mystic sages of the sort romanticized by Martin Buber in his *Tales of the Hasidim*—Kafka was a *Wunderrebbe*, an ecstatic visionary in the tradition of the Baal Shem Tov, the founder of Hasidism, and his great-grandson, Reb Nachman of Bratislav, a tormented sage known for his cryptic parables. His narrative forbears surely also include such Biblical models as the Book of Jonah, the ancient Hebrew nightmare account of a petrified prophet swallowed by the physical manifestation of his own cosmic Angst, a text read in temple on Yom Kippur, the Day of Atonement, that would have been familiar even to assimilated Jews like the Kafkas who seldom otherwise set foot in the synagogue.

Equal parts German and Jewish, Kafka's is a hybrid imagination, in which Jonah's Leviathan couples with the frog prince of the Brothers Grimm to spawn the monstrous bug of "The Metamorphosis."

*

There are so many conflicting claims on Kafka's posthumous literary legacy that one is sometimes tempted to think of him as a kind of secular saint whose relics (in this case texts and manuscripts) are hotly contested by diverse constituencies.

Born under the double eagle of the Austro-Hungarian Empire, Austrians may claim him as one of their own. Prague, the capital of the Czech Republic, a city Kafka once described with considerable ambivalence as "a dear little mother with sharp claws," touts him today as an illustrious native son, his memory bracketed neatly by the plaque on his birthplace and the tombstone over his place of eternal restlessness. His work is taught alongside that of Bertolt Brecht, Thomas Mann, Robert Musil (another fellow Austrian), Rainer Maria Rilke (another Prague native), Joseph Roth, and other canonical masters of modern German letters. Some Jewish scholars emphasize his Semitic sensibility, with spiritual roots imbedded in the mystical tradition of the Kabala and its popular reawakening in the Hasidic tradition. The reader need only consider the Diaspora opus: Polish language stories of Bruno Schulz, the early Hebrew tales of S. Y. Agnon, the Russian narratives of Isaac Babel, the surreal Yiddish yarns of the Russian-born *Der Nister* (aka Pinchus Kahonovich), and the *insolite* French narratives of Georges Perec to extract the transcendent extra-lingual Jewish element of a literary foreign legion to which Kafka unquestionably also belongs. Yiddishists laud his fondness for a troop of itinerant Yiddish actors and his feel for their "*Heimischkeit*" (roughly Jewish soulfulness) in a culture inimical to overt Jewish ways. Zionists claim him as a fellow traveler, who studied Hebrew toward the end of his life and imagined escaping to Palestine, that is, when he was not dreaming of absconding to Berlin. He was also an avid vegetarian and health food enthusiast, and a devout "Fletcherizer," a convinced disciple of the American health food enthusiast, Horace Fletcher, who insisted on the virtues of mastication, advocating chewing each mouthful up to a hundred times a minute. A man torn by conflicting tendencies, sexual desire and countervailing repression, often unable to make up his mind, neurotics the world over justifiably claim him as their patron saint, a precursor of the young Woody Allen.

Ignoring Kafka's written instructions specified, in a letter found after his death, to burn all his unpublished work, including diaries, manuscripts, letters, and sketches, his friend, literary executor and self-appointed amanuensis, the Prague-born, German-speaking Jewish writer Max Brod (1884-1968) lugged a suitcase full of his papers along on his escape to Palestine, later judiciously releasing them in small book-length batches to seed, fuel and nurture a Kafka cult. Brod left the remaining papers after his own death to an assistant, Esther Hoffe, whose heirs subsequently created an international legal conundrum, subdividing and selling off some of the contents—which Brod had bequeathed in its entirety to the National Library of Israel, in Jerusalem—to the Museum of Modern Literature, in Marburg, Germany.

*

Collective and individual fear and doubt are surely not the sole province of the Jews, nor is the state of perpetual insecurity rife with neuroses labeled and analyzed by Kafka's Viennese-Jewish contemporary, Sigmund Freud, a Jewish monopoly. Seeing himself as a scientist first and foremost, Freud sought to pass the irrational under the microscope of rational scrutiny and thereby tame it. But Kafka, a consummate *Dichter* in the German sense, part poet, part visionary, recognized the irrational as a discrete realm unto itself and made no attempt to ensnare it in the straitjacket of reason. Dark as his musings are, they blow the manhole cover off the unconscious, and so, paradoxically, reduce the pressure of human consciousness.

This eloquent plaint of a solitary soul from the provincial periphery of a once powerful empire which he lived to see collapse around him, muttered in a linguistic composite of German precision and Jewish longing, would prove prophetic. Ostensibly an escape into the bunker of the unconscious, Kafka's prose cries out, Cassandra-like, predicting the advent of a time when the sentence would be literally tattooed in the victim's skin, the language of Goethe and Kant reduced to insipid sayings on the gates of prison camps, in which people are metamorphosed into vermin fit for extermination.

*

But Kafka was not always the object of universal approbation, the mythic articulator of the unspeakable, as he is recognized today. In his lifetime he remained essentially a writer's writer, the author of a few slender volumes of enigmatic prose known primarily to a small coterie of German-speaking Jewish intimates in Prague, a reputation that seeped out to a few like-minded souls in Vienna and Berlin, thanks to the reviews of Kurt Tucholsky and the tireless promotion of Max Brod, but stopped short at the cultural and linguistic border crossing.

Posterity owes a profound debt of gratitude to his Czech translator and sometime lover Milena Jesenská, who took the first steps to get the word out in translations that Kafka, himself fluent enough to read and write love letters in perfect Czech, approved and prized. In a stirring obituary published in the Czech language newspaper, *Národnílisty*, she aptly described him as "a sage afraid of life." Referring to his physical and spiritual response to his lung disease, she wrote: "It gave him a nearly miraculous finesse and intellectual purity to the point of terrible intransigence." Keenly attune to his strengths and weaknesses, she noted: "He had a singular and profound knowledge of the world, he was a singular and profound world unto himself." Of writings that baffled most of his contemporary readers she aptly observed: "They are true, naked and sad, and even where his mode of expression is symbolic, are almost naturalistic." And finally of his astounding opus she concluded: "All of his books depict the horrors of the mysterious incomprehensible, the senseless mistakes that pit man against man; he was a man and an artist of such a fearful awareness that he heard signals of impending peril where others, deaf to the truth, felt safe and secure."

Other posthumous praise came from German writers and critics, including Walter Benjamin, Bertolt Brecht, Alfred Döblin, Hermann Hesse, Siegfried Krakauer, Klaus Mann, Thomas Mann, Herbert Marcuse, and Rainer Maria Rilke, who helped spread the word.

Kafka's young friend and protégé, Dr. Robert Klopstock first translated his stories into Hungarian. Bruno Schulz and Jorge Luis Borges transposed the prose into peerless Polish and Spanish, respectively, the latter thereby heralding a generation of Magical Realists half a world away. André Gide read Kafka in the original German, and Alexandre Vialatte transplanted his Judeo-Teutonic syllables into the Gallic lines, first publishing his version of "The Metamorphosis" in 1928 in Gide's prestigious literary journal, *La Nouvelle Revue Francaise*.

English language readers have the Orkney Island-born poet, novelist and translator, Edwin Muir, and his wife Willa (née Anderson), recipients of the Johann Heinrich Voss Translation Award, to thank for first transmitting the mysteries of Kafka into our hybrid Anglo-Saxon-Norman tongue. Other respected English translators who have each given it a go include: Anthea Bell, Susan Bernofsky, Mark Harman, Breon Mitchell, Joachim Neugroschel, Idris Parry, and Malcolm Pasley. Ross Banjamin is presently in the process of translating the sum total of the extant journals.

*

What then impels yet another *Übersetzer* to tackle Kafka?

I once heard the translator likened to a musician or an actor, and think there is some truth to the comparison. Both apply artistry, insight, cunning and craft, working from a track, a musical score, a script of dialogue, or a string of sentences, jotted down by a sentient being in another time, place and tongue, attempting to listen in, as it were, to the whisper and howl of the original, to capture an echo of that voice, and by reformulating rhythm and meaning to tap the heartbeat and reanimate the breath enveloped by the silence of eternity. Beethoven and Bach have been interpreted countless times before, so have Calderon, Shakespeare, and Racine, which does not keep new conductors and instrumentalists, directors and actors from taking a crack at it.

Having tried my pen, and by some accounts succeeded at transmitting the spirit and essence of Chamisso, the Brothers Grimm, Musil, Heine and Kleist, among other German prose masters, I felt it was time to return to one of the first writers who made me gasp.

As to the selection, my sole criteria was amazement. Jill Schoolman, my perfect publisher, accorded me the incomparable freedom of permitting me to dip into the entire opus, to find and translate whatever struck my fancy, including finished tales, long and short, some published by the author in his lifetime, some issued posthumously by Max Brod, and narrative nuggets from the journals and letters with a clearly demarcated beginning and end and such a pressing imminence that one is inclined to believe that Kafka might have salvaged and polished them for publication had he lived.

Translating Kafka for me is a bit like looking back at a first love, an attachment saved from sentimentality and necrophilia by a corpus of work in need of no facelifts or taxidermy to entice, still as alive and relevant as any musings of an eloquent insomniac committed to extreme particularity of expression. I give you the precious nuggets of a goldminer in the caves of the unconscious.

Inverted Anonymity: The Mindful Farce of Mynona[1]

"Who is Mynona? Almost incomprehensible: either very good or very bad. I will have to read more by this author," wrote the implacable Viennese critic Karl Kraus upon first discovering a text of his published in 1910 in *Der Sturm*, a leading Berlin-based literary review of Expressionist writing. After reading another text in the next issue, Kraus concluded: "Mynona is very fine. Who is this?"

*

> "His long, lean, beardless face was dominated in profile by his unabashedly protruding pointed nose. Around his craggy features, marked by an ugliness that strained to correct itself, hovered a severity merciless to lies that might also be seen as self-effacing mirth. Since these contradictions canceled each other out rather than cross-fertilizing, he came across as bizarre and banal."

This is how Mynona mercilessly described a character modeled after himself in a roman à clef, *Graue Magie* (*Gray Magic*), published in 1922.

Mynona relished enigma:

> "I searched for a pseudonym that would permit me to remain as anonymously opaque as possible, of which

1 This essay was first published as the introduction to *The Creator, a fantasy*, by Mynona (aka Salomo Friedlaender), translated by Peter Wortsman, Wakefield Press, Cambridge, Mass., 2014

> one could not even suspect the sex; a pseudonym that could just as well serve as a first name. It came to me in a snap—"Mynona." "Anonym" (anonymous) read backwards; a feminine name, but as such rendered suspect by the "y" in the first syllable. Quite rightly, therefore, did Professor Bartels, of Weimar, a venerable authority, take me for a lovely Jewess. Would I be less misguided to presume he is a German of Aryan blood?"

In the inverted anonymity of his penname, Mynona, aka Salomo Friedlaender, was toying with and perhaps unwittingly predicting his fate. A philosopher-satirist-fabulist likened in his day to Voltaire, a self-styled "synthesis of Kant and clown (Chaplin)," as he dubbed himself in a letter to his publisher, Kurt Wolff—also the publisher of Franz Kafka, with whom he was sometimes mentioned in the same breath—an active member, along with Raoul Haussmann, Herwarth Walden (aka Georg Lewin), Else Lasker-Schüler, Alfred Kubin, and Georg Grosz, of the German literary and artistic avant-garde that thrived between WWI and II, a literary iconoclast and forerunner of the Dadaists, the author known as Mynona has been essentially erased from memory.

Born on May 4, 1871 into a bourgeois Jewish family, his father a cultivated doctor, his mother a woman of musical talent and refinement, in the backwater town of Gollantsch in the Prussian Province of Posen on the border with Poland, to which it was re-annexed following World War II, Friedlaender lived to witness and suffer the total collapse of the enlightened German civility to which he had committed himself heart and soul, fleeing to Paris, where he managed to avoid deportation by being bedridden, too sick to move, and where he died in penury on September 9, 1946, a year after the end of the war.

The quintessential intellectual Jewish *Luftmensch*, his life comprised a bundle of contradictions of which he was all too well aware. After attempting to please his father by undertaking, first the study of medicine, then dentistry, thereafter working briefly for a photographic studio, all futile efforts abandoned forthwith, he ultimately pursued the study of philosophy, flirted with Nietzsche and Schopenhauer, then fell under the influence of Kant and one of his modern interpreters, Ernst Marcus (1856-1928), and produced a substantial corpus of serious philosophical works, the best known of which are: *Friedrich Nietzsche, An Intellectual Biography* (1911), *Schöpferische Indifferenz* (*Creative Indifference*), 1918; a pedagogical textbook, *Kant für Kinder* (*Kant for Children*), 1924; and *Das magische Ich*, (*The Magical I*), 2001, a posthumously published work completed in French exile, which he considered his magnum opus.

But Friedlaender/Mynona drew equal inspiration from the hilarious legends of the mythical residents of Chelm, the Jewish hamlet of *meshuganah*, and their German counterparts, the Schildbürger, a realm of licensed madness, where people sow salt in their fields and gather daylight in buckets to illuminate their town hall in which they'd neglected to cut windows. Parallel to his philosophical writing, a raucous Mr. Hyde to his meditative Dr. Jekyll, under the penname Mynona he produced novellas, novels, and art criticism, including the first monograph on the painter Georg Grosz. But he was best known for a vast body of short prose texts he called "*Grotesken*" (grotesques) which he presented at various avant-garde venues of the day, including the Neopathetisches Cabaret in Berlin, the unofficial clubhouse of the Expressionist poets, published in Der Sturm, Die Aktion, and other leading avant-garde journals, and subsequently collected in more than 20 volumes.

A contemporary commentator left a vivid description of a Mynona reading at the Kunstverein Erfurt, in 1926:

> "A man of medium height, in his mid-fifties, with thick white hair, his face and broad forehead radiated much kindness and brilliance, much unsentimental love of life and merriment that comes from within—that serenity pressed out of struggle and pain. Tilting his head forward to peer at his manuscript in hand, he appears in profile a bit like the young Voltaire, but without the latter's acid and gall [...] Mynona is his own best interpreter. He reads splendidly and accentuates well. His choicest gems are often hidden in his afterthoughts. Reading, he half sweeps them under the table, where, of course, they have the strongest effect, since the offhanded is always more powerful than the outright remark. Each piece elicits spontaneous applause. For an hour every audience member felt himself as if soaking in a delightful hot bubble bath."

His writing attracted the attention, and later sparked the friendship of, among others, the philosopher and theologian Martin Buber, and the artist Alfred Kubin, who illustrated a number of his works. His comic satirical texts entered the repertoire of such Berlin cabaret performers as Resi Langer, Rudolf Blümner and Ludwig Hardt. In 1931 Mynona was invited to celebrate his sixtieth birthday with a radio broadcast in which he read aloud his raucous grotesque "*Gebratenes Sphinxfleisch*" (Roast Sphinx).

*

Having been painfully introverted as a child, so much so as to arouse the serious concern of his parents who sent him off to boarding school to try to make him shape up and conform to social norms, Friedlaender sought psychic refuge in the imagination, staking out an internal territory to which he alone had privileged access. "My theme is the inner world, my I, in comparison with which all human external life, my own included, seems grotesque," he wrote in a posthumously published autobiographical sketch entitled I, 2003. As a child he delighted in reading works of fantasy, fairy tales, in particular from *A Thousand and One Arabian Nights*, and his absolute favorite, the science fiction of Jules Verne. As an adult, he expanded his select roster of kindred spirits to include those he dubbed "bizarre authors," notably E.T.A. Hoffmann, de Quincey, Poe, Rabelais, Swift, Sterne, Jean Paul, and his contemporary and friend, the satirical humorist, Paul Scheerbart.

Like a number of his contemporaries and followers in the literary avant-garde of the early 20th century, the Expressionists, the Dadaists, and later the Surrealists, Friedlaender/Mynona was a lifelong explorer in the quicksand of the unconscious, seeking to tease the limits and bridge the cognitive gap between waking and dreaming, between the instinctive and the learned, between the innermost I and the acclimatized we. Yet whereas such notable contemporaries as the Expressionist poets Georg Heym and Georg Trakl and the great master of the prose parable, Franz Kafka, drilled directly into the fundament of dreams, tapping its potent sap to escape the mundane and reveal the dark irrational undercurrents of consciousness, Friedlaender/Mynona investigated the subjective with the cool-headed sobriety of a philosopher and the visionary daring of a mystic. There was more than a little Cabala and Swedenborg mixed in with his Kant. Here is how he put his philosophical stance in the aforementioned autobiographical sketch, I:

> "To be human means to be an angel in the body of a beast, and every man is afforded the option to freely transpose the emphasis from beast back to angel, from natural man to man of reason, even if true advantage of this freedom may never have been taken. This freedom is the hallmark of humanity, and it should and must one day be possible, not to emancipate the angel from the beast, but to free the angel from subservience to the beast."

Writing in a beastly time, a brief window of shaky civility between the wholesale trench butchery of World War I and the mass deportation and extermination of World War II, it may seem a futile exercise to pursue the angelic. But what else is literature than a futile attempt to hoodwink the Grim Reaper and his determined human henchmen and hold on to a fleeting angelic flicker before the beast bears its claws.

*

A word about the text at hand.

Initially conceived as part of a book of grotesques collectively titled *Das widerspenstige Brautbett* (*The Intractable Bridal Bed*), accepted for publication but later withdrawn by the author from the Verlag Georg Müller, Mynona issued his novella *The Creator* in 1919 in seven installments in supplementary pages to *Der Einzige* (The One and Only), a journal he co-edited with his brother-in-law Anselm Ruest (aka Ernst Samuel), pitching it with a wink of unabashed hyperbole in a notice to readers as "the most profound magical experiment since Nostradamus."

Following some initial, and perhaps justifiable, objections on the part of the publisher, Kurt Wolff, as to the imbalance between the lush sensual fantasy of the first part and the theoretical philosophical ruminations that freight the second part, the novella was subsequently reissued alone in 1920 in the series *Schwarze Bücher*, an imprint of the Kurt Wolff Verlag, with illustrations commissioned by Alfred Kubin (included in the present text).

The manipulation of the unconscious was in the air. Robert Wiene's landmark Expressionist horror film about a hypnotist's diabolical experiments in mind control "*Das Kabinett des Dr. Caligari*" (The Cabinet of Dr. Caligari) came out that same year. And in the political arena, the National Socialists tapped Teutonic myth and archaic notions drudged up from the German collective unconscious to seduce the German electorate.

To set the tenor of his tale and anchor it in philosophical discourse, Mynona picked an epigram from Kant's metaphysical examination of the spirit, *Träume eines Geistersehers* (Dreams of a Spirit-Seer), elsewhere in which the 18th century critic of pure reason freely confessed: "I do not know if *Geister* [ghosts] even exist, what's more, I do not even know what the word *Geist* really means."

The somewhat autobiographically conceived protagonist of the novella, Gumprecht Weiss, an intellectual who has withdrawn from a life of libertinage to pursue his solitary philosophical ruminations, first dreams up, then encounters, the figment of his imagination in the flesh, an enticing young woman named Elvira. She, as it turns out, has escaped the clutches of her uncle, the Baron, who has been using her as a guinea pig in his metaphysical experiments. But the Baron catches up with them, and promptly entices Gumprecht and Elvira to come with him to his laboratory in a tower, shades of Faust's tower, to willingly engage in an experiment to bridge the divide between waking consciousness and the creative wellspring of dream by entering a mirror engineered to bend and blend reality. Like the looking glass in "Snow White," this one, too, establishes the truth, but unlike the *Märchen* mirror it joins the seer and the seen, the inside and the outside, the subjective and the objective, the I and the thou, along with the it.

I will leave it to the reader to discover the upshot.

Not a popular success, selling few copies when it first appeared, this philosophical fable pitched by the publisher as "the fulfillment of a poetic-philosophical miracle —; a station farther on the imaginative train of thought of Hoffmann, Villiers, Poe, etc.," was nevertheless appraised and appreciated by a number of critics. Writing in the *Prager Presse*, Paul Hatvani opined:

> "We know the unbridled, albeit temporally bound, imagination of Mynona. It can be downright pedantic in its logic: never leaving the realm of philosophical reflection; Mynona always proceeds deductively from the idea underlying his premise to the thing at hand. He is, so to speak, an inverted Plato. His worldview is built on nervous irritations: he is a Jules Verne of the soul …"

After giving this fair enough assessment of the strengths and weaknesses of the text, the critic goes on to praise it as:

> "… in the most *geistig* [roughly intellectual] sense, a riveting read. Since the Romantics, since E.T.A. Hoffmann, there has been no other work of German literature that has, like this one, managed to evoke the atmosphere of philosophical insight. […] But the book should be read and treasured, like everything else this extraordinary and pure thinker has given us."

*

The novella inspired a film scenario, "*Traumwandlerin*" (Dream Wanderer) by Franz Fischer, but the movie never got made. On the prompting of an intermediary, a fellow émigré, Dr. Victor Grubwieser, produced an English translation, but the translation never made it into print.

Salomo Friedlaender/Mynona never had a self-appointed literary amanuensis, like Kafka's bosom buddy Max Brod, to cultivate and resurrect his reputation. In presenting this slender volume, in which the publisher and I have decided to also include the translation of a short grotesque on a kindred theme, "*Die langweilige Brautnacht*" (The Wearisome Wedding Night), to an English speaking readership, this translator, who has elsewhere already situated Mynona's work in a German tradition of the enigmatic, herewith hopes to call upon the laws of poetic justice and leave it to a jury of discriminating readers to assess the merits of Mynona's prose, and if found tantalizing, compelling, and innocent of guile, to pluck the author out of the limbo of anonymity and put his words back in circulation.

Posthumous Papers Revisited[1]

"What matters to me," Robert Musil wrote in a diary notation dated 1910, "is the passionate energy of the idea."

What matters to us is the product of that passion tapped like a fermented sap from his overripe mind, a blend of deeply felt thoughts and dispassionately reasoned feelings filtered through vivid metaphors rooted in a life from which Musil maintained a lifelong remove. Steeped in military science, engineering, mathematics, philosophy and behavioral psychology, each sentence is a poetic treatise unto itself, taking aim like a sharpshooter's rifle, whirring like a well-oiled engine, fitted with the perfect balance of a theorem, a rigorously reasoned philosophical substrata, and keen psychological insight, the whole capped off with the mysticism of a skeptic. It's a rich dish indeed, the mark of a true *Dichter*, that untranslatable German composite of poet and philosopher with a sprinkling of the prophet and a touch of the fanatic.

What are we to make, for instance, of the following sentence from "Flypaper," the first piece in *Posthumous Papers of a Living Author*, a dark meditation on flies stuck fast to the stuff of their undoing? Imagining the insect's conundrum on first fathoming its fastened state, Musil puts himself (and us) in its place:

> "It's a very quiet, disconcerting sensation, as though while walking in the dark we were to step on something with our naked souls, nothing more than a soft, warm, unavoidable obstruction, and yet something

1 This essay was first published as the afterword to *Posthumous Papers of a Living Author*, by Robert Musil, third edition of the translation by Peter Wortsman, Archipelago Books, NYC, 2006

> into which, little by little, the awesome human essence flows, recognized as a hand that just happens to be lying there, and with five ever more decipherable fingers, holds us tight."

Consummate Musil, it's a sentence replete with grammatical subordination and plenty of Kant, in which the abstract melds inscrutably with the particular, a sentence in which Aesop meets Nosferatu, in which the physical suddenly turns meta, the real sur-real, conjuring up a vivid, albeit unimaginable, picture, an indissoluble capsule of seeing and feeling and thinking. It's as if Kant himself, impersonating an anthropomorphic fly for the edification of imagined progeny, got trapped in the telling of a Grimm fairy tale and never made it past the once-upon-a-time.

*

Born in the provincial town of Klagenfurt, Austria, in 1880, the son of a "clear-headed," albeit rigid, academic engineer and a "curiously muddled mother, like slumbering hair upon a handsome face," (according to another diary notation), Robert Musil took a circuitous educational path, attending military boarding school and, to his parents' great chagrin, promptly abandoning a career in the military, only to pursue and drop studies in mathematics, engineering, philosophy and behavioral psychology, respectively. Conscripted as an officer in the Imperial Austrian army during World War I, he edited a military newspaper. A brief stint as a drama critic after the War was one of his last attempts at gainful employment before finally settling into the uncertain life of an independent author.

While his first book, *Die Verwirrungen des Zöglings Törless* (Young Törless), a novel published in 1906, was an immediate and smashing success, subsequent works were less well received. Two volumes of short fiction, *Vereinigungen* (literally *Unions*, but which I preferred in my translation to render as *Intimate Ties...*), 1911, and *Drei Frauen* (Three Women), 1924, received respectable notice but did not sell well. A play, "*Die Schwärmer*" (The Enthusiasts), 1921, was honored with the prestigious Kleist Prize two years later, but bombed at the box office. Another play, "*Vincenz und die Freundin Bedetuender Männer*" (Vincenz and the Girlfriend of Influential Men), 1923, didn't do much better. Undaunted, Musil devoted much of the rest of his waking consciousness for the remainder of his days to the composition of his epic novel, *Der Mann Ohne Eigenschaften* (The Man Without Qualities), a work often compared in its breadth of vision and innovative structure to James Joyce's *Ulysses* and Marcel Proust's *A la recherche du temps perdu* (In Search of Time Past). The first volume was published in 1931 to much acclaim but modest sales, followed by another installment in 1933, the same year Hitler came to power—an inauspicious year for serious intellectual endeavors in the German language.

Though essentially apolitical, Musil was constitutionally averse to the philistinism of the Third Reich. His wife Martha's Jewish parentage added another complication. The Musils, who resided in Berlin at the time, moved back to Vienna, and thereafter, following Austria's annexation to the Reich, fled to Geneva, where Musil died in 1942. His widow released the unfinished conclusion of his magnum opus in 1943. The entire work was finally issued in three volumes, as edited by Adolf Frisé, from 1952 to 1957. Sophie Wilkins' and Burton Pike's landmark English translation was published in New York in 1995.

In 1935, while laboring on his masterpiece in poor health in destitute Swiss exile, Musil reluctantly allowed the Humanitas Verlag in Zürich to issue a slender compilation of previously published occasional writings. The ironic title he picked, *Nachlass zu Lebzeiten* (Posthumous Papers of a Living Author), reflected the author's profound ambivalence at presenting this reheated platter of this and that while the world he knew was going under and he himself was going nowhere. "To publish nothing but little tales and observations amidst a thundering, groaning world," he wrote in the foreword, "to speak of incidentals when there are so many vital issues; to vent one's anger at phenomena that lie far off the beaten track: this may doubtless appear as weakness to some, and I will readily admit that I had all kind of doubts regarding the decision to publish."

He called it "*mein kleines Lückenbüsser Buch*" (my little stop-gap book), grudgingly acknowledging that "the little parts of which it was to be constructed ... were after all more durable than I had feared." But anyone who has ever indulged in a Viennese *Jause*, or high tea, knows the refined finesse of a Viennese finger sandwich, and no one could prepare and pepper them quite like Musil. If anything, *Posthumous Papers* has aged well. History confirmed the dark prophetic poetry of his parables on dying anthropomorphic flies and the sadistic simian doings on a monkey island at the Roman zoo, so uncannily like a concentration camp:

> "Then the long, indifferent gaze nails its arbitrary victim [...] With the release of a scream, the others rush apart on down the ditch; they flicker dimly about like the damned souls in the flames of purgatory, and gather chattering cheerfully as far from the scene as possible."

In the mini-essays that comprise part two, "Ill-Tempered Observations," Musil takes aim at many of the sacred cows, theories and conceits of his time. He dispels the idyll of peaceful Nature so dear to the Teutonic heart:

> "Are there no seasoned naturalists from whom we can learn that the stalwart oak, today a veritable epitome of solitude, once spread in hordes [...] That the spruce [...] was a relatively recent interloper [...] and where a variety of trees seem to conjure up an image of happy coexistence, they are really scattered combatants, the surviving remnants of enemy hordes crowded together, too tired and exhausted to continue battle!" ("Who Made You, Oh Forest Fair ...?")

He reveals the indecorous truth about the innate invisibility of monuments of which Vienna was so fond:

> "... they are impregnated with something that repels attention, causing the glance to roll right off, like water droplets off an oilcloth, without even pausing for a moment." ("Monuments").

He even dares poke piercing fun at the panacea of psychoanalysis:

> "If ancient man had his Scylla and Charybdis, so modern man has his Wasserman test and Oedipus complex; for if he succeeded in eluding the former, and effectively setting a little offspring on its own two feet, he can be all the more certain that the latter will catch up with his son." ("Threatened Oedipus")

Part three, "Unstorylike Stories," includes a narrative nugget, "A Man Without Character," from the seed out of which the monumental novel erupted like a magic beanstalk.

Musil wraps up the book with a long short story, "The Blackbird," arguably one of the eeriest, most exquisite works of German speculative writing, a product of what the author called "*taghelle Mystik*" (daylight mysticism). In three memories of strange visitations recounted by the narrator to a fictional friend—the first, the flight of a bird, prompting his leaving his wife; the second, a close scrape with death in the form of an aerial dart whizzing his way on the battlefield in World War I; the third, the reappearance of the fateful bird which now identifies itself as the reincarnation of his dead mother—the author manages seamlessly to bridge the great divide between "*Wirklichkeitssinn*" (sense of reality) and what he postulated as "*Möglichkeitssinn*" (sense of possibility), leaving the reader dangling over the abyss of doubt:

> "I had no thoughts of the kind that are supposed to come at death's door, but all my thoughts were rather focused on the future; I can only say that I was certain that in the next second I would feel God's proximity close up to my body—which, after all, is saying quite a bit for someone who hasn't believed in God since the age of eight." ("The Blackbird")

And while Musil did not invent the form of *Kurzprosa* (short prose), he managed to put his own original spin on it, with echoes of Nietzsche, Hoffmann and Poe. Bits and pieces of the book, alternately characterized as prose poems, fairy tales, fables, or just plain prose, subsequently found their way into various anthologies.

Having first shepherded English language readers up the foothills of Musil's *Posthumous Papers of a Living Author* in preparation for the more arduous trek up the intellectual Everest of *The Man Without Qualities*, I would like to deflect a flicker of attention to celebrate this third edition of my translation. In so doing, I admit to feeling a bit like the overlooked Sherpa guide Tenzing Norgay at Sir Edmund Hillary's salute, a bit like a graying gigolo flaunting an old love affair with Norma Jean before she became Marilyn Monroe.

Originally published in the U.S. in 1988, as Volume One of the splendid, albeit short-lived, Eridanos Library, *Posthumous Papers* was reissued in the U.K. by Penguin 20th-century Classics, and, now, a little more than a decade later, has once again been lovingly resurrected on this side of the Atlantic by Archipelago Books.

Musil's little book already enjoyed a considerable following elsewhere, admired as it was in Italy, Spain, and particularly in France, where it had been expertly rendered by the Swiss poet-translator Philippe Jaccottet in 1965.

Still it took some prodding to pry open the American clam. Having published an excerpt in the literary journal *Antaeus*, and a longer selection entitled Pictures, as a workshop project of the Coalition of Publishers for Employment at Cooper Union, both in 1983, I amassed a slew of laudatory rejection letters from various and sundry editors and resolved to bury the translation in a heap of unwanted manuscripts at the bottom of a drawer. Then one day the telephone rang. It was a Mr. Juan Garcia calling from the remote mountain hamlet of Hygiene, Colorado. Mr. Garcia informed me that he and his business associate, Andrea Nasi, had selected my translation to launch their new publishing venture. This on the urging of Juan's father, the Mexican novelist Juan Garcia Ponce, who knew and admired the text in Spanish translation and had even published his own rewriting of "The Blackbird," and on the advice of Ledig Rowohlt, principle of the German publisher Rowohlt Verlag, who knew my English take. And while translations as a rule do poorly in the American literary marketplace, the hot potato that nobody had thought marketable turned out to be a runaway literary hit, a Village Voice "Our Kind of Bestseller," and *New York Times Book Review* "And Bear in Mind" selection, and promptly went through several printings.

Such acclaim for his "little stop-gap book" would have surprised no one more than Musil himself, for whom it was a mere afterthought to his monumental work. But afterthoughts can have a rich afterlife and monuments, as the author himself suggested in a text of the same title, risk invisibility. And whereas big books are often admired from afar and have a way of gathering dust, little books are more readily plucked off the shelf and stuffed into handbag and backpack, from whence they have a pretty good crack at the unconscious.

Preserving the Imprint of the Ineffable in Musil's Prose [1]

Not to tell a story per se, but to evoke the hollow husk of mind and mood in which a story is conceived, born, and incubated; not to deploy the impregnating battering ram of reason, but to embrace the nurturing womb of impressions—this is what the Austrian writer Robert Musil (1880-1942), best known for his unfinished magnum opus *Der Mann ohne Eigenschaften* (The Man Without Qualities), strove for in the two-and-a-half-year-long literary ordeal and crisis of consciousness begun in 1908 that ultimately culminated in his second book, *Vereinigungen*, here translated as *Intimate Ties.* What started out as an attempt to quickly whip off a text to placate an eager publisher stretched into a soul-searching experiment in the course of which, as he wrote in his journal, "I almost drove myself out of my mind." Published in 1911, this loose assemblage of two novellas, both focusing on the woes of troubled female protagonists, defies in form and content any heretofore established notions of literary license.

Written in the wake of the stunning critical and popular success of his debut novel, *Die Verwirrungen des Zöglings Törleß* (The Confusions of Young Törless), this second book, by which Musil hoped to establish his reputation, proved a complete flop. While heralded by a few early Expressionist writers as a pathbreaking work, it was savaged by critics as "chapter after chapter of abstract psychoanalyses" of two "hysterical" women presented in "thick patches of fog." Musil himself retained a lifelong fondness for what he ultimately considered a worthy, albeit failed, experiment. "It is the only one of my books I sometimes

1 This essay first appeared as the afterword to *Intimate Ties*, by Robert Musil, translated by Peter Wortsman, Archipelago Books, Brooklyn, NY, 2019

return to. I can't stand extended passages. But I'll gladly dip into one to two pages anytime," he recalled in a journal notation in 1935. Recognizing that it was far outside the accepted norms of European art, he thought of it rather as a verbal collage, a kind of medieval illuminated manuscript. Today's reader might well view it as hypertext before its time. Its primary fault, Musil allowed half-tongue-in-cheek, was

> "that it had a binding, back cover, pagination. A few pages at a time should be spread out and displayed between glass plates, the selection to be changed every now and then. Then you would see what it is."

Ostensibly, at least on the narrative surface, the first novella, "Die Vollendung der Liebe," here translated as "The Consummation of Love," is about the protracted emotional tug of war leading up to a married woman's infidelity, and the second, "Die Versuchung der stillen Veronika" (The Temptation of Silent Veronica) taps a sexually repressed young woman's traumatic childhood memory of a near tangle with bestiality, her rejection of a would-be lover, and her struggle to formulate a coherent notion of deity. With a psychic Geiger counter Musil goes prospecting in the hearts and minds of his imagined female protagonists conjured up like jinnis from his wife Martha Marcovaldi's early bottled-up recollections.

Read at your own risk. Those expecting a traditional narrative thread may well be frustrated by the near total absence of signposts and touchstones.

The first novella, "The Culmination of Love," offers at least a recognizable emotional build-up. A woman whose husband is too busy to join her reluctantly sets out on a journey in winter, first by train, then by horse-drawn carriage, to visit her daughter from an earlier marriage at a boarding school in the country. Along the way she recalls and alternately savors and disdains the insidious lure of past infidelities in her former marriage, all the while becoming enticed as much by the flavor of memory as by any actual attraction for the pompous windbag who happens to be seated opposite her in the train. Musil captures the inherent Eros of travel, when life flies by through the picture window of a speeding train, the traveler, herself lost in reverie, in a constant state of flux, basks in the passivity of looking and letting the world whisk past, responding to stimuli more by tropism than reason, and all is illusion. Later upon arrival at her destination and finding herself snowed in, she crawls naked on the floor of her hotel room, sniffing the scent of myriad feet on the rug, sensing the stranger waiting outside her door. Before succumbing to his crude advances, or rather to the remembered lure of past advances channeled through him, she previews and savors her disgust, watching him mutter inanities:

> "… and soon she saw nothing but the never-ending rise and fall of his beard, the bobbing beard of a repulsive Billy goat ceaselessly chewing, spitting out a whispered soporific stream of words."

Tina Turner's hit tune "What's Love Got to Do with It?" leaps to mind. But the novella is really about the limitations of language.

> "… her own words sounded strange swimming among strange syllables, like fish flouncing against the cold damp bodies of other fish in the indecipherable whirlpool of opinions. […] Again, she felt that it did not so much matter what people say of themselves, what they manage to put into words, but rather that any real revelation was conveyed in altogether different ways—a smile, a lapse

> into silence, an ear turned inward to the secret murmurings of self."

This, the reader must remember, was written by a man committed heart and soul to words as his primum mobile and literature as his life's work. But in acknowledging the limitations of language, Musil sounds its bottomless depths as few writers have done before or since:

> "For a moment, the great painstakingly plated emotional braid of her being became apparent, fluttering in the distance, like a pallid, practically worthless backdrop to reality. She thought to herself, you draw a line in the sand, any old unbroken line, just to have something to hold onto in the swarm of silently looming things; that is the stuff of our life; like when you keep speaking nonstop, pretending that each word is somehow ineluctably linked to the one before and automatically generates the next, because you fear the moment you allow silence to strip off the pretense of continuity the flimsy construct of self will falter in some unimaginable way and be dissolved by silence; but it is only your fear, your frailty before the terrible, gaping randomness of it all ..."

The second novella, "The Temptation of Silent Veronica," offers far fewer footholds for the reader as psychic rock climber. The heroine, Veronica, lives in a big house with her ageless maiden aunt and two young men, the introvert Johannes, who once contemplated becoming a priest, and the extrovert Demeter, a man of actions, not words, both of whom seek a romantic liaison with her. Traumatized by lingering childhood memories of an encounter with an aroused Saint Bernard dog and the shocking sight of a rooster going at it with hens in the pen, Veronica remains sexually repressed and rejects both suitors. Longing for love, yet fearful of the pain of consummation, she retreats into a state of troubled reverie bordering on madness.

> "Soul is something of the sort for an uncertain pursuit. Throughout her long, dark life Veronica dreaded and yet longed for love, only in dreams did it sometimes turn out as she wished. Powerful and plodding as they are, actual occurrences slip away and yet seem to seep inside; they hurt, but like something you do to yourself; they mortify, but just barely: mortification flies off like a restless cloud and nobody else notices; mortification dissipates like the rapture of a dark cloud … She kept wavering between Johannes and Demeter … And dreams do not reside inside the self, nor are they fragments of reality, they camber out their own nook in a burst of complete feeling, and that's where they reside, hovering, weightless, like a liquid seeping out. That's how you give yourself to a beloved in dreams, like a liquid seeping out; with an altered sense of space; for the waking soul is a bottomless hollow, making its contour go lumpy like bubbles in ice."

This is as much as we are told, or rather let to surmise from a highly refracted narrative.

But like the first novella, this one, too, serves Musil as a lush platform for a meditation on the limitations of language:

> "… but once having been uttered every word was viewed from a distance, as if from a broad perspective and accompanied by that remarkably resonant understanding that

> everyday doings attain crowded together on the stage of life and piled up helter-skelter on the gravel strewn ground, suddenly looming as signposts on an otherwise invisible pathway. Like a gossamer silken mask, it draped everything in a light, silver gray mist, and shifted about as if in anticipation of being ripped apart; straining her eyes, it flickered before her, as if shaken by invisible blows."

The silken mask in question is, of course, a reference to the legend of the Veil of Veronica, the apocryphal saint who, encountering Christ along the Via Dolorosa on his way to be crucified, mercifully proffers a cloth to wipe his blood, sweat and tears, retaining an imprint of his face. An alleged copy of the veil that Musil may well have seen and been inspired by hangs in the Schatzkammer of Sacred and Secular Treasures in the Hofburg Palace in Vienna.

For Musil, language is that most precious treasure, that cloth soaked in blood, sweat and tears, preserving the imprint of the ineffable.

Together these two texts comprise an attempt to paint an internal psychic landscape as much sensed as seen. Whether or not Musil succeeded, a question each reader will ultimately have to answer for him- or herself, it is a rich and daring experiment that broke new ground.

A word about the translation.

Each sentence meanders in the German according to a logic of its own, sometimes ignoring, sometimes subverting standard rules of grammar and syntax to wrap itself around a sentient mind and portray reality from the inside out. The primary challenge for the English translator obliged to follow in the author's footsteps, emulate and transpose his dance steps into a coherent routine, is how in another language to follow the fever chart of emotion, let the English words echo the ungainly awkwardness of consciousness, and in the process even to risk translating badly, as the writer risked writing badly, and so risk displeasing the reader. Not every train of thought arrives at the station, some get sidetracked along the way and stall for lack of tracks.

The effect is an oftentimes bewildering flood of language let loose, unfettered syntax, sentences freed of the need to tell, a true-to-life string of uncertainties, and as such a realistic portrayal of the messy business of living.

When Kathrin Rosenfield, a noted Austrian literary scholar living in Brazil, who, with the help of her erstwhile companion, Lawrence Flores Pereira, himself a celebrated scholar and translator, both dear friends, translated the little book into Portuguese, challenged me to tackle it in English, I hesitated at first. I had had a bit of a success with my English translation of Musil's last book, *Nachlaß zu Lebzeiten*, in my rendering, *Posthumous Papers of a Living Author*, now in its third edition (Eridanos, 1988; Penguin Modern Classics, 1995; Archipelago Books, 2006)—excerpted yet a fourth time in *Flypaper* (Penguin Mini-Classics, 2011). Ordinarily I never translate two books by the same writer. But Kathrin being Kathrin and Musil being Musil, I took up the challenge, in part as a project to propose to the *Österreichische Gesellschaft für Literatur* (Austrian Society for Literature) to land a fellowship in Vienna.

I got the fellowship and fumbled through the translation.

Permit me to confess that I cursed my friends Kathrin and Lawrence, Musil, and myself countless times along the way for my having been foolhardy enough to even attempt the task of channeling Musil's idiosyncratic German into semi-intelligible English, and was about to give up more than once.

Even the title proved a knotty dilemma. *Vereinigungen* ought literally to be translated as *Unions*. But lest the unknowing prospective reader misconstrue Musil's slender volume as an exposé on trade unions or a prophetic look forward at the European Union, I had to find a title that would evoke both the texture of the prose and the thematic dialectic of intimacy and estrangement. So, I settled on *Intimate Ties*, though I might well have gone for *Intimate Distance*.

I have already quoted a few examples of the many impossibly long and convoluted sentences on which I almost choked in translation. I will not here dwell on the discordant strings of similes, metaphors, and other figures of speech, and all the subsidiary clauses I had to wade through and transpose into an equivalent English so as to faithfully render the style of the telling and the soul of the story. I admit that I cried out with joy and relief when I was done, putting myself metaphorically in the sandals of Lawrence of Arabia after crossing the impassable Nefud Desert and first catching sight of the sparkling waters off the Red Sea port of Aqaba.

I hope that the reader will derive some pleasure from my pains.

Orpheus Raising Hell: Memories of the late Aleksander Kulisiewicz[1]

The late Aleksander Kulisiewicz (Aleks to his friends) lived in a world turned topsy turvy. While others did backward somersaults of denial to compensate for the rude disruption to their everyday lives, turning a blind eye to the unsightly reality, thereby deflecting attention from themselves and feigning normalcy, Aleks had the effrontery (foolish or courageous—take your pick) to stand upright and look the lies and liars in the eye.

Neither Jew nor Gypsy, Communist, homosexual, Jehovah's Witness, high-profile Polish intellectual or other likely candidate for the Nazi roster of undesirables, he could, like most of his contemporaries, have kept his mouth shut and bit his tongue to still the hunger and disgust, but Aleks stuck out his tongue.

"*Genug Hitler, Heil Butter!*" (Enough Hitler, Heil Butter!) he wrote in an anonymous jibe entitled "Homemade Hitlerisms" in a student newspaper subsequently traced by the Gestapo back to its author. He was arrested in 1939, at the age of 22, and sent to Sachsenhausen concentration camp, the grim finishing school, where he spent the next five years (or more precisely, 66 months) in Hell, and found his true calling as a modern-day Orpheus, a troubadour of the unutterable. In 54 of his own songs composed and first performed surreptitiously during his incarceration, Aleks snubbed his nose at the German authorities to amuse and boost the morale of his fellow inmates. He also committed to memory hundreds of other songs and poems gathered from those who suspected that their own end was near.

1 This essay was commissioned by the U.S. Holocaust Memorial Museum, in Washington, D.C., and first published on their website, in 2008, and reissued in abbreviated form on the liner notes of "Ballads and Broadsides, Aleksander Kulsiewicz," a CD produced by the museum that same year.

Following an informant's denunciation and the subsequent brutal interrogation, he was injected with diphtheria bacilli to shut him up for good. But thanks to medicines smuggled into sickbay, Aleks lived to go on singing.

Following liberation, back in his native Kraków, once the tragic farce of the Third Reich had played itself out and amnesia was the new norm, Aleks once again found himself out of step with the times. While postwar Poland engaged in a whole new regimen of compliance and denial dictated by Moscow, Aleks took his cues from conscience and memory. And though the doctors at the TB clinic where he was laid up diagnosed his restless muttering as a mark of madness, more indulgent nurses took dictation. Out poured 617 songs. He once suggested that the resolve "to spit out the songs as long as I have the breath left in my lungs to do so" may well have helped him battle the deadly bacilli. The disembodied voices deposited in his memory clamored to be heard. For Aleks, the will to live was inextricably bound up with the need to remember.

"There was a time when I wanted to forget about all this and live a normal life," he confided, "but at night these songs kept coming back to me." At the cost of his livelihood, the professional journalistic career he'd commenced following his convalescence, and at the cost of his marriage—what woman in her right mind could stand to share her husband with a bevy of bellowing hellhounds?—Aleks took his music to the stage.

At one of his first public appearances at a festival in Italy in 1965, "*Le Musiche della Resistenza*" (Music of the Resistance), Neo-Fascists planted a bomb, which, fortunately, was discovered and defused in the nick of time. He went on to sing his songs throughout Europe, with frequent appearances in Germany (East and West), where he always emphasized that "the youth are not guilty, only the bastards who committed the crimes."

Aleks was not out to settle any scores. His single-minded purpose was to deliver the precious messages with which he'd been entrusted. Accepting no remuneration, except travel expenses, he sang on till death finally silenced him in 1982.

I was privileged to meet and interview Aleks in Warsaw in 1975 and subsequently published a short profile, "A Singer From Hell."[2] The article stirred some interest and a reader in Milwaukee with connections in Jewish cultural circles arranged to bring him to the States for a concert tour. In New York, I introduced him to the late Moe Asch, founder of Folkways Records, for whom Aleks taped and I produced the album, *Songs From the Depths of Hell* (Folkways, 1978; reissued by Smithsonian Folkways in 1993), which included historical liner notes to each song and my translations.

While in New York, Aleks stayed in my parents' house. Of his visit, I remember most vividly one Passover Seder, his first, I believe. The Yarmulkah sat ever so slightly off kilter on the crown of his big head with gray hairs poking forth helter-skelter like weeds beneath a welcome mat. Our's has always been a free-wheeling Seder with plenty of laughter and mayhem mixed in with the ritual. Aleks felt very much at home. His wide open face glowed with an almost boyish glee. My father took pains to explain every last detail. Aleks soaked it all up and could, I'm quite sure, thereafter, have sung the traditional Passover folk songs by heart. He basked in the family circle of affection, especially that of my aunt Risa, who did not, alas, return his romantic interest. (His sober life's mission notwithstanding, Alex remained a hopeless romantic. He had once in his youth run off with a circus to follow a dancing girl he fancied, and hadn't lost his eye for the ladies.)

"This is the bread of poverty," my father pointed to the matzah, the unleavened bread, reading aloud from the Haggadah, the

2 *Sing Out! The Folk Song Magazine* Vol. 26, No. 3, 1977

sacred script of that holiday of liberation. "Let all who are hungry enter and eat ... This year we are slaves, next year may we be free men." The words were greatly enriched by the presence of our guest.

"Remember, Aleks?" I asked. It was the same bread of poverty he'd acquired, god knows how, in Warsaw Pact Poland, and pulled out of a drawer to break with me the day we met.

Aleks nodded and for a fleeting instant the veil of sadness lifted and he smiled.

Permit me a personal digression and reflection here, if only to establish my credibility as a source.

Age 21 at the time of my first meeting with Aleks, armed with a faulty tape recorder and a fellowship from the Thomas J. Watson Foundation—I spent a year traveling around Eastern Europe digging into the unhappy history that sent my Viennese-Jewish parents packing.

Among the many issues that troubled me at the time was the worthiness and worth of civilization in general, and Western Civilization in particular, in the wake of that total collapse of conscience and accountability we call the Holocaust—a man-made cataclysm unique in extent, not intent (ethnic cleansing is still in vogue). I questioned the intrinsic value of artistic creation of whatever derivation—for Germany was not the only place where leaders and their lackeys fiddled while the world burned. If the sublime symphonies of Beethoven merely served to soothe and anaesthetize the planners and executioners in between transports—the infamous Joseph Mengele, devil doctor of Auschwitz, was a great Beethoven fan!—then concert halls, I reasoned, are little better than ante-rooms to crematoria. Hermann Goering, Hitler's right-hand man, was an astute connoisseur of the artwork he stole from the finest museums, which he prized along with his pet leopard and his morphine fix.

The actor and director Gustaf Gründgens (later fictionalized in the Istvan Szabo movie "Mephisto") managed to tailor Goethe's "Faust" to the taste of his Mephistopholean audience. Had not Luigi Pirandello, the great Italian playwright and novelist, and Ezra Pound, America's most erudite modern bard, played for the Black Shirts?

Had not a twisted artistry itself played an unsettling role in a world order conceived by Hitler himself, a would-be painter with a passion for Wagnerian opera; a world order propagandized by a two-bit novelist with literary pretensions, Dr. Joseph Goebbels; built to last by the Fuehrer's personal architect, Albert Speer; and filmed for optimal effect and a wink at posterity by the sinister cinematic genius Leni Riefenstahl? What Hollywood studio set could compete for nostalgic appeal with the potted flowers and rural train station facade at Bergen Belsen, or was it Treblinka? Indeed, one might well read the very schema of the concentration camps as a grand spectacle à la D.W. Griffith with a cast of millions: a Roman Coliseum with Jews in place of early Christians in the pit, or a Ring Cycle staged with wild operatic excess and wit—"To Each His Own," read the diabolical tongue-in-cheek logo above the entrance to Sachenshausen, "Work Makes You Free," read the sign over the portal at Auschwitz—terrific entertainment value for a select audience.

And beyond any question of compliance, complacency or complicity, there remained the troubling fact of the impotence of art as an antidote to evil. Even such sublime verse as Rainer Maria Rilke's "Sonnets to Orpheus," poetic harbinger of things to come, which I had learned by heart in college and loved to declaim, seemed to me, in the light of what followed, little more than a perfumed fart subsumed by the blast of the furnaces. (Remember, I was 21 at the time and might, therefore, be forgiven such a strident stance.)

In the many interviews I conducted in the course of my research throughout Eastern Europe and Israel with men and women who had survived the pit of civilization, I kept coming back to the same question: Did anyone pause to make music, art, poetry at the threshold of death? A few of my respondents remembered stray verses, a tune hummed, a popular prewar ditty that served as a piece of flotsam in the flood, a tenuous straw to suck. Most often, however, they just shrugged and threw up their hands. "Who the hell had time for such frivolous nonsense? We were busy staying alive!"

All responses seemed to support my suspicion that art was at best nothing but a vanity dresser full of costume jewellry, at worst a cunning camouflage for atrocities, canned music to jam out the screams. Then a cultivated doctor in Krakow, himself a survivor whose name I can't recall, suggested I look up Aleksander Kulisiewicz.

Rather than rehash and risk dulling the vivid impression of that first encounter, I quote freely from my 1977 recollection, "A Singer From Hell:"[3]

> "Warsaw. A hotel room. A suitcase, a singer and myself. We break bread together. The dry, hard bread of affliction. Matzah in Warsaw 1975.
>
> Aleks stutters German, "Lager Deutsch," the lingua franca of Sachsenhausen, the Nazi concentration camp in which he spent six years. His sad, soft eyes have not forgotten what they saw. At 59, Aleksander Kulisiewicz, born in Krakow, Poland, is the oldest and perhaps sole surviving concentration camp singer. His songs—so many disembodied voices—are the only real survivors.

3 Op cit

Some of them he wrote; others he remembered, each with a face and a story. "Aleks," someone whispers, "is there room in your head for my song too?"

"Now," Aleks sighs, "I have to go back … there." He shuts his eyes. Silence. Then like a faraway echo, a deep voice floods the room. It moans in basso profundo a terrible-beautiful song. "Lullaby for My Little Son in the Crematorium." This is no lullaby to fall asleep on. This is Aaron Liebeskind's song. The young clock-maker from Bilgoraj, who watched in Treblinka while they shot his wife Edith, while they swung his little boy head-first against a wall. The man who tried to sing his son awake. Who could not and turned gray over-night. Who fled Treblinka and, with a borrowed name, found his way to Berlin. Who was arrested again, sent to Sachsenhausen and on to Auschwitz. Who could not finally escape the gas.

I glance down at my tape-recorder. The spools are not turning. I look closer. They have not been turning. They have recorded nothing. I groan and feel sick in the stomach. Aleks finishes his song. He looks from me to the machine. I am about to cry. He takes a deep breath and speaks without anger. "Don't think I sing for you or for myself … No! … I sing for Aaron Liebeskind." We fix the spools. He sings the song again from the begin-ning with even greater tenderness.

An astounding performer—though the word, "per-former," with its underlying hint of counterfeit affect, belied the painful honesty of his "act," and he never knowingly tried to astound—Aleks was a one-man choir-orchestra who never needed a microphone to fill a space of whatever size with his voice. He spilled his guts and gave his all every time he opened his mouth, whether on an outdoor stage, in a concert hall, a recording studio, or a hotel room.

Rage, joy, terror, revulsion, love and longing, all these emotions and more welled up in his dark, sunken eyes and colored his infinitely flexible, mellifluous baritone voice. The effect was admittedly a bit uncanny, like that of a medium at a seance. Aleks was a macabre ventriloquist who could bring forth a complete musical spectrum of voices from the pit of his gut. Enjoined not to applaud, the listener had no other recourse but to tremble.

"Every time I sing I return to this damned concentration camp," he once wrote. "Once again I have to experience this, not only to reproduce the sounds, but also all the horror included in the songs. I must not be an actor. The line between documentary retrospection and the singer's theatrical art growing into mannerism is very tenuous. In Germany, they would say: 'What a good actor!' Nobody would believe the authenticity."

In none of the songs in his repertoire is this versatility of range and painstaking authenticity more evident than in Aleks' seering rendition of "*Jüeddischer Todessang*" (Jewish Deathsong), a work written and orchestrated by his fellow Sachsenhausen inmate, the German-Jewish composer Rosebery d'Arguto (aka Martin Rosenberg, 1890-1942), who organized and directed a clandestine Jewish camp choir. All 25 singers and their director were later sent off to Auschwitz and silenced in the gas chamber. Aleks was the only surviving witness to the last rehearsal in 1942. Suddenly SS-men burst into the barracks screaming, "Alle raus!" (Everybody out!), as Aleks recalls in his version of the song, which manages to evoke, not only every voice in the choir, from tenor to bass, but also the thump of the human heart, the creak of the floorboards, the shriek of the SS, and the deathlike silence that followed.

Perhaps the most striking (and for us, indeed, unsettling) feature of the songs he himself wrote in Sachsenhausen is the comic element. His own lyrics can get raucous and downright raunchy, as in "Heil, Sachsenhausen!," in which the singer, "a shit-caked Polish clod," imagines buying himself "a nice German girl":

> "She, the sweet young mommy.
> Me, the stupid daddy,
> We'll make a few striped babies—
> Black and white and red!"

Things can also get side-splittingly hilarious, as in "Mister C," in which a mythic Mister C (Churchill) snuffs out his cigar and proposes to pay for Adolf's funeral, these words written in 1940, when the end was nowhere in sight. In the camp, we must imagine Aleks as a tragi-comic clown, a Charlie Chaplin in pinstripes who could elicit tears or titters with a wink or a yowl. And while he discouraged applause at his postwar performances and a chuckle would have been unthinkable, mirth was surely the richest gift he gave to his comrades, a riproaring belly laugh that ventilated their pent up rage and let them at least pretend to be alive.

Even death could be a quasi-comic relief, an escape hatch, as he once implied in a letter:

> "In the camp I had much, so much to do with death—endlessly. I was, among other tasks, a corpse-bearer. On occasion, we carted off people who appeared to be

> dead and afterwards, in the cellar where we stacked them, suddenly came back to life. There was nothing awful about this for us. We were so damned hardened. And in each case, these 99% dead told us (or indicated with their lips) that we should let them die, they were mad that we'd awakened them. One of them said: 'It was so pleasant ...'"

In the camp, Aleks longed for the future with the trompe l'oeil of laughter as the only escape from a suffocating present. Afterwards, he looked back in grief to embrace the inescapable and reaffirm life. A latter-day Orpheus, Aleks peered fearlessly into the pit, eyes and ears open wide, to retrieve in each of his songs the imprint of life as the consummate memento of love. "To believe in love in a concentration camp, that was not easy," he recalled. "But we had to believe." Thus the eerie surreal vision of a song like "The Living Stones," anonymously composed in the quarry of the camp Mauthhausen-Gusen, in Austria:

> "We are the living stones
> goddamned alive to hell.
> Though slaves we still must believe
> in people, in people and love ..."

You may by now have gathered that my once wavering faith in the value of cultural artifact, Occidental or other, has since returned, fortified in large part by Aleks' example. What are we humans but scavengers in the great rubble heap of history, memory-burdened creatures re-building our anthills at the site of past destruction? (Every morning I peer out the window in search of the felled Twin Towers that once filled the view.) Our very DNA, the recipe of our survival as a species, is a recycled gift from the dead. Or as Aleks put it in a letter to my mother mourning my father's death: "What remains of us all? Only memory."

Now Aleks is the stuff of memory too. He wafts forth in the odor of musty brown envelopes pockmarked with faded postage stamps from pre-Walesa Polska. He crumbles between my fingers as I shuffle through his letters, most written in long hand on brittle acidic sheets of Warsaw Pact paper.

I experienced a sudden burst of déja vu at the library of the U.S. Holocaust Memorial Museum in Washington, where I sat one afternoon in March, 2002, perusing the Polish index to the holdings of The Aleksander Kulisiwicz Collection to stoke my more than 20-year-old recollections of the man. The index made reference to a "Konzert" in New York. What New York concert? As far as I could remember, Aleks' only public appearance in the New York Metropolitan Area was a performance he gave at Nassau Community College on November 5, 1979, at which I presented and interpreted for him. Imagine my surprise when the first audible voice on the tape to which the Polish index made reference turned out to be my own.

And then it came back in a rush, the impromptu concert I'd arranged in 1979 at my Greenwich Village studio packed to the rafters with a Downtown crowd of artists, actors and writers, seated cross-legged on the parquet floor, leaning against the walls and spilling out through the open door into the hallway and down the stairs, listening, speechless, practically breathless, clinging to Aleks' every sung and spoken word. The walls took a while to stop shaking. Aleks himself savored the memory. As he later recalled in a letter with all the pride of a masterful performer and a hint of black humor: "*Ich hab' sie fertig gemacht, nichtwar!*" (I knocked 'em dead, didn't I!)

*

Back to the airy realm of art and letters, without which we mortals would never be able to digest bitter reality. The cow has a second stomach to help grind the grass. We depend on poetry and art.

In "The Singing Bone," a lesser known, albeit profound, fairy tale of the Brothers Grimm, a wandering shepherd-turned-minstrel finds a little white bone out of which he carves a mouthpiece for his flute or horn. But the bone won't play the tune the minstrel intends, it has its own repertoire:

> "Oh dear little shepherd boy,
> The bone you blow on knows no joy,
> My brother slayed me.
> Beneath the bridge he laid me.
> All for the wild boar's hide,
> To make the king's daughter his bride."[4]

As I wrote in a previous essay:

> "No mere accommodating instrument this, no cheap pennywhistle to accompany idle chatter, no mouthpiece for a ditty—the bone cannot help but echo the cries of the misdeed that did its 'I' in. The shepherd's breath, like an author's ink or an archeologist's glue, literally re-members the dismembered."

Aleks accompanied himself on such an enchanted instrument. "I don't play it," he once said of his guitar, "it plays me." Sometimes the guitar played sympathetic comrade to his lonely voice, sometimes a clown to mock the futility of his song, sometimes a taskmaster whipping the crooning slave shackled to it, sometimes

4 *Kinder- und Hausmärchen der Brüder Grimm*, 1812. The translation is my own.

a rhythmic, ominous reminder of the end. The guitar had a history of its own—several histories! Aleks' accounts of the instrument's origins varied. (Every true artist inevitably weaves a web of mystery around himself to hide behind and enhance his myth.) In one version, Aleks liked to tell, it belonged to an old Jew, a merchant or a musician, who took it with him on his last tour to destinations unknown. "You won't be needing this where you're going," an SS-guard snickered, and relieved the old man of his burden. The same guard, later detailed to Sachsenhausen, panicked as the Allied armies approached. "Hold this!" he said to Aleks. The guard disappeared and Aleks held on to the guitar. A somewhat more prosaic provenance might well have been the depot of abandoned objects immediately following the camp's liberation. Wherever he got the guitar, none who heard it play can deny the richness of its timbre and the haunting music Aleks was able to coax out of its belly. Part Sancho Panza, part Rosinante, the guitar was his true companion in life.

Aleks is gone now, but we've got his music, his singing bones, still ringing in our ears. The ordinary world keeps tilting to the left and to the right, blindly following the marching orders of demagogues of every ilk. No music meant for easy listening, these songs were written and sung to raise hell.

Translating the Surreal (Or Doing the DADA Dance): On Coming up with an English Take on Kurt Schwitters' "The Onion"[1]

What better way to illustrate the quandaries of translation than by reflecting on coming up with an English take on "Die Zwiebel (Merzgedicht 8)"/"The Onion (Merzpoem 8)," a virtuoso verbal collage by the great German DADA doodler-scribbler-warbler Kurt Schwitters (1887-1948).

A total artist, equally adept at multiple media, Schwitters' assemblages, in whatever form, whether visual, sculptural, poetic, dramatic or oral, have always struck a deeply personal note in me. First, because of that curious harmony he achieves, despite the apparent dissonance, an artistic ordering, which, rather than deny the disorder by shrewd dissembling, embraces the chaotic. And second, because his assemblages comprise the shattered bits and pieces of a German Zeitgeist, in which, as the American-born son of refugees from Hitler's insidious organizing principle, I see the reflection, or rather, the refraction, of my own divided psyche. For me, his visual and verbal building blocks, the metro tickets, popular clichés and advertising slogans, all speak to a strangely familiar, and oddly comforting, German chaos. As such, I have always found Schwitters to be one of the most realistic artists, able to portray better than any naturalist the true face of the 20th-century.

While best known as a master of the visual collage, Schwitters also worked—or rather, played—with words throughout his life. Play was for him a simultaneously whimsical and eminently

1 An earlier version of this text was first presented as a talk to a gathering of literary translators, hosted by Breon Mitchell, Director Emeritus of the Lilly Library and Professor Emeritus of Comparative Literature, at the Lilly Library, University of Indiana, in Bloomington, Ind., on March 8, 2007

serious pursuit, the guiding principle of his life. "*Wir spielen bis uns der Tod abholt.*" (We play till death hauls us away), he put it in a letter to a friend, from his voluntary English exile—a dictum perhaps best understood in opposition to the one engraved in bold block letters above the portal to Auschwitz and Dachau: "*Arbeit Macht Frei.*" (Work makes you free.)

My attachment to Schwitters' wit is, furthermore, founded in a fondness I inherited from my late beloved father for "*blödeln,*" or the practice of nonsense, and for the "*Blödler,*" the practitioners thereof.[2] Schwitters raised nonsense from child's play to a high art form—though he would surely have scorned any such distinction, for who's to say that child's play isn't serious, and what else is high art but licensed child's play with a price tag attached!

Here is how Schwitters put his passion for verbal nonsense:

> "Letters, syllables, words, sentences are elements of the poetic art. Poetry arises from a comparative appraisal of these elements. Sense is only essential if appraised as a factor. I weigh sense against nonsense. I prefer nonsense, but that is a purely personal matter. I felt bad for nonsense that it was until now so seldom informed by art, that's why I love nonsense."[3]

His nonsense always appears to have a perfectly sensible substrata, wherewith he pulls the carpet of reason out from under our feet. Consider this snippet of prose, "Wir leben 25 Minuten zu spät" ("We Live 25 Minutes Too Late"):

---

2 By curious coincidence, Schwitters and my father were both interned as German speakers, side by side with suspected Nazis in a prison camp on the Isle of Man.
3 "Anna Blume und ich," Zürich: Verlag der Arche, 1965

> "We live 25 minutes too late, that is if you're looking at it from the right. Considered from the left, life is 20 minutes too short. Too late and too short, so much for our left and right fate. But viewed from above we're as flat as a primer, and beheld from below we're as tall as a cylinder. Fixed full in the face we reveal our retrospect, ass backward the belly looms, the belly, yes, alas. Snow melting between our toes will tick off a terrible toothache stilled only when the sun burns down directly on the brain. But that's how bright ideas are born, one of which will do to record here such wisdoms as these."[4]

I sought rhythms and rhymes in the English to echo, not copy, the German.

Note the belly reference:

> "Fixed full in the face we reveal our retrospect, ass backward, the belly looms, the belly, yes, alas."

I must admit that I savored this particular detail, since it immediately brought to mind, not only my father's brand of nonsense, but also his impressive potbelly, which he affectionately dubbed his "*Backhändlfriedhof*," (fried chicken cemetery), and where he lay to rest many a New Jersey pullet. An inveterate "*Blödler*" of eminently serious bent, whenever my father lost his patience and swiped at me for flubbing my Latin declensions or mispronouncing my French in our Sunday morning lessons, as was his wont, I was, by prior agreement, permitted to draw a little man on the elastic ledger of his great belly, one pen stroke at a time for each word of the following rhyme:

4 My translation of this poetic text was originally published in Verse, Spring 1996

"Punkti, Punkti, Beistrich, Strich,
Ist das nicht ein Rundgesicht?
An dem Kopf zwei Ohren,
Ist das Kind gebohren.
Handi Handi, Haxi Haxi,
Ist das nicht der kleine Maxi?"

Roughly:

Period, period, comma, comma,
Isn't that a fine round face?
On the head, two ears,
And the child is born.
Handy, handy, leggy leggy,
Isn't that little Maxi?)

You get the picture.

Schwitters once again toys with the straitjacket, or, in this case, the stranglehold, of time in another prose snippet, "*Schwandote*," which I translated as "Swansnatch:"

> The famous 'fine art painter, Kurt Schwitters, poet of Anna Blume and Schnauze Bauze,' well known back home in Hanover, still lives in England, a refugee from Hitler's henchmen. On June 2, he happened to be seated in a rowboat on the Grasmere, an idyllic little lake swimming with swans, like in Tchaikovsky's "Swan Lake," ballet music, you get it. He was absorbed by nature, painting the landscape. Beside him lay his trusty pocket-watch, still from Hanover. A swan swum up without a sound, and suddenly he heard a noisy clamor as if someone were gasping for air. He looked

toward the hubbub and spotted a swan straining to swallow his pocket watch. Well, according to English law, all swans and their holdings are untouchable, the sole property of the Crown, and so the poor Dadaist could not get his watch back, and in any case the swan hissed at him in a very uppity fashion and swam off. Kurt Schwitters asked a physician if the swan could get sick from eating a watch. 'Possibly,' replied the physician, Dr. Johnston, 'if the watch lands in the appendix. It is more likely, however, that he would release the watch into the Grasmere in the natural fashion, from the rear. Or else … he might digest it, except for the glass.' Then the good doctor gave the hapless painter his own watch and chain by way of indemnity.[5]

1946

The text may well contain a subtle ironic reference to Schwitters' naturalistic portraits and landscapes, by which he earned his living in English exile.

But back to "The Onion," composed a quarter century before, in 1919, around the time Schwitters first rediscovered the collage (with which the French Cubists and Italian Futurists had been toying) as an artistic prison-break from the canvas. 1919 was a good year for collage-making, as Germany had just finished tearing itself (and all of Europe) apart in the continental conflagration of "The Great War" and began the arduous task of reassembling itself from scratch.

"The Onion" is the account of an execution as anti-marriage, erotic act and reverse birth-giving, the consummation of a dissection rather than a coupling, but with the same cheesy ceremonial lingo and euphemized Eros as that of a wedding ceremony. The

5 From *Eile ist des Witzes Weile*, by Kurt Schwitters, Reclam, Stuttgart, 1987

text is strewn with popular sayings and political slogans and snippets of advertising taken out of context and, so, drained of their sales potential and rendered purely poetic. The butcher is the standby for the preacher. The snippy little princess is white-robed like a bride. The soon-to-be-sacrificed and then re-constituted narrator is a stand-in for the groom. Shades of "The Golem," 1920, a silent horror classic of a reconstituted monster, a precursor of Frankenstein, shades of the Expressionists' notion of the "New Man," shades of Kafka's "In the Penal Colony," coincidentally published the same year, "The Onion" also seems to suggest a cultural dissimulation. When peeled apart, though the onion induces tears, there's nothing left in the middle—which might well be construed as a metaphor of war-torn Europe.

When Schwitters writes: (in my translation) "I had them call the king. 'Your Majesty, I commend to you my beautiful body! My corpse is in your hands!" his contemporary reader could not help but recall the wholesale slaughter of the just completed Great War, in which millions were compelled to sacrifice themselves in the trenches and on the battlefields—with nothing left but tears. In a sense, Schwitters, the collagist, does with ordinary logic and language, what the Kaiser did with the body of his typical subject: he deliberately mangles it. Standard syntax, Schwitters seems to playfully suggest, no longer suffices to render the shredded reality.

The playfulness of Schwitters' shockingly violent imagery is best understood in the context of the children's literature of the day, like the cautionary tales in *Struwwelpeter*,[6] in which an ominous tailor snips off the thumbs of a boy who refuses to

---

6 *Struwelpeter*, a book of cautionary tales for children, by Heinrich Hoffmann, 1845; translated in 1891 by Mark Twain as Slovenly Peter, not published until 1935, 25 years after Twain's death

stop sucking them, and the ill-fated exploits of Wilhelm Busch's cartoon characters, *Max und Moritz*[7] (the direct inspiration for the comic book series, *The Katzenjammer Kids*), who end up falling through a grinder and being baked into two loaves of bread.

The translator is obliged to address and resolve two dilemmas: How do you render the surreal outside its original syntactical and cultural context? And since DADA was, in principle, an attack against sense, should a faithful translation merely reproduce the stream of seeming nonsense or attempt to render its underlying spirit and wit?

7 *Max und Moritz—Eine Bubengeschichte in sieben Streichen*, written and illustrated by Wilhelm Busch, 1865

Qui es tu, Federman?
An Intimate Reading of *La fourure de ma tante Rachel*[1]

Raymond Federman[2] was a phenomenon of nature, a talking tidal wave, a Franco-American tsunami with a wicked dip, a hurricane howling in the hard drive of a computer, a closet earthquake erupting way off the Richter Scale of American Letters. So how come the forecasters aren't busy plotting his course, predicting when and where he'll strike next?

Defying categorization, Federman perplexes the experts who can't quite figure out where he's coming from. American by adoption, French by birth, Jewish by memory, ballsy by bent, he is really the unrecognized poet laureate of the No Man's Land between France and forgetting, and though he has lived for decades practically within earshot of Niagara Falls (the great wet crack in the North American continent) and has written his best-known work in the American idiom, Federman also writes in his native French. His real literary voice is a blend of both tongues, emitting *twofold vibrations*,[3] always playing it *double or nothing*,[4] as the narrator and protagonist of his latest novel, *La fourure de ma tante Rachel*, written and published in French (Circé Editeur, Strasbourg, 1996) explains:

> Yes yes, that's it, I write mostly in English, but sometimes also in French when I get the urge. All the same, I must tell you, it isn't easy writing in a language other

1 This essay originally appeared in FEDERMAN FROM A TO X-X-X-X (*A Raymond Federman Casebook*), edits. Larry McCaffrey and Doug Rice, San Diego State University Press, San Diego, CA, 1998; reprinted in *The Laugh that Laughs at the Laugh Laughing*, a special issue of the *Journal of Experimental Fiction*, Macon, GA, 2002.
2 The author was fortunate to count Raymond Federman (1928-2009) as a friend.
3 *The Twofold Vibration*, a novel by Raymond Federman (Indiana University Press, 1982)
4 *Double or Nothing*, a novel by Raymond Federman (Swallow Press, 1976)

> than your own, it isn't easy at all to adopt words that aren't your own, words that resist your best effort because they're strangers to you. But you do learn to love them, these words, you manage to make them your own. A little like a mother hen who has lost her chicks and adopts a duckling. Ignoring his yellow down and his flat bill, she teaches him to sift through the sand and to peck at the English words in what I write, but of course without ever forgetting my mother tongue.

And later in the same package:

> You see how I sometimes mix up these two tongues I have rattling in my mouth, these two tongues that keep playing hide 'n seek and often play tricks on me … As Gilles Deleuze put it so well, the creation of a style in a foreign language passes through different stages, the first of which is a decomposition of the mother tongue which soon becomes convulsive, starts stammering, stuttering, becoming something else, subsequently to reemerge as a new tongue, a new syntax. Well, that's what happened to me, and the novel I'm in the process of writing …

The French, who can't forgive linguistic defection, think of him as an American turncoat, if they think of him at all (though his 1974 novel, *Amer Eldorado*, originally written in French, was nominated for the prestigious Prix Medicis). He is popular in translation in Germany, where his Post-Modernist phrasing and playful seriousness (or serious playfulness) appeal to a Post-War generation, bursting the straitjacket of outdated structures. But back home in the States, plot and character development are still the sine-qua-non of serious fiction, the novel is a sales pitch, and experiments are strictly for the test tube. Here Federman is slotted in the Avant-Garde, that great literary landfill of the critically unapproved.

*

The scenario of much of his work, known to a devoted coterie of reader-listeners, keeps tapping the portable epiphany of a little French boy of Jewish ancestry, thrust by his mother in a closet to elude round-up and deportation, what Federman has called "the closet experience," the egg of his rebirth and the eruption of consciousness. But his real subject is breath, the breath it takes to blow a horn or tell a tale, the breath of a scream, a cry of ecstasy or a belly laugh, the breath of life. His real element is not ink but air.

Having first learned self-expression on the saxophone from Black buddies in Detroit, blowing long, sultry riffs on the saxophone in a jazz band before falling for the lure of language, his novels retain the fluid musicality of oral literature. Restless on the page, despite the carefully crafted surface, the words tap a primal intra-lingual pulse. And while the conventional reader may be put off by his leapfrogging "Post-Modern" prose line, modulated more by breath than by any standard punctuation—Federman tolerates commas, but abhors periods for the suffocating closure they denote—there is something unquestionably archaic in his Post-Modernity, a return to the erotic roots of storytelling, the groping of a naked tongue in search of a willing ear.

Federman puts it bluntly in *La fourure de ma tante Rachel* (literally "My Aunt Rachel's Fur," though a racier English rendering of the title might be "My Aunt Rachel's Muff"). "After all, as everyone knows," Federman reminds, "creation, literary or other, can't happen without excitation, you've got to get a hard-on before you can fuck ..."

*

In *La fourure*, Federman plays his childhood tongue with a fierce assurance and virtuoso effect. The boundless pleasure given and taken in the telling of this tale is tempered some by the compulsion of the teller, a fear of silence, and by the simultaneous thrill and embarrassment the reader feels at the imposition of such intimacy with a stranger. The plot, loosely speaking, spirals round the return of a young man to his native France after the War and the memories stirred up by the inverse of nostalgia. Lest the prospective reader fear a somber accounting of atrocities à la Elie Wiesel, he may breathe a sigh of relief. Federman's inferno is peppered with plenty of purgatory and sweetened with intimations of paradise. If there's any literary influence here, it's strictly Rabelaisian.

A memorable passage recounting a young boy's wartime experience as a farmhand in hiding focuses on the natural cycle. Here's a healthy helping in translation:

> so here I am on this farm during the occupation. can you picture me planting, cultivating the earth, I don't know a thing about agriculture, but lemme tell you, you sure learn quickly on a farm [...] up at five in the morning to milk the cows, shovel the manure out of the barn, feed the pigs, the chickens, the ducks, the rabbits, the whole menagerie of those more or less domesticated creatures that spend their life doing nothing but feeding and shitting all the time until we eat them and

> defecate in turn, boy is there ever a lot of shit on a farm, tons and tons of it, but you know it's still a pretty good system nature, yeah it's just amazing how it functions, how it keeps renewing itself with shit, you see first you cultivate the earth to make all things grow, hay, wheat, the plants you stuff your animals with to fatten them up so that afterwards we can slaughter and stuff ourselves with them, but before they die my god do these animals ever shit, and then we shit too after devouring them, and eventually all that shit is returned to the earth to enrich it to make things that grow in it bigger and more nourishing, bigger on account of the manure, and so it goes until the end of time, or until we human beings are destroyed by nature, or until we destroy ourselves, oh what a beautiful system nature is, it keeps jumpstarting itself with shit …

But Federman's meditation on nature is not restricted to feeding and elimination. Copulation and death complete the cycle:

> Oh yes on that farm I saw how easy it was to fuck and die, the animals that's all they did, kept mounting each other all the time, and every day there was at least one creature that croaked, either from fatigue, or age, or because we had to kill it so that we could eat its meat, death was always around on that farm, it's really such a simple thing death, but sometimes you know it's kind 'o funny too, you should've seen the time the farmer's wife killed a chicken for her stew, she grabbed a great big kitchen knife in one hand, wedged the chicken between her plump knees and held its head, with the other hand stretching its neck, and swish swash there

> goes the head, when I saw it for the first time I almost gagged … of course it bleeds, what do you think, that chickens don't have blood like us, but the funniest thing is that even beheaded, the chicken still struggles a few seconds before dropping dead, and one time, see, it was hard, but after my farmer's wife lobbed the head off a chicken the chicken fidgeted about so furiously it managed to slip free of her fat knees and it fell to ground, so here's this chicken without a head that starts hotfooting it 'round the kitchen beating its wings […] you see how simple and downright tiresome death can be …

Now Federman dwells a brief moment on the boy's sense of solitude, only to segway into his witnessing a quickie in the kitchen between the mailman and the farmer's wife, just like the livestock, which subsequently inspires the boy's own sexual initiation with the farmer's wife:

> so I said to her, without thinking, just like that, I said to her, if Monsieur le mailman can do it why can't I … yeah sure, that's exactly what I said to her, so she turned red in the face, but she didn't say a word, she just put a finger to her lips, the index, with a wink to make me comprehend that I'd better keep my mouth shut and not breathe a word about this […] I was almost asleep when I felt a hand slip in under the covers and fondle my prick till it stiffened and …

Copulation and death. The same hand that cuts the chicken's throat caresses your prick. It's all part of the natural life cycle.

No *Painted Bird* this! No Kosinskian inventory of evil!

What stuns a reader of these reminiscences is not the ordeal of survival, nor the unspoken horror of what the boy must have gone through. Nor are we taken aback by the vivid description of all natural functions. The contemporary reader is accustomed to excess.

La fourure shocks, not with its subject but with its tone, the unabashed "in your face" intimacy it presumes with the reader.

English lacks any syntactical distinction between the formal and the intimate form of address. An American will freely address his wife, his boss, his best friend, or a total stranger on a first-name basis and mean nothing by it, whereas for a Frenchman crossing the line of demarcation between *vous* and *tu* instantly alters the psychic climate from Arctic to tropical. The absence of that distinction, while it's always implicit in Federman's English language opus, may, unbeknownst to its readers, ever so slightly detract from its effect. There is no such confusion in Federman's French. To say "*tu*" to a stranger is to presume some kind of intimacy.

From its opening line, *La fourure* is addressed to a fictional *tu*: "*Ah tu veux savoir … tu veux savoir pourquoi je suis rentreé en France après dix ans d'Amérique* …" (So, you want to know why I returned to France after ten years in America …")

That "*tu*" has a dual role. He is an actual character in the novel, a professional listener, the narrator's initially nameless foil or sidekick, the compliant, passive, listening ear to the narrator's incessantly wagging tongue (a foil, who only in the very last paragraph identifies himself as Federman, the narrator's double). He is also, of course, a stand-in for the reader-listener bending over the book in his lap who can close it or toss it aside whenever he likes. Readers take books to bed. This fact is not lost on Federman.

It is this second *tu*, let's call him *tu*2, whom the author is obliged to tease and entertain, to lure away from the myriad distractions of life, and hold for the next two hundred pages.

Of course, *tu*2 knows what he's getting into. He's bored with himself, his wife (husband or partner), the kids, the mundane troubles and annoyances from which the novel offers an escape in print. In addition to which, the erotic elements of *La fourure* offer a vicarious affair. But the author-narrator-*Je*-I has to watch it, lest the game get out of hand:

> Okay, hold it, that's enough, I better not go too far or else you'll excite yourself like a bull and won't be able to listen any longer …

Needless to say, the writer-narrator-*Je*-I is also simultaneously addressing a third incarnation of *tu*, *tu*3, a stand-in for himself. This is what Federman calls "the happy catastrophe when I tell my tales," the ever-present risk of overstimulating oneself, from concentration to masturbation. A pleasant risk to which any author worth his salt will sometimes succumb.

Now let me, a particular reader-listener-respondent-*tu*—call me *tu*4, if you like—confess something to you, *tu*5: This book embarrasses me. The author-narrator-*Je*-I gets so close I can almost feel his hot breath in my ear.

Say, keep me out of it, will you, Federman! This is all your fantasy, not mine! Sure, your aunt Rachel gives me the hots, and so do the society girl Sucette and the nymphomaniac Judy you fucked for 48 hours straight way back when in Detroit! If writing is an erotic act, then what is reading, Raymond, old *tu*3? So, what kind of polymorphous perverse role-playing are we engaged in here? And that includes you out there, *tu*5, wherever you are! And while we're at it, that includes the prurient eye of the publisher, Claude Lutz, *tu*6—you old lecher, you must get your vicarious kicks from the books you publish, or why else would you publish them! And hey, you Peeping Tom, Eckhard

Gerdes, *tu7*, invisible editor of this volume, you're in on it too, so don't you go sneaking off into anonymity.

The literary enterprise is one big virtual orgy! Which is, of course, what keeps us coming! But at least it's safe sex, you say, what with the book cover and binding functioning as an effective condom.

Another confession, while we're at it. Let me admit that I've had unsafe communion with this text. I mean, I've never actually rubbed up against the book, if that's what you're thinking. (It hasn't yet been published at the time of the writing of this response.)

I've had two secret trysts with the naked text. Once, while having it read to me through a long Sunday afternoon by the author, in Buffalo, an exhilarating, albeit infantilizing, experience. And a second time, reading through a preliminary draft of the ms. late at night in insomniac fits and spurts, it having been mailed to me by the author for my response.

In both cases, the text (not yet bound into a book) was still a loose, slippery, uncontrolled substance, threatening at any moment to spill over into my life.

Which brings me back to the intersection of oral literature and the novel, the locus of Raymond Federman's premeditated intralingual transgressions. Or as Walter Benjamin put it in his essay "The Storyteller, Reflections on the Works of Nikolai Leskov:"

> A man listening to a story is in the company of the storyteller; even a man reading one shares this companionship. The reader of the novel, however, is isolated, more so than any other reader.

La fourure embraces the reader, leaving him breathless. "I just can't put it down!" you commonly say of a book that grabs you. In this case, "*It* just can't put *me* down!" might be more apt!

Oh yes, I forgot. I had a third encounter, when the author came to read aloud from the then still unpublished book to an intimate audience at the Maison Française, NYU, in New York. The real thing straight from the horse's mouth!

What's that you say? So, what about Aunt Rachel's muff? What a dirty mind you have! Go buy a copy of the book and find out for yourself!

Oh, but you don't speak French?

Well, I'm afraid you'll just have to wait for the book to come out in English! Of course, there's always Berlitz. Or better yet, for optimal effect, take your teacher and the text to bed!

Six Fragments in Pursuit of Fiction's Roots and Fruits[1]

1.

Preparing for today's discussion of "Postmodern Theoretical Ramblings," I dutifully had a dream. I will call it "The Dream of the Things Left Behind." An untuned guitar whose strings are out to strangle me. Books in which the homeless have taken up temporary residence. I try to shake a few favorite classics free of this alien presence, but instead, loose letters drop out in droves like dead bugs. In the dream, serious authors are ordered to shave off their beards. But when I report for my compulsory shearing, I am met by derisive laughter.—"Put that pathetic tuft back where it belongs!" I am told.

2.

In "The Singing Bone," one of the most telling and least well-known fairy tales of the Brothers Grimm, a wandering shepherd-cum-minstrel finds a little white bone out of which he carves a mouthpiece for his horn. But the bone has its own agenda:

> Oh, dear little shepherd boy,
> The bone you blow on knows no joy.
> My brother slayed me,
> Beneath the bridge he laid me.
> All for the wild boar' hide,
> To make the king's daughter his bride.

No mere accommodating object this, no mouthpiece on which to play an idle ditty—the bone cannot help but echo the cries

1 Remarks originally delivered at a roundtable discussion on "Fiction Yesterday Today and Tomorrow," in conjunction with the New Fiction Festival, organized by Raymond Federman, at SUNY Buffalo, April 17, 1994

of the misdeed that did its "*I*" in. The shepherd's breath, like an author's ink or an archeologist's glue, re-members the dismembered. Implicated as accessories to the crime of forgetting, lest we turn a deaf ear to the song, the shepherd who unwittingly plays it, the king who hears it, the storyteller who tells the tale, the Brothers Grimm who transcribe and retell it, generations of readers, I, and now you, simultaneously reveal truths and derive considerable pleasure by recycling the song, keeping it in circulation. I could well imagine a contemporary rap version set in Harlem, South-Central LA, or Chicago's South Side Grand Crossing, with sneakers that belonged to the murdered brother dangling from a traffic light in lieu of the bone. This is the essence of fiction.

3.

What else is fiction, but a selective recycling! Like a murderer returning to the scene of the crime to relive the thrill of the kill. Like a dog sniffing out those sentient nooks and crannies where other canines already did it, lifting a leg to do it again. Like the Church of San Clemente in Rome, a kind of archeological seven-layer cake of sanctuaries, a church atop a church, atop a Temple of Mithras, the one piggybacked on top of the other. Like an author who goes back and scours old notebooks for impressions, stray remarks overheard and observations noted, fragments waiting to be reconstituted into a whole. The focus and format may change, depending on fashion and whimsy. But the function, whether for tomorrow's avant-gardes or yesterday's traditionals, remains essentially that of a talking tombstone, a singing bone.

4.

Off-beat, so-called experimental fiction, we are told by those in the know, is old hat. The public craves "true confessions," "biography," "fact." An Indianapolis realtor, the father of an old flame, once took me to task, solemnly informing me that for his money, Tom Wolfe was the only writer worth reading, because what he wrote was real. Mr. Wolfe, in turn, an ardent proponent of the "real estate" school of writing, whose fiction is grounded in "new" journalism has himself publicly lambasted all fictional fooling around. More recently, a finger-wagging self-styled arbiter of taste, a book reviewer took me to task in a review of *A Modern Way to Die*, my first book of short fiction, for failing to "delve for the beauty in the real," strongly advising me to "drop all the nonsense," "get with the Nasty Nineties," and "tell it like it is."

Taking this critic's advice to heart, I rushed off to the "True Crime" section of my local B. Dalton's and read up on the little mementos the Long Island serial killer liked to take from his victims, trinkets which finally told the story that did him in. Singing bones. Then I turned to my favorite source of current events, *The World Weekly News*,[2] which I peruse religiously while waiting on line at the supermarket. The headlines alone are imaginative masterpieces: "Super Genius Dazzles Docs: Boy with 2 Brains," "Farmer Shoots 23-Pound Grasshopper," "Werewolf Battles Cops in Alabama," "First Photo of Human Soul," "Satan's Face in Hurricane Andrew! Evil Image Appears in Storm Clouds Over Miami—Call it what you will, ficto-fact or facto-fiction! The call of the wild is alive and well at A&P!

5.

So, how do we explain the stubborn conservatism of American letters? How curious in the cradle of the American Dream that we should relegate the dreaming instinct to the supermarket tabloid!

2 *The Weekly World News* ceased publication in print tabloid form in 2007, but is still publishing online.

In the largely realistic American literary tradition, fantasy is generally disdained as a trifle or a cop-out, good for such low-brow literary forms as science fiction and comic books, but not worthy of a serious adult reader's attention. We may analyze our dreams to death on the couch, but heaven help the Anglo-Saxon scribbler who taps what the French poet Gérard de Nerval called "*une seconde vie*" ("a second life"), a realm previously prospected by the great American dream miner, Edgar Allen Poe. (Perhaps one reason the French get away with delving into the surreal and the fantastic in their literature is that they use the same word, "*expérience*," for "experience and experiment." The Latins, the Eastern Europeans and various and sundry Third Worlders are permitted to sound off, flip their lids, get gone in print—though I am, quite frankly, inclined to suspect a little insidious cultural chauvinism on the part of contemporary American publishers who promote a free-wheeling Magical Realism from abroad while still demanding the old stiff upper lip of the hacks back home. An African American author or two may get away with flights of fancy! Myth runs through their blood, after all, they can't help it. But the good ole boys really ought to know better! Maybe somebody ought to remind the multinational marketeers of culture that Julio Cortazar helped kick off Latin American Magical Realism in Buenos Aires by translating Poe—who, in turn, knew his E.T.A. Hoffmann and Brothers Grimm—who knew their *1001 Arabian Nights*—who knew their *Odyssey* and *Panchatantra*, etc. Let me take this train of thought one step further, outside the rarefied realm of the literary. Could it be that if we Americans kept less of a tight lid on what we allow ourselves to imagine, we'd have less of a need to shoot up and blow each other's brains out.

6.

The distinction between fact and fiction, in any case, may well be mute. Best to let the two realms spill freely and fertilize each other, as they always have.

Shortly after publishing "It,"[3] my imaginary account of a football field full of prehistoric slop discovered in Nevada (surely the most whimsical, farfetched fantasy I'd ever dreamed up—or so I thought) until I read in *The New York Times* about a massive, mysterious, pre-Ice Age fungus growing under the desert in the Southwest.

So long as the chickens keep laying their eggs, who cares which came first?

For my bread-and-butter job on the staff of a medical journal, I recently interviewed a microsurgeon testing an experimental procedure to transplant the ears of a young mouse onto an aged rodent. (So that's how Mickey manages to remain forever young!) Severed limbs and even vital organs, the microsurgeon predicts, will one day grow back out of stimulated stem cells. Shades of Frankenstein! Sing on, bone!

I also interviewed a celebrated urologist-collector of arcane objects, whose prize possessions include Lincoln's blood-stained collar, Göring's cyanide capsule with which he precluded the gallows, the bullet that killed JFK, and Napoleon's penis. Then French President Jacques Chirac refused his gracious offer to return it to the body at *Les Invalide*, in Paris.

Is fanciful fiction dead?

Yes, and doing quite well, thank you.

But before we cry Wolf(e) and hurl Finnegan's bones into the bonfire of the inanities, I suggest we scrap the traditional "any

3 It was first published in Blue Light Red Light (a magazine of speculative fiction and thearts), NYC,1991; and subsequently included in A Modern Way to Die, small stories & microtales, published by Fromm Int'l, 1991.

resemblance between person, etc." disclaimer on novels, and add instead, in big bold letters: ORIGINAL! NOT FROM CONCENTRATE! ALL NATURAL INGREDIENTS!—and who knows, maybe the book will make it to market, sandwiched in between Tom Wolfe, Twinkies, and *The World Weekly News*.

Small Wonder[1]

A Reflection on the Short Form

An atom of matter is all it takes to make a pretty big bang. E=MC2, the concise epic of the 20th century, is three letters and a number long. The same compressed, impatient age that spawned the transistor and the computer chip, the acronym, the one-minute commercial, the sound bite and the photo-op, also contrived its own narrative form, a story in a hurry—call it short-short, sudden or flash fiction—general consensus appears to have coalesced around the latter. Bastard child of the prose poem and the wise crack, illegitimate heir to the parable and the allegory, this mongrel darling was raised on a varied diet of the coarse and the genteel, brash big city bus bumper ads, political campaign jargon, dream talk, surrealist tricks and over the counter painkiller packaging copy. Ever anxious for a quick fix of meaning, sometimes posing as a poem, sometimes as a story, it steals its strength from legitimate forms only to sabotage any underpinnings of legitimacy. Soon enough, tomorrow maybe, it will be categorized, anthologized, neutered and defanged for popular consumption and the college curriculum. But for the time being it still retains a delinquent edge like a foot print in wet cement.

1 Brief introductory remarks delivered at "Small Wonders," an evening of short-short fictions, co-curated (with Pete Cherches), at Fales Library, New York University, October 17, 1996

Language Belongs to All its Practitioners
An Afterword

Whereas dictionaries support the fiction of verbal stasis, and institutions charged with maintaining linguistic purity, like France's Académie Française, are charged with the futile task of guarding against all immodest advances on the mother tongue, language is, in fact, a big, sloppy, ever-evolving, free-for-all. Words evolved from a prehistoric series of systemtized grunts and onomotopeic commands. Language belongs to all of its practitioners, the proficient and the faulty, the linguist and the new immigrant inadvertently spiking accepted formulations with alien elements, the poet deliberately toying with sense and structure, the kids on the street spinning new idioms, the newborn mouthing its first syllables based on its mother's mutterings and the muttered last words of the dying.

However much grammarians may grit their teeth at perceived missteps, mistakes, mispronunciations, and other affronts to proper speech, language keeps evolving. So, too, do the media of linguistic expression, from cave walls to stone tablets, to scrolls, to illuminated manuscripts, to printed incunabula, from movable type to digitalized tracts on computer screens and audiobooks, and whatever forms they may come up with in the future.

I have built my life around the printed word and retain a fetishistic attachment to the book as object. Upon entering the reading room on a recent visit with my wife to the Bibliothèque Mazarine in Paris, founded in 1643, the oldest public library in France, a veritable sanctuary of books, I fathomed that our marital bond is based in part on our shared attachment to books, that we are links in a chain of communication, and that whereas words will live on, the book as we know it is surely an endangered species.

Saddened as a bookmaker to acknowledge it's demise, I have learned from my son Jacques that there are other equally valid modes of communication, including spoken word and video. Socrates, he reminded me, never jotted down a word, he just liked to talk. Technology lacking, we owe the preservation of his wisecracks to the seemingly flawless memory and compulsive hypergraphic bent of Plato. Rooted in systems of pictorial signs, like Aztec and Egyptian hieroglyphs and Chinese pictograms etched in stone and inscribed on scrolls, computer icons may well reach back to the pictorial roots of language. Storytelling in one form or another will live on. Children still crave bedtime stories, as do their progenitors. Publishers contracts nowadays generally include terms relating to technologies not yet invented. I'm fine with whatever word-bundling mode they may come up with, so long as the story gets told.

New York
July 11, 2024

P.S.

Flipped open by day, as if the walls wore sunglasses, lowered and locked at night, the ubiquitous green metal lids of the *bouquinistes*, the used and antiquarian book stalls that line the sidewalk along the River Seine, in Paris, have been peddling the printed word for several centuries. In 1991 they were officially recognized as an essential part of the "*paysage Parisien*" (Parisian landscape) and collectively designated a UNESCO World Heritage site.

On a recent stroll I happened upon and could not resist snapping pictures of signs clipped onto the front of one such book box.

Reading Makes You Less of a Dick.
Buy Books!!!

Acknowledgements

It is difficult to pinpoint and acknowledge influences in one's life. This is particularly true for a writer who draws on any and every stimulus, from a beloved book, to a shred of conversation overheard in passing, to a morsel of undigested memory. That having been said, I am beholden above all to three teachers.

My septalingual father, Alfred Wortsman (1914-1979) was my first teacher who liked nothing better than to spend Sunday mornings tutoring his offspring in French, his preferred language, and German, his native tongue. Though I would oftentimes have preferred to have been left to my own devices, to play or read, or just loll about, unbeknownst to me back then, his passion for languages, French in particular, helped pave the way for my life for the past 40 years and counting with my French wife.

The late Allen Grossman (1932-2014), poet and educator, taught generations of starry-eyed undergraduates, like myself, not only how to read like your life depended on it, but also, and above all, how to mine and process the meaning of what you read. In his sometimes inscrutable, but always thrilling lectures, he made the Big Books speak. Oedipus, Odysseus, and Achilles leapt like human cannonballs through the thick skin of our self-absorbed adolescent minds, with him holding the loop. Grossman's sobering grade of B-/C+ on my first class paper would have been devastating, had it not been accompanied by the words scribbled below: "It's a wonder how badly you write and how well you speak in class!" It was just the encouraging virtual kick in the ass I needed to shock me into consciousness and help me bridge the gap between thought and word.

And though nowadays the very idea of a Euro-phalo-centric literary canon, with a marked preference for the books of white males to the exclusion of all others, is justifiably called into question, the current tendency to scrap the classics simply because they are just that, and to dump *The Odyssey*, *The Divine Comedy* and *Hamlet* into the dustbin of time, is an aberration not all that different from the Taliban blowing up colossal ancient statues of Buddha because the message they convey no longer fits the new dominant dogma. The worthy imperative to shed new light on the words of the overlooked does not justify gagging the great poets and sages of old; it just means the old boys need to move over to make room at the table for everyone else.

Grossman was remarkable in his ability to convey to young minds the thrill of reading. Notwithstanding the inherent "epistemological hopelessness" of the human condition—a Grosssmanism I still do not fully fathom, but that any erstwhile Grossman-acolyte would immediately recognize as the catchphrase of the master)—he demanded that we take the words of the Bible, the Baghavad Gita, the Illiad and the Odyssey et al to heart and to mind.

The late Phillip Rahv (1908-1973), essayist and astute literary critic, and co-founder of *The Partisan Review*, was another kettle of fish. At the late stage of his life at which I encountered him, Rahv delivered his lectures in an almost inaudible growl, rarely looking up from his singed and tattered notes, having no doubt concluded that intellectual jousting with us illiterate babes just wasn't worth the effort. Still, there was something inspirational in the way he wagged his finger, wiped his nose, thumped the desk to make a point, and dumped the ash of the Chesterfield cigarettes forever dangling from his lips into the central drawer of the desk at which he sat—something epic and monumental, some resounding echo of the snowy streets of Dostoyevsky's St. Petersburg and the frenetic ferment of Delmore Schwartz's

Greenwich Village. What he offered was a living link back to the source. An unprecedented A+ and barely legible, scribbled remarks that a paper I wrote on Henry James was publishable was to me a ticket to the big leagues.

Other Books by Peter Wortsman

Fiction

A Modern Way to Die, smallstories and microtales, Fromm Publishing International, New York, 1991; paperback edition, Fromm Publishing International, New York; second edition, Pelekinesis, Claremont, Cal., 2019
Cold Earth Wanderers, a novel, Pelekinesis Press, Claremont, Cal., 2014
Footprints in Wet Cement, a collection of short prose, Pelekinesis Press, Claremont, Cal., 2017
Stimme und Atem/Out of Breath … Out of Mind, a bilingual German-English collection of short fiction, PalmArt Press, Berlin, 2019

Nonfiction

Ghost Dance in Berlin, A Rhapsody in Gray, a travel memoir, Travelers' Tales/Solas House, Palo Alto, Cal., 2012; *Geistertanz in Berlin*, a German translation, Palm Art Press, Berlin, 2021
The Caring Heirs of Dr. Samuel Bard (Selected Profiles of Distinguished Graduates at the Columbia University Vagelos College of Physicians and Surgeons), Columbia University Press, April 2019
Epiphany of a Middle-Aged Pilgrim, essays in lieu of a memoir, Pelekinesis, 2021

Poetry

Borrowed Words, cutup poems, Bamboo Dart Press, 2022
Driftwood at the River's Edge, cutup poems, Bamboo Dart Press, 2023
The Laboratory of Time, cutup poems, Bamboo Dart Press, 2025

Collaborations

it-t=i, text by Peter Wortsman, art by Harold Wortsman, limited edition, here and now press, Brooklyn, NY, 2004
New York, NY, 1978, photographs by Jean-Luc Dubin, text by Peter Wortsman, translated from the original English into French by Claudie Bernard, Les Éditions Dumerchez, Creil, France, 2016
Einblattdruck Nr. 170, Der Müll Tanzt einen Walzer mit dem Wind / The Garbage Waltzes with the Wind, a broadsheet, with print by Harold Wortsman, Palm Art Press, Berlin, 2020
Odd Birds & Fat Cats, An Urban Bestiary, text by Peter Wortsman, art by Aurélie Bernard Wortsman, Turtle Point Press, Brooklyn, NY, 2024

Plays

Wo Man Bücher Verbrennt … Reuchlins Streit um das jüdische Schrifttum, the German translation of my play Burning Words, translated from the English by Peter Torberg, Kulturhaus Osterfeld, Pforzheim, Germany, 2014;
The Tattooed Man Tells All, bilingual English/German edition, Palm Art Press, 2024

Translations

Songs from the Depths of Hell (Sung by Aleksander Kulisiewicz), album of songs from the nazi concentration camps, produced, annotated, and translated by Peter Wortsman, Folkways, New York, 1978; reissued by Smithsonian Folkways, Smithsonian Institute, Washington D.C., 1993.

Sadly Whisper the Leaves of the Willow: Polish Partisan and Folk Songs (Sung by Aleksander Kulisiewicz), produced, annotated and translated by Peter Wortsman, Folkways, New York, 1980; reissued on audio cassette by Smithsonian Folkways, Smithsonian Institute, Washington D.C., 1993

Pictures, by Robert Musil, Cooper Union, New York, 1983

German Essays in Art History, Gert Schiff, ed., The German Library, Volume 79, Crossroad/Continuum, New York, 1988 (I translated most of the volume)

Posthumous Papers of a Living Author, by Robert Musil, Volume One of Eridanos Library, Eridanos, Hygiene, CO, 1988; second edition, Penguin 20th Century Classics, Penguin U.K., London, 1995; third edition, Archipelago Books, NYC, 2006; *Flypaper*, (a selection from my translation of *Posthumous Papers of a Living Author*), Penguin Mini-Classics, Penguin Books, London, UK, 2011

Max Beckmann: Tradition as a Problem in Modern Art, by Hans Belting, Timken Publishers, Inc., New York, 1989

69 Ways to Play the Blues, by Jürg Laederach, Semiotext(e), Foreign Agents Series, New York, 1990

Peter Schlemiel, The Man Who Sold His Shadow, by Adelbert von Chamisso, a new translation with an introduction, Fromm International Publishing Co., New York, 1993

Recommendation Whether to Confiscate, Destroy and Burn All Jewish Books, a classic call for tolerance, by Johannes Reuchlin, translated, edited and with my foreword, The Paulist Press, Mahwah, NJ, 2000

Tales of the German Imagination, from The Brothers Grimm to Ingeborg Bachmann, an anthology, selected, edited, and translated, and with an introduction by Peter Wortsman, Penguin Classics, London, U.K. and New York, NY

Telegrams of the Soul, Selected Prose of Peter Altenberg, selected, translated and with an afterward by Peter Wortsman, Archipelago Books, NY, 2005

Travel Pictures, by Heinrich Heine, Archipelago Books, Brooklyn, NY, 2008

Selected Short Prose of Heinrich von Kleist, Archipelago Books, Brooklyn, NY, 2010

Selected Tales of the Brothers Grimm, a new selection and translation, illustrated with paintings by contemporary Haitian artists, Archipelago Books, Brooklyn, NY, 2013

The Creator, a fantasy, by Mynona (aka Salomo Friedlaender), Wakefield Press, Cambridge, Mass., 2014

Konundrum, Selected Prose of Franz Kafka, a new selection and translation, Archipelago Books, Brooklyn, NY, 2016

The Sandman, by E.T.A. Hoffmann, a new translation, Penguin Little Black Classics, Penguin Classics, UK, 2016; bilingual Chinese/English edition, 2019
Hinkemann, a tragedy, by Ernst Toller, a new translation, Berlinica Books, Berlin/New York, 2019
Intimate Ties, by Robert Musil, a new translation, Archipelago Books, Brooklyn, NY, 2019
The Golden Pot, and other Tales of the Uncanny, by E.T.A. Hoffmann, a new translation, Archipelago Books, Brooklyn, NY, 2023
I Just Let Life Rain Down on Me, Selected Letters and Refletions of Rahel Levin Varnhagen, selected, edited and translated by Peter Wortsman, Seagull Books, Kolkata, India, 2024

First Edition 2026, PalmArtPress, Berlin

ISBN: 978-3-96258-233-3

Cover fotos: Peter Wortsman
Design: Catharine J. Nicely
Layout: NicelyMedia
Printed in Europe

PalmArtPress
Verlegerin: Catharine J. Nicely
Pfalzburger Str. 69, 10719 Berlin
www.palmartpress.com

Selected books from PalmArtPress

Peter Wortsman
Stimme und Atem – *Out of Breath, Out of Mind*
ISBN: 978-3-96258-034-6
330 Pages, Essays, Hardcover, German/English

Peter Wortsman
The Tattooed Man Tells All / Der Tätowierte Mann
ISBN: 978-3-96258-164-0
180 Pages, Play, Softcover/Flaps, German/English

Martina J. Kohl
FAMILY MATTERS – *Of Life in Two Worlds*
ISBN: 978-3-96258-143-5
244 Pages, Novel, Softcover/Flaps, English

Kevin McAleer
L.A. KID
ISBN: 978-3-96258-193-0
316 Pages, Novel, Softcover/Flaps, English

Dennis McCort
The Golden Pot – *A Fairytale for Our Time*
ISBN: 978-3-96258-109-1
300 Pages, Softcover/Flaps, English

Patricia Paweletz
Tracing the Past in the Present – *En Route to Gaby Glückselig in New York*
ISBN: 978-3-96258-169-5
180 Pages, Non-Fiction, English

YoYo
One Man's Decision to Become a Tree
ISBN: 978-3-96258-136-7
268 Pages, Four Novellas, Softcover/Flaps, English

Rüdiger Görner
The Marble Song
ISBN: 978-3-96258-079-7
280 Pages, Softcover/Flaps, English

Thomas Poeschel
Indian Miniatures
ISBN: 978-3-941524-77-4
76 Pages, Essay, Hardcover, Englisch

Mitya New
Beyond Mount Kailash
ISBN: 978-3-96258-210-4
320 Pages, Novel, English

Sophia Alexandra
Summer on the Subway
ISBN: 978-3-96258-152-7
118 Pages, Poetry, English

Kyricacos Efthymiou
The Red Horse – ***Eighteen Short Stories***
ISBN: 978-3-96258-237-1
70 Pages, Poetry, Hardcover, English

Michael Hampe
The Wilderness. The Soul. Nothingness – *About the Real Life*
ISBN: 978-3-96258-150-3
390 Pages, Phil. Novel, English

Wolf Christian Schröder
Five Minutes before the World Was Made
ISBN: 978-3-96258-233-3
342 Pages, Novel, Translation: Dennis McCort, Softcover/flaps, English

John Berger
garden on my cheek
ISBN: 978-3-941524-77-4
Paintings by Liane Birnberg
60 Pages, Poetry/Art, Softcover/Flaps, English

Michael Hannon
Between Nothing and Nothing at All – ***Zwischen Nichts und überhaupt Nichts***
ISBN: 978-3-96258-236-4
90 Pages, Poetry, Hardcover, with images by William T. Wiley, English

Peter Wortsman

Dubbed a "20th-century Brother Grimm" (Bloomsbury Review) and "a delinquent Hans Christian Andersen" (by playwright Mark O'Donnell), Peter Wortsman is the author of works of fiction and nonfiction, stage plays, poetry, travel writing, and indefinable forms, most recently *Odd Birds & Fat Cats (An Urban Bestiary)*, created in collaboration with his daughter, Aurélie Bernard Wortsman, his words, her art (Turtle Point Press, 2024). Also a critically-acclaimed translator from German, his English takes include the anthology *Tales from the German Imagination* (Penguin Classics, UK, 2013), which he also compiled, and most recently, *The Golden Pot, and other tales of the uncanny*, by E.T.A.Hoffmann (Archipelago Books, 2023), shortlisted for the Helene and Kurt Wolff Translation Prize. A former fellow of the Fulbright Foundation (1973), The Thomas J. Watson Foundation (1974), and a Holtzbrinck Fellow at the American Academy in Berlin (2010), his writing has been honored with the Beard's Fund Short Story Award (1985) and an Independent Publishers Book Award (2014).

Photo © Ricky Owens